Aretism

Aretism

An Ancient Sports Philosophy for the Modern Sports World

M. Andrew Holowchak and Heather L. Reid

LEXINGTON BOOKS
Lanham • Boulder • New York • Toronto • Plymouth, UK

Published by Lexington Books
A wholly owned subsidary of The Rowman & Littlefield Publishing Group, Inc.
4501 Forbes Boulevard, Suite 200, Lanham, Maryland 20706
www.lexingtonbooks.com

Estover Road, Plymouth PL6 7PY, United Kingdom

British Library Cataloguing in Publication Information Available

Library of Congress Cataloging-in-Publication Data

The hardback edition of this book was previously catalogued by the Library of Congress as follows:

Holowchak, Mark, 1958–
Aretism an ancient sports philosophy for the modern sports world / M. Andrew Holowchak and Heather L. Reid.
    p. cm.
 Includes bibliographical references and index.
 1. Sports—Philosophy. 2. Physical fitness—Philosophy. 3. Sports—Sociological aspects. 4. Competition (Psychology) I. Reid, Heather Lynne, 1963– II. Title.
GV706.H64 2011
796.01—dc22

2011007245

ISBN 978-0-7391-4881-5 (cloth : alk. paper)
ISBN 978-0-7391-8208-6 (paper : alk. paper)
ISBN 978-0-7391-6914-8 (electronic)

Printed in the United States of America

Holowchak dedicates this book to the loving memory of his maternal grandmother Theophilia, in whom he first recognized the courage of dedication to duty and the beauty of solidity of character.

Γνήσια ἰσχύς ἐν γυναίκα.

Reid also dedicates this book to her maternal grandmother Clara, who always told her that she could do anything.

Contents

Preface

M. Andrew Holowchak

"God alone is worthy of supreme seriousness, but man is made God's plaything
and that is the best part of him. Therefore every man and woman should live
life accordingly, and play the noblest games and be of another mind from what
they are at present... For they deem war a serious thing, though in war there is
neither play nor culture worthy of the name, which are the things *we* deem most
serious. Hence all must live in peace as well as they possibly can. What, then,
is the right way of living? Life must be lived as play, playing certain games,
making sacrifices, singing and dancing, and then a man will be able to
propitiate the gods, and defend himself against his enemies, and win in the
contest." Plato, *Laws,* 803a ff.

IN EARLY AUGUST OF 2004, PROFFESOR REID AND I attended a conference
in Pyrgos, Greece—very near to the ancient Olympic site. As the games
were shortly to be held in Athens later in the month, the theme of the
conference, suggested to the conference organizers by Reid, was the Greek
contribution to competitive sport. There was considerable discussion at the
conference of just what the Olympic ideal, today called "Olympism,"[1] would
have meant to the early Greeks as a competitive ideal as well as discussion of
what Olympism means to us today.

Throughout the conference, we were especially struck by the modern
Olympic motto—"Citius, Altius, Fortius" ("Faster, Higher, Stronger")—
displayed beneath the dais and inspired by the "Muscular Christianity" of its
day. The slogan seemed oddly out of place, when considered in the context of
ancient Greek thought. It also seemed to be a poor slogan to capture the essence
of the Olympic creed for the modern games, which reads: "The most important
thing in the Olympic Games is not to win but to take part, just as the most
important thing in life is not the triumph but the struggle. The essential thing is
not to have conquered but to have fought well." The modern Olympic creed is a
beautiful statement to the effect that victory in sport as well as in life is in the
effort, not in the ranking. It is also a creed that seems to reflect better the Greco-
Roman ethical systems—characterized by *aretē* (in general, "excellence" or,

when characterizing psychical excellence, "virtue") and sketched early on in Homer and Hesiod in the eight century B.C. and elaborated on fully in the ethical treatises of Aristotle and the Stoics of Greece and Italy much later. As former athletes now academically immersed in ancient Greek thought, we were troubled by the tension between the slogan and the creed, and we began to discuss the similarities and differences between ancient and modern competitive sport.

In ancient Greek competitive sport, athletes would endure great hardships through training in their quest to win. The Greek word *athleō* means "I contend" or "I fight for a prize," yet it also means "I suffer" or "I endure." The contests in which athletes competed were called *agōnes* ("places of combat," "arenas," "contests," "labors," or "struggles"), from which we derive our word "agony." That spirit of laboring, struggling, or contending for some prize—a spirit that permeated Greek society—is today called "agonism."

What was the prize that pushed athletes to labor as they did at the Olympic Games or any of the many other religious festivals that sprang up later? Consider what the poet Bacchylides says, in a victory song, about Pytheas of Aegina, winner of an athletic event called pankration (a vicious mix of boxing and wrestling) at the games of Nemea:

> Now, beside the altar of Zeus, the mightiest ruler, the garlands of glory-bringing Nikē (goddess of victory) nurture dazzling fame for men throughout their lives—anyway, for a few—and when the gloomy cloud of death covers them over, the everlasting fame (*kleos*) of their fine deed is left behind, immutable and secure.[2]

Or consider what the Theban poet Pindar wrote about young Hippocleas of Thessaly, the winner of the boy's double-stadium footrace at the ancient Pythian Games:

> He, who is free from pain of heart, may truly be divine. Yet, as poets say, he is happy and is a theme for their song, who gains the greatest prizes by being victorious through his hands or the prowess of his feet and through courage and strength. He is also happy and is a theme for their song who, while still alive, sees his young son win more than one Pythian crown. He cannot climb the brazen heaven, but, given all the bright achievements that mortals can achieve, he can reach the supreme limit of that voyage.[3]

Thus, those athletes that competed at a large festival, like Olympia, and returned home victorious could be at least assured some measure of lasting, godlike fame—*kleos*. Some, like the pancratist Arrhichion (see chapter 1), earned *kleos* by snatching victory, during competition, at the cost of his life.

The promise of fame still drives athletes today. Competitive sport is just one of many enduring agonistic aspects of human society, where mortals can, if they rise above others through exceptional deeds, "escape the grave" as it were. They become immortal or, at least, as immortal as is humanly possible. Jeffrey Seagrave writes: "The language of sport reflects our efforts to control matters of life and death—in short, to control our fate. Sport is a social drama...but it is also a cultural drama, and it demonstrates how a group draws on rituals and symbols as well as language to face a crisis, the ultimate crisis of its existentiale."[4] For Seagrave, victory in sport is conquest of life over death—an affirmation of human existence through competitive tasks. John Izod adds that identification with sport's heroes is a semi-religious activity that is fundamentally libidinal.

> [T]he adulation of sporting heroes arises in part from unconscious desires and impulses. Because the search for personal power through identification with the image of a hero is often led by the libido in this way...it could be described as a quasi-religious activity.... Like the hero of Greek myths, today's sport's heroes confront all conceivable external hardships as well as their deepest doubts and fears.[5]

Yet the paths modern athletes take to achieve athletic fame often come at a high price—perhaps too high a price. Many athletes choose sports, like Mixed Martial Arts or cliff jumping, where great risk is part of the contest. Some, like race-car driver Dale Earnhart or boxer Duk Koo Kim, wind up paying the ultimate price for their *kleos*. In less dangerous sports, others bring harm on to themselves through unsafe training aids (e.g., using performance drugs or harmful performance-enhancing techniques). For instance, Olympic weightlifters often use dangerous plyometric techniques, such as jumping down from a tall staircase and catching themselves in the squatting position, to develop explosive, out-of-the-hole strength at the cost of long-term bodily damage to tendons, ligaments, muscle tissue, and bones. Consider also track star Florence Griffith-Joyner. She gained the title of the fastest woman to have ever lived at the price of premature death, if the suspicions about her use of performance drugs are true. Finally, many athletes bring harm to others. That often happens directly, as when a player on one team deliberately tries to injure a player on another team, or indirectly, as when an athlete, who is a hero to thousands of fans, behaves in a way that is morally reprehensible, whether on or off the field. Tiger Woods' infidelities spring to mind.

There are two striking dissimilarities between ancient Greek contests and today's athletic events. Each concerns agonism. First, Greek sport embraced agonism as an absolute ideal. By this we mean that Greek contest had a definite end or limit—victory as the first place on a given day—and all victors historically were considered to be of the same rank. Modern athletic agonism, in contrast, is relativistic and unendingly agonistic—to coin a term we shall be using much, "panagonistic." There are contests within contests, through addiction to statistical data, and seasonal as well as historical struggles through comparisons between athletes and between teams that never reach a conclusion. Second, Greek agonism, as an absolute ideal, was limited by Greek religiosity. Athletic festivals were first and foremost religious festivals in honor of a particular deity—like Zeus, his wife Hera, or Apollo. Athletes were continually reminded by statues and the very oaths they took that they were human, not divine, and that their skills were on display foremost to honor the gods. The victor in a contest was the *protoagonistēs*—first in the struggle on a given day, but never able to transcend the struggle like a god. The panagonism of modern competitive sport seems driven by an open-ended commercial paradigm in which the most visible athletes promote themselves through pompous, arrogant displays while competing. Such displays ensure celebrity status by inviting critical discussion on ESPN and guaranteeing product endorsements. The Greeks had a cautionary word for that type of unbounded arrogance—"hubris." Let me elaborate on both dissimilarities.

Agonism vs. Panagonism. The Greeks kept official records of their victors, but no official records of time, distance, or other statistics. Wrestler Milo of Croton, for instance, is known to have won six times at six different Olympic Games—a record perhaps never to be broken. No other records have been kept about Milo's victories. That suggests that victory for the Greeks was something absolute, not itself to be ranked among other victories by other athletes or even among other victories by the same athlete. Taking the first position marked an end or limit to Greek competitiveness—at least until another competition. Thus Greek agonism, stressed the achievement of excellence relative to an absolute ideal, victory itself, rather than to a particular time or statistic.

In contrast, taking the first position in some event today marks no such end of competition, as athletic contests are multi-faceted. There are, as it were, numerous contests within a single contest. Through statistical analyses and (sometimes rational) debate, victories and victors are ranked. Statistical components come into play to rank, for instance, team against team, player against player, player against team, and even the same team against itself and the same player against himself. What was the greatest World Series of all time? Was Annika Sorrenstam better than Babe Didrikson? Was the 2009 Stanley Cup the greatest series ever played? Was Jim Thorpe the greatest athlete? Victories and victors can even be contested. What would have happened to the Chicago Cubs in the 2003 NLCS, if the fan had not interfered with the pop fly ball down the left-field line at the concession stand? Were the Tennessee Titans, who lost Super Bowl XXXIV by one foot on the final play of the game, just as good as or even better than the St. Louis Rams that year? Victory, today, is not absolute and the result is that a relativistic and restless agonism has come to permeate competitive sport at all levels.

Religious vs. Commercial Agonism. Greek agonism was also cosmically limited, as it were, because Greek contests were essentially religious. The second-century-A.D. historian Pausanias tells us that athletes who competed at Olympia and persons associated with them had to swear an oath to Zeus Horkios (Zeus Oath God) that "in nothing would they sin against the Olympic Games."[6] Dedicatory poems—honoring athletes and written by Simonides, Pindar, and Bacchylides—show clearly human deference to deity. Pindar writes of Epharmostus of Opus on his Olympic victory in wrestling, 468 B.C.:

> What comes through Nature (i.e., through Deity) is always best, but many men have striven to win their fame through merit that comes from mere training. Yet that in which Deity has no part (i.e., mere training) is no worse for being buried in silence. Still some roads lead farther than others, and not all of us can prosper in a single path of work. The heights of skill are steep, but, while offering this prize of song, with a ringing shout, I boldly declare that our hero has by the blessing of the heaven been born with deftness of hand and litheness of limb. With valor in his glance, our hero has been crowned by his victory at the altar of Ajax[7] at the banquet of the son of Oileus.[8]

Everything in Greek contest speaks of a deference of human skill to that of divine skill. Greeks were amply reminded at all times—especially at their games and through their oracles—first, that they were humans and not gods and, second, that their talents were god-given.[9]

Today's athletic competitions, of course, have been secularized and commercialized. Many athletes today think of themselves as, if not deities, superhuman beings with superhuman talents and demand to be treated thus. They see the commercial value in letting others know that. They conduct themselves, both on and off the "playing field," as if they are above the rules of sport, the laws of their country, and even the moral considerations that bind all human beings. In some sense, they are. No matter what trouble those pampered players get into—today, basketball player Gilbert Arenas and football quarterbacks Ben Rothlisberger and Michael Vick spring to mind—owners always find a place for them on a team and fans still flock to see them play. The goal here is profit and not some divine ideal; hubris and other transgressions are easily sacrificed on the altar of Mammon.

Thoughts such as those permeated our conversations in Ancient Olympia. Some of the problems discussed at the conference—the prevalence of cheating, violence, self-promotion, and performance-enhancement through drugs—seemed themselves by-products of today's panagonistic paradigm. Yet that is a paradigm, we were sure, that ancient Greek culture could not have accepted.

The panagonism of today is captured by what we call the Martial/Commercial model (MC model) of competitive sport. This model, based historically on the notion that competitive sport is a form of war-play (chapters 1-5), comprises nine MC ideals: sport as warlike play, manliness, inflexible justice, winning as the end, strength and speed, domination, individualism, instrumentation, and closure (chapter 6). The MC model seems to be widely, though not universally, accepted by critics, competitors, and fans of sport today. The ends of the MC model—e.g., glory, money, enduring fame—are largely to be found outside of its practice.

The thesis of this book, given the widespread acceptance of MC ideals, is that the MC quest for victory can and often does come at too high a price. With the amount of money involved in competitive sport today, the message more than ever before redounds: Sport is war and one must do whatever it takes to win. As former University of Miami tight end Kellen Winslow said chillingly after a frustrating loss to Tennessee in 2003: "It's war! They're out to kill you, so I'm out there to kill them. We don't care about anybody but this U[niversity]! … I'm a fucking soldier!" That attitude is also illustrated by the stabbing of tennis star Monica Selles by a fan of Stephi Graff; the rampant use of performance drugs in many types of sports; the needless self-promotion of football stars like Terrell Owens and "Neon" Deion Sanders; Pete Rose's gambling on baseball; and even the arrogance of golf superstar Veejay Singh, who refused to compete in a tournament in which female star Annika Sorenstam was admitted to play. Thus, MC ideals are neither just characteristic of sports designated as combative—like rugby, football, baseball, and hockey—nor are they confined to events that feature only men.

Yet those undesirable consequences militate against condonation or sanction, at least implicitly, of MC sport. Something else is lost, or at least given to neglect, that should be widely promoted in competitive sport—the aesthetic and recreational dimensions, which we capture in what we call the AR model of sport. An aesthetic approach to competitive sport is not just a gut-level, sensationalist response to events as they happen—the momentary thrill as someone on your team slam-dunks the basketball or the satisfaction that comes with knowing your team won, however undeserving they might have been of victory. It is a rational approach to competitive sport that requires, for fullest appreciation, a subtler attitude toward participating or viewing. It is the intellectual enjoyment of a smartly pitched 4-3 victory by pitcher Justin Verlander on a day that it is apparent that he does not have his best stuff. It is recognition of the efficiency of form of former vaulter Sergey Bubka in the pole vault, an event which he dominated for some 15 years. It is the sheer power and presence of Serena Williams, when she takes the court and is on her game. It is the beauty of a skilfully orchestrated, time-consuming drive by New England quarterback Tom Brady to run down the final three minutes of the clock and end the game. It is the stubborn refusal of strongman legend Žydrūnas Savickas to make maximal use of his legs, while he pushes up a 480-pound log over his head with triceps and deltoids. Neglect of such features, which seldom show up in statistics, is a regrettable consequence of today's panagonistic ideal.

For all those reasons, the traditional MC model of competitive sport needs substantial rethinking. What is beautiful in competitive sport needs to be put on a level playing field with what is bestial, because competitive sport is at least as much about beauty as it is about bestiality.

To that end, we propose a revival of the ancient Greek athletic spirit, focused on excellence, what the Greeks called *aretē*. This model, which we call "Aretism," draws a balance between the inflexible instrumentalism of the MC sports culture and the pliable playfulness of aesthetic, recreational models in today's critical literature, where athletic activity is its own end, to recover the personal, social, and global benefits of sport.

Aretism comprises four parts. The first part, "Brief History of Competitive Sport," begins with the historical evolution of competitive sports from its early roots in Sumerian, Greek, and Roman cultures to the present commercialization of sport (chapters 1 through 5). History shows a definite link between competitive sport and war—a relationship that is still strong today.

Part Two, "The MC Model of Competitive Sport," begins by listing the most general features of MC sport, what we take to be the received view of competitive sport today, and then turning to an examination of nine particular features of it. The remaining chapters of this part, chapters 7 through 11, look at some of the problems linked with MC competition—use of performance drugs, the obsession with performance enhancement, aggression and violence, self-promotion, and infatuation with statistical data.

Part Three, "The AR Model of Competitive Sport," considers the alternative aesthetic, recreational approach often proposed as an antidote to the MC practice of sport today. Chapters 13 through 16 analyze different, non-competitive theses about beauty in sport: aesthetical spectacle, integrity in competition, economy of performance, and unity. Those elements are important considerations for a philosophical view of competitive sport as a socially sanctioned, ethically sensitive activity, but they leave too much behind to stand on their own.

The final part, "Aretism," spells out specific normative principles of competition—principles governing how sport ought to be played—and lays out some practical guidelines for implementing these principles. Chapter 17 analyzes the status of sport: Is it a genuine good? Chapters 18 and 19 cover the normative principles, culminating in a new model of competitive sport, the "Aretic" model, which focuses on development of character in athletes through pursuit of excellence in athletic competitions. Finally, chapters 20 through 22 cover practical guidelines for instantiating the normative principles. One key issue addressed in those chapters is gender equality in sport today.

Thus, *Aretism* is an examination of vital, topical, and hot issues in competitive sport—e.g., gender equity, violence and competition, performance drugs in sport, the overemphasis on winning, self-promotion during competitions, youth sports programs, and the erosion of male identity in macho sports.

Overall, *Aretism* is, in a straightforward sense, a rejection of the panagonism suggested by the modern Olympic slogan "Faster, Higher, Stronger!" for a more moderate, non-relational type of agonism, characterized perhaps by the slogan "Fast, High, Strong!" which is tempered by aesthetic and AR models of sport—a mean that better reflects the modern Olympic creed's emphasis on striving and excellence. The modern Olympics recognize the *aretē* of all competitors and reward of the top-three competitors, not merely the top competitor. As Aristotle himself said, "And just as Olympic prizes are not for the finest and strongest, but for the contestants—since it is only these who win—the same is true in life; among the fine and good people, only those who act correctly win the prize."[10]

Before closing, we turn to a translational issue. The Greek work *aretē* is ambiguous. When used in relation to humans, it means excellence of a physical or psychical sort. The Theban poet Pindar, for example, uses *aretē* to characterize the physical excellence of athletes that have excelled in religio-athletic festivals like the Olympic or Delphic Games. Plato and Aristotle, for example, use *aretē* to characterize a person's virtue or equanimity. To preserve the ambiguity of *aretē*—as aretism is both a commitment to the physical excellence of competitive athleticism as well as to the cultivation of virtue along the way—we prefer throughout not to translate the term.

Notes

1. A term that was coined by Coubertin in drawing up the revival.

2. Bacchylides, *Epinician Odes and Dithyrambs of Bacchylides*, trans. David R. Slavitt (Philadelphia: University of Pennsylvania Press, 1998), 56.

3. Pindar, *Olympian Odes, Pythian Odes*, trans. William H. Race, Loeb Classical LIbrary (Cambridge: Harvard University Press, 1997) "Pythian Ode" X.22-30.

4. Jeffrey O. Segrave, "A Matter of Life and Death: Some Thoughts on the Language of Sport," *Philosophy of Sport: Critical Readings, Crucial Issues*, ed. M. Andrew Holowchak (Upper Saddle River, NJ: Prentice-Hall, 2000), 61-62.

5. John Izod, "Television Sports and the Sacrificial Hero," *Philosophy of Sport: Critical Readings, Crucial Issues*, ed. M. Andrew Holowchak (Upper Saddle River, NJ: Prentice-Hall, 2000), 380-381.

6. Pausanias, *Guide to Greece* V, ed. R.E. Wycherley, Loeb Classical Library (Cambridge: Harvard University Press, 1935) xxiv.9.

7. One of the great Greek heroes of Troy.

8. Pindar, "Olympian Ode" IX.100-112.

9. For more on the Greek attitude towards the gods, called "apotropaism," see M. Andrew Holowchak, *Happiness and Greek Ethical Thought* (London: Continuum Books, 2004), xvii-xxi.

10. Aristotle, *Nicomachean Ethics*, 2nd ed., trans. Terrence Irwin (Indianapolis: Hackett Publishing Company, Inc., 1999), 1099a4-6.

PART I
How Did Sports Get Here from There?

Chapter 1
The Roots of Competitive Sport

"When the gods created Gilgamesh they gave him a perfect body. Shamash the glorious sun endowed him with beauty, Adad the god of the storm endowed him with courage, the great gods made his beauty perfect, surpassing all others, terrifying like a great wild bull. Two thirds they made him god and one third man." *The Epic of Gilgamesh*

T HIS CHAPTER OFFERS A BRIEF ACCOUNT of the early roots of competitive sport by examining contest and excellence in the Babylonian epic *Gilgamesh* and the Greek epic *Iliad* as well as in Greek and Roman cultures.

Sumerian Justice through Contest & Conquest

Gilgamesh is the oldest existing epic. Thus, it is likely that there is much more that is fantastic than factual about it. Still it is one of the most moving stories ever told and it give us valuable information about a civilization that existed several thousands of years ago—ancient Babylonia. For the purposes of this undertaking, it reveals much about Sumerian play and contest. It also gives us some indication about how virtue and friendship factor into an understanding of each. So, it is perhaps not so untoward that our historical sketch of sport should begin, as it were, ahistorically.

Gilgamesh is a Sumerian tale of a great and handsome ruler named Gilgamesh, who has the desires and abilities of a god, but the destiny of a man. As king of the Mesopotamian city Uruk, he proves to be a restless and irresponsible king, whose youthful arrogance and appetite know no bounds. "His lust leaves no virgin to her lover, neither the warrior's daughter nor the wife of the noble."[1] In response to his excesses, the gods create the bestial Enkidu in the likeness of the god of war, Ninurta, the god of agriculture, Ashnan, and the god of wild animals, Sumukan. Thus, Enkidu is an equal of Gilgamesh and is fashioned to neutralize the king and his vices.

Eventually, the two heroes meet one another, as Gilgamesh is about to enter the bridal bed of another virgin bride in Uruk. A frightful brawl ensues. The brawl is a critical test of pluck. More importantly, it is a test of character and virtue. As the two are destined to become inseparable friends, the victor will win the upper hand in the friendship.

> Mighty Gilgamesh came on and Enkidu met him at the gate. He put out his foot and prevented Gilgamesh from entering the house, so they grappled, holding each other like bulls. They broke the doorposts and the walls shook, they snorted like bulls locked together. They shattered the doorposts and the walls shook. Gilgamesh bent his knee with his foot planted on the ground and with a turn Enkidu was thrown. Then immediately his fury died. When Enkidu was thrown he said to Gilgamesh, "There is not another like you in the world. Ninsun (goddess and mother of Gilgamesh), who is as strong as a wild ox in the byre, she was the mother who bore you, and now you are raised above all men, and Enlil has given you the kingship, for your strength surpasses the strength of men."[2]

Ultimately, the fight is a draw and afterward the two embrace and begin a friendship so enduring and complete that it defies common understanding.

Gilgamesh and Enkidu go on to share many heroic adventures together. On perhaps their most noteworthy adventure, they enter into the Cedar Forest with the intention of confronting and slaying Humbaba, the fearsome god of the forest. Working together, they have strength, cunning, and courage enough to confront and kill the monstrous god. In gruesome combat, Humbaba is beheaded, and the two heroes fell the mighty cedars of the forest and return to Uruk to praise that only gods or godlike men deserve.

After the episode in the Cedar Forest, the goddess of love, Ishtar, confronts Gilgamesh and attempts to seduce him. Citing many ruinous instances where she has used mortals to sate her divine lust, Gilgamesh spurns her advances and thereby remains true to his intimate friend Enkidu. In retaliation, Anu, father of Ishtar and the gods, sends to Uruk the bull of heaven, who has killed hundreds of men with mere snorts. Gilgamesh and Enkidu confront and kill the bull. Enkidu then tears out the right thigh and, tossing it in Ishtar's face, says threateningly, "If I could lay my hands on you, it is this I should do to you, and lash the entrails to your side."[3]

The adventures of the two brave men against the gods Humbaba and Ishtar do not go unnoticed by the other gods and, in consequence, it's decided that Enkidu must die as divine retribution. Upon the death of Enkidu, Gilgamesh grieves bitterly the loss of his friend—perhaps even to a greater extent than one might expect from the loss of a close spouse. After an inordinately lengthy spell of mourning, Gilgamesh begins an agonizing and lengthy search for immortality that ultimately ends futilely. After this grievous quest, he returns to Uruk as a fitful, wise, and compassionate king.

This more than 3000-year-old tale tells us many things about virtue, friendship, and their connection to serious contest in ancient Sumeria. First, each hero's respect and love for the other has to be earned through competence in fighting the other. Greatness of ability and the very magnificence of the brawl between them ensure that the two god-like men will be complete and inseparable friends. For Gilgamesh, there is no woman, not even a goddess, who is an equal, but only a divinely crafted man. The bond of intimacy between the two great friends is clear in the extent and sincerity of Gilgamesh's mourning for his friend. In addition, when the two heroes share adventure, they choose a life-threatening episode that involves a clash to the death with a menacing, frightful god. Their manly courage redounds to the praise of the people of Uruk. Last, Gilgamesh spurns the advances of the beautiful seductress Ishtar, who is depicted as a lustful, opportunistic, and vindictive goddess. Enkidu even threatens her with violence. In the end, Gilgamesh, through virtue tested by competition, defeats not only threatening monsters, but also overcomes his vulnerability to female passion and cunning—the original obstacle to his becoming a great leader. The tale is doubtless a rite of passage for Gilgamesh, who proves through doughty might and bloody deeds his divine-like status and entitlement to rule the people of Uruk. Like friendship, justice in this Sumerian epic is a matter of conquest—victory through strength in serious competition.

Early Greek Agonism

Homer was a poet of early eighth-century Greek antiquity who, most scholars believe, wrote two of the most celebrated epic poems of all time: the *Iliad*, a work that tells about the 10-year Greek siege of Troy (thought to have occurred c. 1250 B.C.), and the *Odyssey*, a story about the 10-years homeward journey of Odysseus, one of the most venerable Greek heroes of the Trojan expedition. Both the Trojan War and Odysseus' struggles are examples of what the Greeks called *agōn*, contest or struggle. Agonism, the belief that life is characterized and given meaning by such contests and struggles, is often associated with the ancient Greeks.[4]

In Book XXIII of Homer's *Iliad*, the poet describes another form of *agon*, celebratory funeral games (Greek, *agones*) for the fallen warrior Patroclus, a close friend of the greatest Greek soldier Achilles. After the Greeks burn Patroclus' body, Achilles readies the mourners for competitive events in honor of their deceased companion. The events include a chariot race, a boxing match, a wrestling event, a footrace, hand-to-hand combat with shields and spears, an iron-discus toss, an archery event, and spear-throwing.

The depiction of these events is highly competitive and, because honor is at stake, deadly serious. For instance, when the prizes for wrestling are announced—a large tripod for standing over a fire for the winner and a woman who is skilled in domestic chores for the second man—huge Ajax, son of Telamon, and thickly muscled Odysseus square off in preparation for brutal contest.

> Both champions, belted tight, stepped into the ring and grappling each other hard with big burly arms, locked like rafters a master builder bolts together, slanting into a pitched roof to fight the ripping winds. And their backbones creaked as scuffling hands tugged for submission-holds and sweat streamed down their spines and clusters of raw welts broke out on ribs and shoulders slippery, red with blood, and still they grappled, harder, locking for victory, locked for that burnished tripod: Odysseus no more able to trip and bring to ground his man than Ajax could—Odysseus' brawn held out.[5]

The mighty battle between these two heroes is ultimately called a draw and ended before serious exhaustion or injury could occur.

The vividly depicted events in Book XXIII give us many clues about early Greek culture and its love of athletic competition. Most importantly, if formal contest arose out of funeral celebrations such as this, as many scholars think, then athletic prowess for Greeks was valued as a means to demonstrate one's virtue and honor. Funeral contests functioned initially as a meritocratic way to distribute the deceased's property as prizes. However, in *Iliad* the prizes are not Patroclos' possessions, but rather tokens of social honor.[6] Athletic competition was related partly to prowess in war, but more importantly it was a way to negotiate honor among social equals, specifically males of noble descent.[7]

The agonistic clash of heroes that fills the pages of Homer's *Iliad* had an extraordinary impact on subsequent Greek culture. The *Iliad* was a mirror of the early Greek ethical code. Life, for early Greeks, was a hard and endless struggle and a young boy would learn about the battle for and conquest of Troy as a means of indoctrinating him in proper, manly behavior for everyday life and preparing him for the inevitability of contest and the possibility of war. In fact, the Greek word for "courage," *andreia*, comes from the Greek word for man, *anēr*.[8] Being courageous meant having a manly, ready-for-contest disposition. Later Greek ethical codes—such as those of Plato, Aristotle, and Diogenes of Sinope—incorporated that sense of agonism in their views of what it was to strive for a good life. Two examples will suffice. First, the city-state of Sparta, after the reforms of Lycurgus, became a war-centered city-state. Preparing them to dedicate themselves to the city's successive war efforts, athletics was instituted as an important part of a Spartan education for both boys and girls. Second, Alexander the Great, whose love of competitive battle enabled him to conquer the mighty Persian Empire and much of India, carried an annotated copy of the

Iliad with him on his military campaigns. Overall, Greek culture was inescapably agonistic.[9]

Though the events described in *Iliad* depict Greek life as it probably was hundreds of years before Homer, by the time of Homer early in the eighth century B.C., formal athletic festivals began to spring up throughout Greek culture. They were predominantly religious festivals—with prayer, sacrifices, and recitals by philosophers, orators, and poets—where athletic competitions in honor of a particular deity took place.

The first of these was the Olympic festival, which is generally considered to have begun in 776 B.C.[10] The festival was a multi-day religious gathering in honor of Zeus, king of the Olympian gods, that featured a variety athletic events. There were the running races, boxing, wrestling, pancratium (a particularly brutal event that combined elements of boxing and wrestling), chariot and horse races, the discus and javelin throws, and jumping. Boys as well as men participated.[11]

At this and later religious competitions, athletes took training and victory very seriously. Olympic contestants were required to arrive at Elis, the city in charge of organizing the festival, 30 days before the beginning of the games. They had to swear an oath that they had been training for at least 10 months, and during the month at Elis anyone who seemed unworthy of contest was excluded before the Games began.[12] Honoring the god through athletics required at least as serious an approach as fighting in war. Indeed, athletic games could be as deadly as war.

A Greek father tells his son the story of Arrhichion's deadly victory in the pancratium, while the two look at a painting of this fateful bout. The pancratist, while being choked to death, applies a kick to his opponent's right leg, which leaves it dangling, and grabs him by the groin to force a concession. At the moment of victory, however, Arrhichion dies from suffocation. His Olympic crown is awarded posthumously. Of the various techniques used in pancratium, the father speaks:

> What about the wrestling technique? Well, my boy, people who contend in the pancratium use the dangerous type of wrestling for they have to employ moves where they fall backward which are not safe for the wrestler, and holds by which one who has fallen can still win, and they must have skill in strangling various ways at various times, and they also use wrestling strokes against the ankle and twist the hand of the person preparing to strike them or to jump upon them. All such, then, is the business of the pancratium, with the exception only of biting and gouging. The Lacedaemonians allow even this practice, training themselves hard, I suppose, for war, but the Elean contests (i.e., Olympic Games) prohibit this but do approve of strangling.[13]

Cities, seeking for themselves the honor and pride (and possibly divine favor) associated with victory, took the Games very seriously. One city in Italy, Croton, is especially noteworthy. From 588 to 484 B.C., Crotoniates, winning 12 of 27 contests, dominated the stade race (a straight sprint the length of the stadium, roughly 200 meters) at Olympia. In this same span of time, Crotoniates won 23 of the 109 known victories in all events contested. From 532 to 516 B.C., Milo of Croton won every Olympic wrestling wreath before finally losing in 512 B.C. to a fellow Crotoniate who refused to come to close quarters with him.[14] After 484 B.C., however, there is not a single known instance of a Crotoniate victory in the Olympic Games. Why? Scholar David Young effectively argues that Croton must have recruited athletes and rewarded them monetarily for superior performance. The absence of victors after 484 B.C. is easily explained by lack of financial backing for athletes. When the money disappeared, so too did the athletes.[15]

Women were not allowed to compete at Olympia, and married women were even excluded from attendance. The prohibition probably has its origin in an early cult of Heracles located on the site. Women were not allowed to enter sanctuaries of Heracles or participate in his worship because it was believed that female presence could harm or diminish the power of warriors, heroes, and presumably athletes.[16] Unmarried females seem to have participated in other games and there were ritual races for girls in several Hellenic locales, including the track at Olympia.[17] But the reason for excluding women from Heracles' sanctuaries belies the underlying belief that females were not fit for true Greek agonism and the excellence it demanded.

Despite their exclusion from the site, women were allowed to breed horses for the chariot race in the Olympics. In one story, Cyniska, the daughter of the Spartan king Archidamus, entered her horses into the race and won. (The owner was declared the winner of horse races, not the rider.) But it is unlikely Cyniska's crown was taken as evidence of her *aretē*. According to one account, Archidamus pressured his daughter to enter only to show that horseracing, since women could win, was a matter of wealth more than virtue.[18]

Roman "Gorification" of Greek Sports

Greek athletics survived the Roman conquest of Greece in 146 B.C. and established themselves in many eastern Roman cities. Athletes made a handsome living by training for and doing well in these competitions. By the first century B.C., the four main Greek contests—the Olympic Games for Zeus and the later-formed Pythian Games at Apollo's sanctuary at Delphi (586 or 582 B.C.), the Nemean Games for Zeus at Nemea and later at Argos (573 B.C.), and the Isthmian Games for Poseidon at the Isthmus of Corinth (582 B.C.)—became known at the *periodos* or circuit. Victory in such events was so prestigious for Greek city-states, that winners would receive such lucrative prizes as a grant for life from the public treasury. The aura of excellence and celebrity that surrounded great athletes attracted even emperors. Nero himself competed at Olympia, Delphi, and Isthmia and "won"—doubtless through the prerogative being emperor—1,808 crowns.[19] Records of his sham victories were later expunged.

In the first century B.C., Julius Caesar rebuilt the Circus Maximus in Rome, an enormous stadium that accommodated over 250,000 people. In 45 B.C., he held triumphal games that included chariot races, athletic competitions, mock naval battles, animal fights, and a competitive war reenactment. In 72 A.D., Vespasian began construction of the Coliseum, which held as many as 60,000 spectators, and Titus finished it eight years later. This was utilized mainly for man-against-man gladiatorial combat (Latin, *munera*) and the hunting of animals (Latin, *venationes*).

Greek-style athletics still flourished in the Eastern Roman Republic, but the attitude toward contest in Rome was different. Sport for Romans was that in which conquered people, not conquerors, contested.[20] The agonistic excellences displayed were generally the same, but when Romans watched athletic events, they watched slaves, foreigners, and even criminals compete. Only rarely did Roman citizens themselves participate. The reasons for that are not exactly clear; perhaps nobles feared failure in the public arena, perhaps they thought sport too frivolous a use of their time. To be sure, they put sport to clever political use. Their events provided entertainment or escape from the congestion and moil of daily Roman routine. At the same time public execution in the arena was a straightforward means of ridding the city of undesirables.

The Latin word for sporting events, *ludi* ("games"), reflects the relative Roman lack of agonistic spirit. Greek *agōnes,* in contrast, did more than free up people from the daily life-struggle through entertainment; it mirrored their daily life-struggle—indeed their philosophy of life. At the Greek festivals, competitors were well respected and admired Greeks—usually of good standing—who were amply rewarded upon victory. In short, the Greek and Roman attitudes toward sport were incommensurable.[21]

The focal point of Roman sportive entertainment was the gladiatorial contest, which was a fight between armed competitors which sometimes ended in death. Gladiators varied in type. Some were outfitted with heavy helmets, swords and shields, and protective leg and arm armor. Others fought nearly naked and moved quickly to defend themselves with lighter arms such as daggers and nets. Successful gladiators achieved great fame; their fighting skill and bravery in the face of death overshadowed their lowly social status and made them highly admired, even erotic figures.

During the reign of Augustus (27 B.C.-14 A.D.), most gladiators were prisoners or slaves, some of whom were deliberately thrown into the amphitheater to be slaughtered as a means of social control.[22] Eventually impoverished free men contended, as did members of the Roman nobility, who sought great fame. These gory competitions were so popular that Nero in 63 A.D. introduced female gladiatorial combat. While formal athletic festivals ended as early as the late fourth century A.D., during the reign of Theodosius I, gladiatorial combats continued at the Coliseum well into the fifth century.

In the early history of sport, we can see not only the fundamental link between athleticism and conceptions of human excellence, but also the stark contrast between sport as a deadly serious activity where participation is essential for honor, and sport as recreation—an entertaining escape from the serious part of life, best left to those unworthy of important tasks. Regrettably, the phenomenon of female gladiators in Rome probably had more to do with the entertainment value of such a novelty than any enlightenment of attitudes about females' fighting skill and their access to agonistic conceptions of virtue. As we shall see, however, these early models of sport bore within them the seeds for positive change.

Notes

1. N.K. Sanders, *The Epic of Gilgamesh* (New York: Penguin Books, 1972), 62.

2. Sanders, *Gilgamesh*, 69.

3. Sanders, *Gilgamesh*, 88.

4. See especially Jacob Burkhardt, *The Greeks and Greek Civilization,* trans. Sheila Stern (New York: St. Martin's Press, 1998).

5. XXIII.789-800. Homer, *Iliad*, trans. Robert Fagles (New York: Penguin Books, 1990).

6. Ben Brown, "Homer, Funeral Contests and the Origins of the Greek City," *Sport and Festival in the Ancient Greek World,* ed. David J. Phillips and David Pritchard (Swansea: The Classical Press of Wales, 2003), 123-162.

7. Females, foreigners, and slaves were generally excluded both from athletics and the conception of *aretē* (excellence) associated with it.

8. In Attic Greek dialect, derivative substantives and adjectives were formed by taking the genitive root of a noun and adding the appropriate substantive or adjectival endings. The genitive root of *anēr* is *andr-*.

9. Females, with a few notable exceptions, were thought agonistically inferior and believed to be incapable of full-fledged excellence (*aretē*). Note that Achilles is offered a woman who is skilled in domestic tasks as a prize second to a tripod. Atalanta and the Amazons are mythological exceptions. Plato and Epicurus are philosophical exceptions. Plato, in *Republic*, argued that women should take an active role in his ideal city, and Epicurus, some years later, developed his own society of friends, called the "Garden," within Athens. The Garden openly welcomed women to study philosophy.

10. This is on the authority of Hippias of Elis of the fifth century B.C. This authority, however, was challenged even in antiquity. Current evidence points to an even earlier

date for athletic activity at Olympia. Many other religious athletic festivals followed that of Olympia.

11. Boys events were added at Olympia in 632 B.C.

12. Mark Golden, *Sport and Society in Ancient Greece* (Cambridge University Press, 1998), 15.

13. Philostratus, *Imagines* (Leipzig, 1893), II.6.

14. He won the boy's wreath at Olympia in 540 B.C. and numerous victories at other religious festivals.

15. David C. Young, *The Olympic Myth of Greek Amateur Athletics* (Chicago: Ares Publishers, Inc., 1985), 134-146.

16. John Mouratidis, "Heracles at Olympia and the Exclusion of Women from the Ancient Olympic Games," *Journal of Sport History* vol. 11, no. 3, 1984, 41-55. 55.

17. There was a festival for girls in honor of Zeus's wife Hera held at Olympia. At this festival, three classes of maidens competed in a footrace that was roughly one-sixth shorter than the men's stade race. A tantalizing suggestion is that this is because the foot of an average Greek woman was approximately one-sixth smaller to the foot of an average Greek man. See David C. Romano, "The Ancient Stadium: Athletes and Aretē," *The Ancient World: Athletics in Antiquity*, Vol. VII, nos. 1 & 2 (Chicago: Ares Publishers, Inc. 1983), 14.

18. The Greek word for excellence is *aretē*. This word was used to describe moral excellence or virtue, athletic excellence, and even a type of excellence that belongs to inanimate objects, such as couches or chariots.

19. Golden, *Sport and Society*, 11.

20. Peter C. McIntosh, "The Sociology of Sport in the Ancient World." *The Sports Process: A Comparative and Developmental Approach,* ed. Eric Dunning et al. (Indianapolis: Human Kinetics Publishers, 1993), 31.

21. M. Andrew Holowchak, "Early Greek Influence on Sport: Romanization and Decline of Athletic Festivals." *Milo* 4, Vol. 4, 1996.

22. Peter C. McIntosh, "The Sociology of Sport in the Ancient World," *The Sports Process: A Comparative and Developmental Approach,* ed, Eric Dunning et al. (Indianapolis: Human Kinetics Publishers, 1993), 32.

Chapter 2
Medieval, Renaissance, and Enlightenment Sport

"But if anyone is anxious to wrestle, to run or to jump with peasants, then he ought, in my opinion, to do it casually, out of *noblesse obligé*, so to say, and certainly not in competition with them; and he should be almost certain of winning, or else not take part at all, for it is too sad and shocking, and quite undignified, when a gentleman is seen to be beaten by a peasant, especially in wrestling-match." Baldesar Castiglione, *The Courtier*

N THE MIDDLE AGES, THE NON-RELIGIOUS, theatrical nature of the Roman "glorification" of sport was mitigated and given a medieval makeover. Mock fighting through jousts and melees alleviated boredom and reproduced the excitement of war. Contestants vied for honor and for female attention. Sporting activities in Renaissance culture were more than pastimes. They brought back the Greek aretic ideals of a sound body as well as a sound mind. Nevertheless, *aretē* was to be had only through ostentation, not through true excellence of body and soul. The seventeenth and eighteenth centuries marked a return to competitive sports as serious activities. The gentry of Europe tended to engage in the sorts of sporting activities that distanced them from commoners—e.g., tennis and fencing—while the commoners played ball games that were rigorous and rough. In Britain, the gentry attended and participated in both violent (e.g., pugilism) and lighter competitions (e.g., hunting). The turn to sport as serious play, which characterized this era of history, set the stage for the modern attitude toward sport that came to fruition in the industrial age of the nineteenth century.

This chapter is a brief sketch of sport in the Middle Ages, the Renaissance, and the seventeenth and eighteenth centuries.

The Medieval Tournament

In the Middle Ages (c. 1000-1400 A.D.), sporting activities shed the religious significance they had in ancient Greece and eventually became a playful imitation of that bygone age. With perhaps the aim of relieving boredom, they took an aesthetic and recreational turn. Yet sports retained their association with nobility, because the demonstration of one's aristocratic status seems to have become their main purpose. To serve that end, lower classes were prevented from competing against their superiors and sports were changed in such a way that success depended more upon wealth and status than training and talent. In the main, taking sports and games too seriously was considered to be beneath a true gentleman.

Sport's turn away from war in the Middle Ages also meant that distinctions of class trumped distinctions of sex. Women of high rank were engaged in many of the activities in which men were engaged: board games, hawking, storytelling, conversation, singing, and dancing. Women were even involved, at least as the objects of motivation, in the twelfth-century martial and chivalric social festivals.

Competitive events at social festivals were exceptions to the frivolity of sporting activities and game-playing. They were taken seriously. Here men of noble birth engaged in competitive jousting and melees, not only to demonstrate their prowess and physical skills, but also to contend for social honor and for the attention and reward of a suitable woman of character.

Jousting consisted of two knights that charged each other with lances on horseback in an effort to unseat the other. In the late medieval period, a points-system came into being. Whereas unseating an opponent made one an unqualified champion, a sharp blow to the breast was worth one point, while a "clean" blow to the head, which sometimes decapitated an opponent, was worth two points.[1] Thus, jousting was a brutal test of aristocratic mettle and character that had a highly desirable, though merely domestic, prize as incentive. Winning a joust or even displaying the proper nobility in defeat could earn a knight a beautiful lady for life.

A melee was an even more violent form of contest. Two sides of combatants on horseback would wield dull-edged swords at each other in mock battle. Though the battle was mock, contestants often had individual scores to settle and swords were sometimes intentionally sharpened to settle them. A tournament in 1249 A.D. near Cologne, for instance, found 60 knights dead or moribund.[2]

While the earliest medieval tournaments were extremely dangerous contests that often did not differ much from actual war, later contests became more rule-governed and much less dangerous. Competition turned to spectacle as the "frequently deadly mock battles became theatrical performances full of allegorical pageantry" that were as much theatrical tests of suitability for romance as mock tests of fighting ability. Knights would ride into battle with their lady's scarf tied to the tip of their lance and do their best to put on a show of courage and valor before her eyes. Tournament sites accordingly became fantastic and colorful marvels to behold.[3]

In short, contest in the Middle Ages was based on honor, not agonism. Honor was worth fighting for, as it had been in Achilles' day, but honor was gained by affecting the appearance of nobility, through the eyes of a worthy lady, in the face of mock danger. This is evident in the chivalric literature that survives today.

Competition and the battle scars that ensued were signs of great chivalric devotion and nobility—especially for tournament victors. Those victorious were celebrities, but earned no respect for past successes. Those beaten in a battle were shamed. The truly heroic knight preferred death to disgrace.[4]

The mock nature of medieval contests is evidence of boredom and tedium in the Middle Ages during times without war. Contest, thus, probably functioned as a substitute for the excitement of war. Richard Kaepur writes, "Fighting for peace is acceptable to these professional warriors only so long as there is no real danger of a surfeit of peace; they could scarcely cheer any smothering of chances for displays of prowess that so well repay their hard efforts in the bright coinage of honour."[5] Tournaments became the renowned social and sportive events of the time.

More than just a means of overcoming boredom through staged spectacle, chivalric fighting was an indissoluble part of medieval culture. Kaepur says:

> We must recognize how strongly chivalric literature acknowledges the impulse to settle any issue—especially any perceived affront to honour—by couching the lance for the charge or swiftly drawing the sword from the scabbard. Force is regularly presented as the means of getting whatever is wanted, of settling whatever is at issue. Accusations of a more or less judicial nature, of course, lead to a fight, as does assertion of better lineage. But so does assertion that one's lady is fairer than another knight's lady, a request for a knight's name or even an answer to the question, 'Why are you so sad?' Of course, as often as not the fight is over no stated question at all, but simply seems a part of the natural order of the imagined world of chivalry: two knights meet in the forest, they fight.[6]

One has only to consider Cervantes' brilliant lampoon of medieval culture in *Don Quixote*.

Though honor was less matter of a desert through genuine, non-staged tests of character and more a matter of social construction, one's worthiness to contest through chivalric fighting was perceived to be part of the very fabric of nature, rigorously purified of lower-class taint. Knights, marrying below their station, were barred from competition. Those who tried to enter were beaten. Peasants were unconditionally barred. Those who tried to enter were killed.[7]

In summary, the jousts and melees of the Middle Ages betray a culture of honor in which those events, as competitive sports, had a key role. The motivation to compete, however, was not aretic and internal; the rewards of contest, social standing and female companionship, were completely external.

A Renaissance Courtier

The Renaissance was a period of cultural and intellectual rebirth in European society that drew inspiration from the pre-Christian paganism of Greco-Roman culture and the medieval notion of chivalry. Johan Huizinga characterizes the Renaissance culture as a playful, aesthetic game. "If ever an elite, fully conscious of its own merits, sought to segregate itself from the vulgar herd and live life as a game of artistic perfection, that elite was the circle of choice Renaissance spirits."[8] Aristocratic in essence, the movement was also philosophical and had important implications for the Renaissance notion of sportive practice.

Renaissance humanists gave sport a philosophical foundation. They supplanted the Christian abhorrence of the body with early Greek holism—the notion of a balanced, virtuous soul within a healthy body. Having a vigorous, fit, and well-proportioned body became an ideal to be cultivated principally through sports. Thus, sport became a meaningful pastime for cultured aristocrats. Humanists, like Richard Mulcaster in the late 16th century, even pushed for physical education at schools.[9]

Perhaps the best depiction of the Renaissance attitude toward sports and Renaissance values among the well-off is Baldesar Castiglione's *The Courtier*. *The Courtier*, published in 1528, has been called by one scholar "the most representative book of the Renaissance."[10] The work is a justification of the courtier's profession as dutiful companion to a sovereign at court. In it, the Renaissance ideal of dignified elegance, which had its roots in medieval chivalry, merges with an exaggerated sensitivity to appearance.

The true courtier is a man of letters, a devoted servant, a champion of propriety, an elegant aristocrat, and a man of "virtue," but also a warrior, in times of crisis. Always ostentatious, he attends with great care to his appearance—his manner of speech, dress, and even gesticulation—for they are great social measures of his character. He cultivates his noble profile by engaging only in enterprises, including sport, which display his talents and hide his faults. Thus, his attitude toward sports is characteristic of the upper-class Renaissance attitude toward life in general: an aesthetic imitation of ancient ideals.

Castiglione adds that a courtier, during peacetime, ought to know how to manage himself properly in sports that involve weapons. In such sports, he should surpass others in everything, or at least appear to do so. He should be a superior horseman and have an adequate knowledge of horsemanship.

In tourneys, in holding his ground, in forcing his way forward, he should compare with the best of the French; in volleying, in running bulls, in casting
spears and darts, he should be outstanding among Spaniards. But, above all, he
should accompany his every act with a certain grace and fine judgment if he
wishes to earn that universal regard which everyone covets.[11]

Concerning other sports that do not require weapons but do exact much toil,
Castiglione states that hunting is foremost because "in many ways it resembles
warfare." Other important sports whose skills are transferable to war include
swimming, jumping, running, and casting the stone. Additionally, facility with
such sports can build one's reputation—especially at the court. Tennis and
horseback riding are also practicable and worthwhile sports because they display
quickness, agility, and gracefulness.[12]

Sports for the Renaissance courtier, overall, were less a measure of fitness
for battle and more a means of highlighting refined abilities that presumably a
courtier possessed and a commoner lacked.

Since a courtier's reputation was almost exclusively a matter of ostentation,
showing oneself well took diligence and uncommon preparation. Before taking
part in public contests, Castiglione warns, the courtier first must "be so well
equipped as to horses, weapons and dress that nothing is lacking." The slightest
misgiving is grounds for not competing—something anathema to the ancient
Greeks—for there is no excusing a poor performance. Next, he must have a clear
notion of his companions and the audience, since "it would be wholly unbecom-
ing to honor peasants with gentlemanly display."[13]

The ideal is for a courtier to maintain the appearance of elegance, dignity,
nobility and, before all, a definite superiority before commoners. Consequently,
the advantages to be gained by competing with the lower classes are few, while
the disadvantages are many. Castiglione continues:

But if anyone is anxious to wrestle, to run or to jump with peasants, then he
ought, in my opinion, to do it casually, out of *noblesse obligé*, so to say, and
certainly not in competition with them; and he should be almost certain of winning, or else not take part at all, for it is too sad and shocking, and quite undignified, when a gentleman is seen to be beaten by a peasant, especially in wrestling-match. Hence I think it would be as well to abstain, at least when there are
many onlookers, because the advantage in winning is very negligible and the
disadvantages in being beaten very serious.

Castiglione adds that when competing, even if the courtier's performance is outstanding, he should never let others think he has spent much time on practice.[14]
Athletic virtue should appear to be effortless; a matter of natural talent rather
than serious preparation.

The Renaissance attitude, illustrated by Castiglione, represents a distinct shift from concern about excellence to concern about its appearance. Athletic competition becomes a form of aristocratic propaganda rather than an attempt to test and disclose true *aretē*.

Sport in the 17th and 18th Centuries

In 1801, Joseph Strutt wrote *The Sports and Pasttimes of the People of England, Including the Rural and Domestic Recreations, May-Games, Mummeries, Pageants, Processions, and Pompous Spectacles, From the Earliest Period to the Present Time.* This work describes exercises by persons of social rank, generally practiced rural exercises, generally practiced urban exercises, and pastimes appropriate for the seasons—all of which were associated with fairs, wakes, and holidays. For commoners, life was hard, workdays were long, and the opportunities for leisure were few, so their sporting activities reflected their lives. Sporting activities were hard, serious, and often very violent. In contrast, the sporting activities of nobility generally emphasized detachment and frivolity.

In Britain and across Europe in the seventeenth and eighteenth centuries, nobility distanced themselves from laborers by the kinds of games they played and observed. For instance, aristocratic males in Britain hunted, attended cockfights, watched horseracing, and involved themselves in forms of leisured competitive activities in which poor, working people could not participate. Cricket, which emerged in the 1700s, is an illustration. In contrast, the lower classes played various ball games—e.g., knappan, camp ball, hurling, and folk football—many of which were violently contested.[15]

For folk football, an early form of rugby, inflated animals' bladders were used as balls and various natural objects served as boundaries and goals. The game was brutal and bloody. Documented evidence of the violence that attended upon folk football comes as early as the 13th century. Writes Phillip Stubbs in *Anatomy of Abuses* in 1583:

> I protest unto you that it may rather be called a frendly kind of fyghte than a play or recreation <a bloody and muthering practice> than a fellowly sport or pastime. For dooth not everyone lye in waight for his adersarie, seeking to overthrowe him and picke him on his nose, though it be uppon hard stones? In ditch or dale, in valley or hill, or whatever place it be he careth not so he have him down. And he that can serve the most of this fashion, he is counted the only fellow, and who but he?[16]

By 1314, the game was banned by Edward II. Numerous edicts and bans would follow throughout the centuries.

In general, the British attitude toward sport differed from that of Europe. Violence was an accepted part of upper-class competitions. After Oliver Cromwell's Puritanical purge and a period of demise, with the return of Charles II, sport and athletic pastimes reemerged in the latter half of the seventeenth century. The gentry indulged in tame field sports, like the hunting of foxes and cricket, but there was also great fondness of races, and the violent sport of pugilism. While the mostly Methodist middle class in general refrained from sports, the lower classes indulged in them with the same avidity as the higher classes. Overall, the British welcomed the exertion of physical contests with opened arms.

In contrast, by the late eighteenth century across much of Europe, games that involved great physical exertion were on the wane in favor of more leisurely and casual sports like fencing and tennis,[17] which were extremely popular in Italy and France.

With the French and American revolutions, there began a democratization and return to seriousness in sport that continues to the present day. There was a leveling down of classes and a rejection of frivolity. "Liberté, Fraternité Égalité!"—the anthem behind the egalitarianism of the revolutions—did not include women however. Though women were importantly involved in the egalitarian movement, they were entitled to few of its benefits, including the open opportunity to play competitive sports. The 1793 National Convention outlawed women's clubs because political involvement by females was said to lead to hysteria and commotion.[18] Mary Wollstonecraft, living in Paris during much of the revolution, saw the gross injustice of the "egalitarian" movement and responded brilliantly with her *A Vindication of the Rights of Women* in 1792.

In England, no sport characterized male toughness like boxing. Pugilists were symbols of all that was characteristically British and they won the patronage, if not the partnership, of wealthy noblemen. Pugilists were down-to-earth, tough, courageous, meat-eating, and ale-drinking combatants, who were capable of enduring whatever punishment or pain might come their way. In the mid-eighteenth century, pugilist John Broughton, under the auspices of the Duke of Cumberland, became the recognized champion of England and the national symbol of English masculinity and power. Early in the century, women too took to fighting. The *London Times* reported on such matches. Overall, the British love of pugilism was evident in the remarks of Pierce Egan, historian of British pugilism, who said that the British greatly exceed both Greeks and Romans in courage and manliness—i.e., *aretē*—on account of their fighters.[19]

The pageantry of medieval chivalric events found a parallel in titillating and often comical smock racing. This time, women were displaying their "skills," as it were. Young women, breasts uncovered and dressed only in smocks, raced in front of scores of enthusiastic spectators. Winning a smock often meant winning a husband. A correspondent for *The Spectator* wrote, "[N]othing is more usual than for a nimble-footed Wench to get a Husband at the same time she wins a Smock."[20]

Overall, the seventeenth and eighteenth centuries saw the emergence of leisured sportive activities for members of British and European aristocracy. The gentry enjoyed these sports especially because of their casual nature and because such leisured activities distanced them from commoners. Many of sports activities—e.g., pugilism, hunting, and folk football—were still quite brutal and had many affinities to activities related to war.

In all, the resurgence of competitive sport in the seventeenth and eighteenth centuries as serious play, due partly to the egalitarian movement, never reached the heights it would reach in the 19th century. Historian Allen Guttman sums:

> Neither in England nor on the Continent did early modern sports play the leading role allotted to them in antiquity. For the sports of London (and Paris and Berlin) to become as culturally central as the sports of the ancient *polis*, it was necessary to move into the industrial age.[21]

It is to the industrial age that we now turn.

Notes

1. William Baker, *Sports in the Western World* (Totowa, NJ: Rowman & Littlefield, 1982), 50.

2. Baker, *Sports in the Western World,* 50-52.

3. Allen Guttman, *The Erotic in Sports* (New York: Columbia University Press, 1996), 39-40.

4. Richard W. Kaeuper, *Chivalry and Violence in Medieval Europe* (New York: Oxford University Press, 1999), 150-154.

5. Kaeuper, *Chivalry and Violence,* 164-167.

6. Kaeuper, *Chivalry and Violence,* 159-160.

7. Guttmann, *From Ritual to Record,* 30.

8. Johan Huizinga, *Homo Ludens: A Study of the Play Element in Culture* (Boston: Beacon Press, 1955), 180.

9. Baker, *Sports in the Western World,* 61.

10. George Bull, "Introduction," *The Book of the Courtier* (New York: Penguin Books, 1976), 12.

11. Baldesar Castiglione, *The Book of the Courtier* (New York: Penguin Books, 1976), 62-63.

12. Castiglione, *The Book of the Courtier,* 63.

13. Castiglione, *The Book of the Courtier,* 117.

14. Castiglione, *The Book of the Courtier,* 117-118.

15. Philip G. White and Anne B. Vagi, "Rugby in the 19th-Century British Boarding-School System: A Feminist Psychoanalytic Perspective," *Sport, Men, and the Gender*

Order: Critical Feminist Perspectives. Eds. Messner and Sabo (Champaign, IL: Human Kinetics Books, 1990), 70.

16 .P. Marsh, K. Fox, G. Carnibella, J. McCann, and J. Marsh, *Football Violence in Europe*. The Amsterdam Group, 1996, 19.

17. Guttman, *The Erotic in Sports*, 50.

18. Roberta J. Park, "From 'Genteel Diversions' to 'Bruising Peg': Active Pastimes, Exercise, and Sports for Females in Late 17th- and 18th-Century Europe," *Women and Sport: Interdisciplinary Perspectives,* eds. D. Margaret Costa and Sharon R. Guthrie (Champaign, IL: Human Kinetics, 1994), 30.

19. Guttman, *The Erotic in Sports*, 51-53.

20. Guttman, *The Erotic in Sports*, 54.

21. Guttman, *The Erotic in Sports*, 55.

Chapter 3
Compensatory Athleticism

"In the 19th century sport became an industrialized and socialized spectacle in both Britain and America, regulated according to the clock and formidable sets of rules. . . . [S]port was like a mirror held up to a capitalist and industrialized society. Sport became a form of work—tightly controlled, organized according to a division of labour, and relying on corporate endeavour." Roger Horrocks

THE NINETEENTH CENTURY WAS A TIME of tremendous social, economic, and political changes. Sport was transformed accordingly. It turned away from the frivolity and emphasis on appearance, characteristic of the Middle Ages and the Renaissance, and took on a distinctively serious and masculine aura. By the19th century, there were efforts to demonstrate and cultivate manliness through a more serious, better organized, and more industrious approach than existed in the two centuries prior. Sport was, Roger Horrocks sums, "transformed from 'play' to 'work.'"[1]

The 19th Century Socio-Political Climate

By the nineteenth century, geographical expansionism in America reached its limits, cities grew rapidly, and the need for urban resources increased as the number independent farmers and businessmen increased. Autonomous subsistence farming was becoming increasingly impracticable, so alternative means of making a living became necessary. Families were urbanized and the role of women changed. While retaining their domestic role, women also became laborers, religious leaders, political advocates, and even merchants. Overall, male authority decreased.[2]

The results of industrialization both reinvigorated and emasculated men. Among the lower classes, women entered factories and were shown to be quite capable of doing many of the tasks that previously only men had done. Consequently, industrialized work came to be seen as effeminate. In the middle classes, though men dominated politically and economically, women were gaining a social presence hitherto thought unattainable. Thus, empowerment of women led to an unspoken sense of male emasculation. Allen Guttman writes:

> Neither the practice of a profession nor the routines of an office provided many opportunities for the demonstration of courage or the display of brute strength. Middle-class men seem haunted by an unspoken question: "A man in any culture is supposed to be strong, tough, adept and courageous; clearly that was true of primitive hunters and warriors, but is it true of us?"[3]

As history usually shows, social advancement comes at a price. As women gained in power and importance in the first part of the nineteenth century in nondomestic areas of influence, men reacted in the latter half of this century in ways that attempted to demonstrate scientifically the physical and even moral inferiority of women. The Victorian era (1837-1901) and the era of modern sport were taking shape in tandem.

The newfound freedom of women in the early nineteenth century was soon quashed. Increasingly, men objected to the presence of women in sports, and a variety of other areas. They sought and gained restrictions to female social and political mobility. Much of this was politically motivated through sham research and spurious scientific "discoveries" concerning the inferiority of women. Evolutionary science and Malthusian economics were cited as "proof" of this. Declared sexually inferior by the science of the day, women were judged socially incapable. After all, the argument was put forth, women needed to conserve their energy for child-bearing purposes.

One prominent example of the gross injustice to women exists in the early psychoanalytical literature—especially that of Freud. Early study of neurosis was often limited to hysterical women, for neurosis was believed to be a disorder affecting only women. Freud's own studies greatly expanded our understanding of human sexuality, but labored under the presumption of female sexual (and moral) inferiority as a fact to be explained scientifically.

Freud's model, still taken seriously in much of the psycho-sociological literature today, states that female inferiority is a consequence of a lag in psycho-sexual development. The sexual crisis of a boy's life comes to a neat close in normal male development. The boy's lust for his mother is directly addressed by the parents, usually the father, through the threat of castration. The boy takes the threat seriously (after all, women have no penis, so *they* must have been castrated), renounces his mother as the object of his affection, represses his feelings, identifies with his father (his former rival), takes on his father's morality (develops a super-ego or conscience), and thus successfully concludes the most harrowing stage of his life. In contrast, there can be no such closure for a female. Simply said, though she comes to lust after her father, she lacks a penis and so there can be no comparable threat of castration to end the lusting. In consequence, her affection for her father is never wholly renounced and repressed, and her crisis never comes to a close. Without repression, she has no fully developed super-ego and is thus morally inferior.[4]

Moreover, nineteenth-century judicial politics bolstered the "findings" of science. Laws promoted male dominance by reinforcing the natural limits of female social and political influence. In short, the rapid advances made by women in the early part of the century were even more quickly smothered by new scientific "discoveries" of male supremacy and female inferiority.

How all of this impacted early modern sport is a matter of serious scholarly debate. Sociologist Todd Crosset has argued that the nineteenth-century concept of "manliness" was the catalyst for the development of early modern sport. He states, "The same economic and social changes that helped to legitimize male bourgeois power increased the power of women, especially bourgeois women,"[5] Females were excluded at the same time that sports became standardized and formalized. Associations—like England's Soccer Association (1863), the Amateur Athletic Association (1880), and the International Olympic Committee (1894)—were formed. Sports became a place to express the masculinity lauded by the science of the industrial revolution. Unable to affirm their manhood in the workplace, men fell back on a type of "compensatory athleticism, where "man-the-breadwinner" could transform into "man-the-hero."[6]

In 1896, Pierre de Coubertin revived the ancient Olympic Games as a reaction to the wars in Europe of the late nineteenth century and the lost sense of manliness they seemed to reveal. The new Olympics were patterned after games played by middle- and upper-class males at public schools, universities, and private clubs. Sports, by instilling in boys values that were deemed necessary for later life, were seen as a means of indoctrinating young males in the ways of manhood. Boys would acquire aretic character traits like courage, ingenuity, friendships, leadership abilities, and endurance through contests like rugby, cricket, fisticuffs, and running. Football, lacrosse, hockey, track and field, and boxing were called "manly sports,"[7] Coubertin, working to exclude females from the Olympics, said: "It is indecent that the spectators should be exposed to the risk of seeing the body of a woman being smashed before their very eyes. Besides, no matter how toughened a sportswoman may be, her organism is not cut out to sustain certain risks."[8]

Nevertheless, women did gain some element of liberty in Victorian society. Jennifer Hargreaves explains:

> The physical education of women gained considerable ground by widening the definition of how they could legitimately use their bodies, but although the freedom gained had some reality in relation to what went on before, it was a very limited version of being free and natural. Women's freedom to move rested upon the assumption about the different, innate characteristics and needs of men and women.[9]

In all, though females were allowed some measure of competitive expression, female athletes were prisoners of the times: "the freer the activity in terms of bodily and spatial mobility, the more powerful was the opposition, always based on moral and biological criteria,"[10] In the nineteenth century, as women made advances in social presence, sport became the province of males.

The Cradle of Modern Sport

With the social and political changes in the burgeoning capitalism of Britain and the United States, the ideals and values of sportive practice progressively became "industrialized"—i.e., they became more serious, more formalized, and more directly linked to manliness than they had been in the past few centuries. Roger Horrocks writes:

> In the nineteenth century sport became an industrialized and socialized spectacle in both Britain and America, regulated according to the clock and formidable sets of rules. Furthermore, rules were administered by a referee or umpire, acting as the interpreter of law and the dispenser of punishment. . . . [S]port was like a mirror held up to a capitalist and industrialized society. Sport became a form of work—tightly controlled, organized according to a division of labour, and relying on corporate endeavour. . . . [S]port is transformed from 'play' to 'work.'[11]

In Britain by the nineteenth century, sport was deemed an educative tool specifically designed to cultivated those manly qualities that stayed and served the British Empire. Teachers encouraged athleticism because it built men out of boys. R.W. Lewis says:

> Such qualities of manliness and leadership [gained through sport] would help pupils throughout their later lives. This became linked to the other main ideological thread running through the public schools, that of service to the Empire. Team games prepared boys to be men who would serve the imperial community and shoulder the 'white man's burden' with honour. Manliness on the football field could be used to advantage on the battlefield or in dealing with large numbers of unruly natives.[12]

In many colleges and public schools, sport became more important than academic achievement. Reverend J.E.C. Welldon, headmaster of Harrow School from 1881 to 1895, wrote:

> When the athletic games of English Youth are considered in their reference not to physical energy but to moral worth, it would seem that they possess an even higher value than intellectual studies. For learning, however excellent in itself,

does not afford such necessary virtues as promptitude, resource, honour, coop-eration and unselfishness; but these are the soul of English games.[13]

Thus, it was not just play, but English institutionalized play or "Muscular Chris-tianity," which nurtured and advanced "moral worth" and the attributes appropri-ate for English gentlemen.

Industrialized sport fit in well with contemporary social theories: Herbert Spencer's "Social Darwinism, which emphasized competition for limited re-sources and laissez-faire capitalism; John Stuart Mill's libertarianism, which promulgated the relatively free expression of impulses' Francis Galton's views on eugenics; and August Comte's theory of progressive social evolution. Sport would play a major role in cultivating male superiority and the sort of aggressive displays that characterize modern sport. The science and philosophy of the time also paved the road to the sexual, cultural, and racial biases and injustices that still exist today in attenuated form.

Rugby took root at Rugby School in England and then spread to other schools in the 1840s and 1850s. In no time, Oxford and Cambridge embraced the game, which had social significance at several levels. First, it was presumed to allow some outlet for pent-up aggression that was a product of sedentary living. Next, it preserved the traditional conception of masculinity, suppressed in urban-ized society. In addition, it represented some type of rebelliousness to the strict policies of the public schools. Last, it became an exclusive male preserve in a social setting where women were becoming a greater part of the social fabric.[14]

Other games that were enjoyed were soccer, boxing, swimming, rowing, and cricket. Each of these was said to cultivate British manliness. It is certainly not accidental that the emphasis on manliness and male virtues was concurrent with the sublimation and repression of sexual impulse in Victorian society. Male character could only be firmly established independent of the taint of women.

At the same time, Victorian principles pushed women to be lady-like in so-ciety and kept them in the home. Women were thought to be soft, delicate crea-tures whose dainty constitutions made them susceptible to malady and infirmity on a regular basis. Clothes were thereby designed to constrain women's move-ments.

Middle-class women fulfilled their own stereotype of the 'delicate female' who took to her bed with consistent regularity and thus provided confirmation of the dominant medical account that this should be so. Women 'were' manifestly physically and biologically inferior because they actually 'did' swoon, 'were' unable to eat, suffered continual maladies, and consistently expressed passivity and submissiveness in various forms. The acceptance by women of their own incapacitation gave both a humane and moral weighting to the established sci-entific so-called 'facts.'[15]

Appropriate exercises for such delicate constitutions were limited to remedial
gymnastics, massage, and other gentle movements.

The situation was similar in the United States. Theodore Roosevelt championed healthy reform in the United States and called out for civic duty. In "The
Strenuous Life, he says:

> In the last analysis a healthy state can exist only when the men and women who
> make it up lead clean, vigorous, healthy lives; when the children are so trained
> that they shall endeavor, not to shirk difficulties, but to overcome them; not to
> seek ease, but to know how to wrest triumph from toil and risk. The man must
> be glad to do a man's work, to dare and endure and to labor; to keep himself,
> and to keep those dependent upon him. The woman must be the housewife, the
> helpmeet of the homemaker, the wise and fearless mother of healthy children.[16]

Sport, in turn, reinforced these nineteenth-century biases and attempted to
revitalize masculinity and the fractured male identity. By the late nineteenth century, Americans, especially men, were turning fanatically to exercise, health, and
sports. Sports enabled men to cultivate masculinity and to retreat from feminini-
ty.[17] The Boy Scouts, for instance, was founded upon this platform and so was
the YMCA.

In America, baseball was the game that bonded male to male and initiated a
young boy's passage into manhood. Albert Spalding enumerated the following
virtues of the sport in his *America's National Game*: "American Courage, Confidence, Combativeness; American Dash, Discipline, Determination; American
Energy, Eagerness, Enthusiasm; American Pluck, Persistence, Performance;
American Spirit, Sagacity, Success; American Vim, Vigor, Virility,"[18] Baseball
demanded deference to authority and team, while it encouraged individualism
within those parameters. It demanded self-control, while it invigorated the male
body and put a young man's limited energy to use in a sexually efficient fashion.
It was no accident that baseball fell into this role; it was deliberately crafted to
restore virility and vitality in an emasculated nation and to conserve gender, racial, and class hierarchies in a society in which such hierarchies were gradually
eroding.[19]

It is perhaps safe to say that the seriousness, showmanship, hyper-agonism,
and brutishness that often characterizes modern sport is in some measure a consequence of and reaction to the social sense of male emasculation that has its
roots in the nineteenth century. Sport was transformed from play into work and
appropriated as a tool to cultivate and demonstrate the ideal of masculinity erod-
ed by the industrial revolution. It would not be long before sport took another
step toward seriousness and moved from the domestic politics of class and gender to the global politics of nationalism and diplomacy.

Notes

1. Roger Horrocks, *Masculinity in Crisis: Myths, Fantasies and Realities* (New York: St. Martin's Press, 1995), 147.

2. Michael S. Kimmel, "Baseball and the Reconstruction of American Masculinity, 1880-1920." *Sport, Men, and the Gender Order: Critical Feminist Perspectives*, eds. Messner and Sabo (Champaign, IL: Human Kinetics Books, 1990), 57.

3. Allen Guttman, *The Erotic in Sports* (New York: Columbia University Press, 1996), 59.

4. Since women were chiefly responsible for the moral development of children, some early feminists have argued that women were morally superior to men. Thus, women deserved the right to vote in that they were best suited to clean up political corruption. See Kathryn Pyne Addelson, "Equality and Competition: Can Sports Make a Woman of a Girl?" *Women, Philosophy, and Sport: A Collection of New Essays*, ed. Betsy Postow, (Metuchen, NJ: The Scarecrow Press, Inc., 1983), 137.

5. Todd Crosset, "Masculinity, Sexuality, and the Development of Early Modern Sport," *Sport, Men, and the Gender Order: Critical Feminist Perspectives*, eds. Messner and Sabo (Champaign, IL: Human Kinetics Books, 1990), 49.

6. Guttman, *The Erotic in Sports*, 61-62.

7. Bruce Kidd, "The Men's Cultural Centre: Sports and the Dynamic of Women's Oppression/Men's Repression," *Sport, Men, and the Gender Order: Critical Feminist Perspectives*, eds. Messner and Sabo (Champaign, IL: Human Kinetics Books, 1990), 34-35.

8. http://www.womenwarriors.ca/en/history/event.asp?id=113. At this revival of the ancient games, a woman named Melpomene is barred from the official marathon event, but runs it unofficially and completes a time of four hours and 30 minutes.

9. Jennifer Hargreaves, "The Victorian Cult of the Family and the Early Years of Female Sport," *The Sports Process: A Comparative and Developmental Approach*, eds. Eric Dunning et al. (Indianapolis: Human Kinetics Publishers, 1993), 78.

10. Hargreaves, "The Victorian Cult," 80.

11. Horrocks, *Masculinity in Crisis*, 147.

12. R.W. Lewis, "'Touched Pitch and Been Shockingly Defiled': Football, Class, Social Darwinism and Decadence in England, 1880-1914." *Sport in Europe: Politics, Class, Gender*, ed. J.A. Mangan (London: Frank Cass, 1999), 118.

13. Horrocks, *Masculinity in Crisis*, 149.

14. Philip G. White and Anne B. Vagi, "Rugby in the 19th-Century British Boarding-School System: A Feminist Psychoanalytic Perspective," *Sport, Men, and the Gender Order: Critical Feminist Perspectives*, eds. Messner and Sabo (Champaign, IL: Human Kinetics Books, 1990), 70-71.

15. Hargreaves, "The Victorian Cult," 74.

16. Theodore Roosevelt, *The Strenuous Life: Essays and Addresses* (New York: The Century Co., 1901), 3-4.

17. Kimmel, "Baseball and American Masculinity," 59-60.

18. Albert G. Spalding, America's National Game, (New York: American Sports Publishing Co., 1911), 4.

19. Kimmel, "Baseball and American Masculinity," 62-65.

Chapter 4
Sport Propagandized

"Today sport is the one international culture which is developing in accordance with a Communist model...the ethos of the sport mobilization initiated by Stalin in the mid-1930s has become a global standard." John Hoberman

𝕿HE BATTLEFIELD OF SOCIAL DIFFERENCE shifted decidedly in the first part of the twentieth century. From class and gender, the focus shifted to international issues of race and, ultimately, nationalism. Political leaders recognized the value of competitive sport as a vehicle for promoting political ideals—what might be called political panagonism. Consequently, sport was exploited for political purposes and athletes, as political guinea pigs, were subjected to rigorous and severe training programs in an effort to serve political ideals. Excellence in competitive sport was valued only insofar as it could be used to showcase political excellence.

The Olympic Games of 1936

The Berlin Olympic Games of 1936 were a startling and extreme example of the exploitative panagonism that was developing in modern competitive sport. They were a camouflage for Nazi racism, nationalism, and militarism. For Hitler, it was the "game" within the Games that mattered most.

Being awarded the Olympic Games by the International Olympic Committee[1] was a sign of Germany's reemergence in the affairs of the global community. After having been appointed chancellor in 1936, Hitler immediately began a purge of the German nation that excluded Jews, Gypsies, and Blacks from communal affairs. In general, German nationalism was fueled by Hitler's anti-Semitism and the notion of Aryan purity that was cultivated in the minds of German youths. Dissent was not tolerated and opposition was met with confinement in prison camps like the one at Dachau.

Competitive sport was promoted as a means of reinforcing Hitler's political policies and demonstrating Aryan superiority. To facilitate those ends, he appointed Joseph Goebbels as Minister of Propaganda. According to Goebbels, "German sport has only one task: to strengthen the character of the German people, imbuing it with the fight spirit and steadfast camaraderie necessary in the struggle for its existence."[2] The German people were imagined to be the fittest of all peoples for both intellect pursuits and, of course, conquest.[3] Competitive sport for Hitler became a vehicle for demonstrating that fitness. By 1933, an Aryans-only policy was instituted for all German athletic organizations. "Every German athlete should voluntarily participate in strengthening the military might of the German people," said Reich Sports Office Director Hans von Tschammer und Osten. The ancient athletic practice of excluding those presumed unworthy was rearing its head again.

German duplicity, on account of Germany's professing to be a proper host for the Olympic Games of 1936, did not go unnoticed by the rest of the world. These Olympics became a political battlefield and many countries threatened a boycott of them. Ernest Lee Jahncke, an American member of the IOC, openly opposed the United States' participation. In a letter to Count Henri Baillet-Latour, the president of the IOC, he wrote: "Neither Americans nor the representatives of other countries can take part in the Games in Nazi Germany without at least acquiescing in the contempt of the Nazis for fair play and their sordid exploitation of the Games." Jahncke's public stand led to his expulsion from the games.[4] Participation by the United States was eventually decided by a vote of the Amateur Athletic Union by a mere two-and-one-half margin. President Franklin Roosevelt, despite the propaganda, remained politically neutral.

The *Volkischer Beobachter,* the main Nazi newspaper, said this about the possible participation of blacks at the upcoming Olympic Games: "Negroes have no place at an Olympiad.... This is an unparalleled disgrace and degradation, and the ancient Greeks would turn in their graves.... The next Olympic Games will take place in 1936 in Berlin. Hopefully, the men who are responsible ... will know what their duty is. The blacks must be excluded. We expect nothing less."[5]

The Winter Olympics were held from February 6 to 16, while German forces were moving into the demilitarized Rhineland outside of France and a large concentration camp was being constructed 18 miles north of Berlin. To mask the duplicity, Hitler ordered the temporary removal of Berlin's anti-Semitic posters and he minimized the German military presence at the games.

The Summer Olympics began on August 1. American Jesse Owens captured four gold medals and was the hero of the games. Nine other black athletes won medals. Hitler was, most acknowledged, furious at the success of black American athletes. At the end of the summer games, protocol dictated that Hitler should shake the hands of all medal winners. Presumably dreading to congratulate anyone who was non-Aryan, he chose to shake no hands at all. Baldur von

Schirach, quoting Hitler, described the latter's reaction to Black American victories thus: "The Americans ought to be ashamed of themselves for letting their medals be won by Negroes. I myself would never even shake hands with one of them."[6] Wrote Goebbels about the victories of the black Americans, in *Der Angriff* (*The Attack*): "If the American team had not brought along Black auxiliaries ... one would have regarded the Yankees as the biggest disappointment of the Games."[7]

The games went on with few glitches and German deceit, for the most part, was overshadowed by the success and glamour of the games. Still Nazi propaganda did not escape the notice of many who attended the games. Wrote one journalist, William Shirer, on August 16 of 1936 in his diary:

> I'm afraid the Nazis have succeeded with their propaganda. First, the Nazis have run the Games on a lavish scale never before experienced, and this has appealed to the athletes. Second, the Nazis have put up a very good front for the general visitors, especially the big businessmen.

Enthralled by the political success of the games of 1936, Hitler made plans with architect Albert Speers to construct a stadium, to be completed in 1945 and fit for 400,000 spectators, in anticipation of future Olympic contests. Hitler said, "In 1940 the Olympic Games will take place in Tokyo. But thereafter they will take place in Germany for all time to come, in this stadium."[8]

The Stalinist Touch

Two other extreme examples of political panagonism are mid-twentieth-century Soviet Russia and its communist ally, East Germany.

Joseph Stalin was dictator of communist Russia from 1924 to 1953. His dictatorship was cruel and severe and many who opposed him were summarily executed.

Participation in two world wars devastated Russia, which lost nearly one-sixth of its population in World War II alone, and posed a serious threat to Soviet political and social principles during Stalin's dictatorship. Communism as a way of life was at stake and sport was deemed to be an ideal way to showcase communist political and military superiority. Therefore, after World War II, Stalin decided to use sports to propagandize communism and achieve, as it were, legitimacy in eyes of the rest of the progressive world. The Soviets, who had not participated in the Olympic Games since 1912, began to train athletes seriously for future Olympic Games. As N.N. Romanov, head of the Sport Committee in 1947, said, "Our goal is to unceasingly develop (*sic*) physical culture and sport.

It is a mass, popular movement with the goal of establishing the capacity of Soviet athletes to struggle for national and world records for the glory of our homeland."[9] Russia had resisted this move for decades, as it ran counter to the communist ideal of responsible comradeship.

> The responsibilities of good conscious Communists kept the Soviet Union out of the Olympics for many years. When the Bolsheviks came to power in 1917 the Olympics was not exactly their cup of tea. An aristocratic cliché dominated it. They clung to a nobles' and rich boy's notion of amateurs that excluded members of the working class because they did not have allowances or trust accounts large enough to let them train at leisure. No one was really expected to do work. The Bolshevik did not want anything to do with such anti-proletarian nonsense.[10]

Soviet involvement would prove to be a turning point in the modern Olympic Games. As John Hoberman writes, "By joining the [Olympic] movement, the Russians achieved, in a formal sense, a certain kind of moral parity with the rest of the world, since it assumed that a deep interest in sport presupposes wholesome instincts. . . . What is more, they seized the opportunity to turn the Olympic motto of *citius, altius, fortius* into an absolute performance principle which has, inevitably, become the reigning doctrine of world sport."[11] In the Helsinki Olympic Games of 1952, for instance, the Soviets finished second to the United States in the count of medals—76 U.S. medals to 69 Soviet medals—even though they had been away from Olympic competitions for decades.[12] Supported equally by the communist government, Soviet women fared especially well. Ukrainian Larissa Latyanina emerged in women's gymnastics as the dominant figure—a dominance that would last for over a decade—by winning six medals, four of which were gold.

Because of the propagandist value of Olympic competition for communism, the pressure on athletes to win was excessive. For some, the political stress was overwhelming. Olga Korbut, who followed Latyanina in gymnastics and won three gold medals in the 1972 Olympics, retired early due to the disgrace of losing to Romanian gymnast Nadia Comaneci in 1976 and the stress that involved. Others, like Igor Ter Ovanesyan, who broke American Ralph Boston's world record in the long jump and defeated Boston in New York in a face-to-face confrontation in 1963, seemed to thrive under the pressure.

In fact Soviet athletes thrived in a large number of sports, but, as the example of Ovanesyan illustrates, the Soviets took an especial liking to track-and-field events. States Robert Edelman, an expert on Soviet sports:

> The sport that best fit official ideals . . . was track and field. Track's rationalism contrasted with the potentially dangerous romanticism of soccer. The highly technical nature of track made it seem more consistent than soccer with the goals of a "scientific" version of socialism. The precise measurement of time,

distance, and height revealed success or failure just as production statistics had come to demonstrate the success or failure of "socialist construction." Track and field, a sport of specialists, could be seen as the sporting correlate of the newly empowered technical specialists who grew so swiftly in numbers during the late thirties.[13]

Perhaps the greatest Soviet success was showcased through a sporting event that was not in the Olympics and, more surprisingly, one that they did not win— the 1972 Summit Series between Team Canada and Team Russia in hockey. Team Canada was an overwhelming favorite to win the eight-game series, but was shocked when they lost to an explosive Russian team in the first game: 7-3. Canada came back to win the second game, 4-1, and tie the third game, 4-4, but Russia bounced back to win the fourth and fifth game, 5-3 and 5-4, respectively, to go up 3-1-1 after five games. Canada, now in a panic, would have to win each of the last three games to take the series. Miraculously, they did just this, but each game was decided by only one goal and the eighth and final game was won by Canada on a goal by Paul Henderson with only 34 seconds left in the game. Soviet Russia had shown the world's greatest hockey nation that they could take up the game and play it as well as the Canadians. Moreover, they demonstrated to the world a technical approach to the game that emphasized physical conditioning, finesse, and maneuverability instead of the physical force that characterized North-American hockey.

Another communist country to exemplify the anything-goes, panagonistic approach to sport was East Germany in the 1976 Olympic Games. East Germany's women's swim team had an overwhelmingly dominant performance in the pool at these Games. Literally coming from nowhere four years before, East German women won 10 of 11 individual events and 11 of 13 total events in swimming. Their use of performance-enhancing drugs at those games has now been well documented. There is testimony that over 1000 scientists, physicians, and trainers had been involved in experimenting with performance-enhancing drugs on athletes as young as 14 years of age. Often these athletes were not informed that the supplements they were given were steroids.[14] It is clear that East Germany's ambition overall was to keep pace with Soviet Russia and the United States in the medal count of the Olympics. The harmful effects of the drugs on their athletes, it seems, was a small price to pay for the medals, and political clout, "earned."

Overall, the hyper-serious Stalinist approach to competitive sport—through the former Soviet Union and the former Republic of East Germany—was essentially propagandist. It began and was sustained in an effort to showcase communist political and military superiority. According to former Soviet hockey star Anatoly Firsov, a Soviet ambassador to Sweden once remarked to the hockey players, "Guys, if you will win now, we will solve very large political issues."[15] The approach in today's Russia, as evidenced some years ago by Putin's outrage over Canadians Jamie Sale and David Pelletier being awarded a second set of gold medals in the pairs skating at the 2002 Olympics in Salt Lake City,[16] seems to be not much different. Athletic victory is a vehicle for showcasing political superiority.

Yet there is at least one critic who believes that the political panagonistic approach to competitive sport is not a local, but a global phenomenon. John Hoberman states, "Today sport is the one international culture which is developing in accordance with a Communist model.... In this sense, the ethos of the sport mobilization initiated by Stalin in the mid-1930s has become a global standard."[17]

The transformation of sport as a means of affirming boundaries of class, gender, and race to a means of propagandizing political ideals gave it a global and political significance it heretofore did not have. The gain in athletic performance was significant, but so too was the price. Exploitation of athletes for political purposes was also moral exploitation of athletes—treating athletes, in the words of the philosopher Kant, as means and not ends.

Notes

1. Before the Nazi party took power.

2. http://www.jewishvirtuallibrary.org/jsource/Holocaust/olympics.html.

3. Max Schmelling's victory of previously undefeated Joe Louis on June 19 of 1939, just prior to the Olympic Games, only fueled Hitler's nationalist and racism.

4. http://www.jewishvirtuallibrary.org/jsource/Holocaust/olympics.html.

5. Hugh Murray, "Review of Hoberman's *The Olympic Crisis*," *Journal of Sport History*, Vol. 16, No. 1, 106.

6. Dave Kindred, "Hitler was the Master of Olympic Scandal," *The Sporting News*, http://www.sportingnews.com/archives/sports2000/moments/138704.html.

7. http://www.jewishvirtuallibrary.org/jsource/Holocaust/olympics.html.

8. http://www.jewishvirtuallibrary.org/jsource/Holocaust/olympics.html.

9. Robert Edelman, *Serious Fun: A History of Spectator Sports in the USSR* (New York: Oxford University Press, 1993), 122.

10. http://www.pbs.org/redfiles/sports_inv_ins.htm, 3.

11. John Hoberman, *The Olympic Crisis: Sport, Politics, and the Moral Order* (New Rochelle, NY: Aristide O. Caratzas, Publisher, 1986), 10.

12. Ironically, Finland was a country Russia had twice invaded in World War II.

13. Robert Edelman, *Serious Fun: A History of Spectator Sports in the USSR* (New York: Oxford University Press, 1993), 75-76.

14. W. Franke and B. Berendonk, "Hormonal doping and Androgenization of Athletes: A Secret program of the German Democratic Republic Government," Clinical Chemistry, 43:7, 1262-1279.

15. http://www.pbs.org/redfiles/sports/deep/interv/s_int_anatoly_firsov.htm, 5.

16. Putin threatened to pull Russia out of the games in the final few days. He was also outraged because of Sarah Hughes' narrow victory over Russian Irina Slutskaya in the women's individual program.

17. Hoberman, *The Olympic Crisis,* 11.

Chapter 5
Sport Commodified

"I had no prior knowledge of the planned assault on Nancy Kerrigan. I am responsible, however, for failing to report things I learned about the assault when I returned home from Nationals." Tanya Harding

𝕿HE LAST HALF OF THE TWENTIETH CENTURY saw the fall of Soviet Russia, the unification of East and West Germany, and other trends toward global democratization and free-market capitalism. Sport too took a democratic, free-market turn. As democratic reforms leveled down distinctions of class, race, and gender, sport became a means for reconstructing individual identities according to egalitarian principles. It also became a marketable commodity like romance novels, Victorian lampshades, and Hollywood movies. As was the case back in ancient Greek times, it once again made sense to speak of handsomely paid professional athletes. This time, however, it would not be the state that rewarded successful athletes, but consumers through their patronage and sponsorship in a free-market, capitalist system.

This chapter is a look at the commodification of sport. The first part examines commodification of professional and college sports in the United States. The second part examines the rise of violence and sexism in the wake of commodified sport.

Sports and the Free Market

Professional Sports

Sport is big business—especially in the United States. Plunkett Research, Ltd. indicates that the size of the entire U.S. sports industry in 2009 was 411 billion dollars—almost double the size from 2005. That is more than one-eighth of the total U.S. revenue for 2009—2,700 billion dollars. The team sports of baseball, American football, ice hockey, and basketball lead the way.[1]

The U.S. sports-teams industry has roughly 800 organizations. The industry is top-heavy. The topmost 50 organizations—including baseball, football, basketball, and hockey—have 60 percent of the revenue. Football, baseball, and basketball are three of the four most revenue-rich sports in the world. The Premier League of English soccer is the other.[2]

Revenue comes predominantly through admissions (40%), television and radio contracts (40%), advertising and endorsement fees (10%), and concession sales (5%). Teams in smaller markets compete with them in larger markets through local marketing.[3]

Major team sports have training camps, a preseason with exhibition games, a regular season, and a playoff system. MLB has eight teams of 30 that go to the playoffs after the regular season. The NFL has 12 of 32 teams that go to the playoffs. The NHL and NBA, each with 30 teams, have 16 teams that go to the playoffs. In effect, post-season play, especially for the NHL and NBA, comprises a season in itself. A team in the NBA or NHL that makes it to the finals can play over 33 percent more games than a team not making it to the playoffs.

In women's professional team sports, the WNBA is by far the longest running and most successful women's league. It started in 1996 and the league currently features 13 teams—eight of which make it to the playoffs. It has a solid fan base and shows no signs of doing anything but improving over time.

Why is competitive sport so marketable? D. Stanley Eitzen states that humans have a natural propensity to compete. Moreover, competitiveness is instilled in them from infancy and reinforced thereafter by parents and society. Why? People believe that competition motivates children and pushes them toward excellence. Unsurprisingly, those values tie in neatly with the productive aims and consumerist mentality of capitalism. There are, Eitzen notes, negative consequences of competition: fraud, misleading advertising, cheating, and, what is worst, the notions that winning the chief standard of evaluation and that there is only one person or team that wins.[4]

The sports-teams industry is unconcerned about such problems, of course; its function is entertainment and corporate spending through marketing whets consumer demand for team sports and promotes fans' identification with athletes.[5] Overall, the attitude of many concerning competitive sport and athletes is fanatical. The situation has caused at least one critic to argue that fanaticism for athletes—our admiration of winners and contempt for losers—is at bottom fascist.[6]

Mavens exhibit extreme, often uncritical enthusiasm for sports teams and sports figures. Fanaticism generates attachments and attachments mean revenue. Much of the fanaticism is generated by clever marketing. The NBA, for instance, places its marketing dollars in its "superstars," not its winning-most teams. Fans are encouraged to watch Kobe Bryant against LeBron James, not Los Angeles against Cleveland, and spoon-fed the notion that the success of each team is reducible to the success of Bryant and James. Sports like hockey are catching on. The NHL now makes much of games in which Washington's Alexander Ovechkin plays against Pittsburgh's Sidney Crosby. Such marketing gives fans a false view of success in team sports. Promoters and owners do not seem to mind. To them competitive sport is about entertainment and making money doing so.

College Sports

Even educational institutions seem to have adopted the professional sports paradigm—in a big way. A 2004 article in *USA Today* revealed that from 1995 to 2001, spending on college athletics was more than double (up 25%) that of non-athletic spending (10%) at universities. What were the motivations? They listed these: a winning season, increased visibility for schools, and a shot of morale for students and alumni. Most colleges raised tuition and/or cut money from the academic program to pay for athletics. Said David Larimore, professor of education and former athletic director: "Education and athletics are linked in this country. . . . It projects an image, and people come to expect that if a school has a major sports franchise, they also have a major institution attached. So if you want to become invisible, downgrade (athletics) or get out of it."[7]

Schools seem to be choosing visibility. In a more recent study by *USA Today*, 99 of the 120 Football Bowl Subdivision (FBS) schools had on average a 20 percent growth rate from 2005 to 2008—from 685 million dollars to 826 million dollars. At the University of Cincinnati, for instance, subsidies for the athletic program went from 5.6 million dollars in 2005 to 10.7 million dollars in 2008.[8] Cincinnati cashed in big on its investment. In 2010, they went to the Sugar Bowl and played last year's national champion, Florida. That meant immediate visibility for the university. Said Tim Lolli, Student Government President: "Student involvement is up on campus. There's a better feeling on campus, more pride for the university. It's something that connects students to the university other than going to class."[9]

Yet there were immediate costs. The athletic program accumulated 24 million dollars of debt. It drew in 2010 from university funds for one-third of its athletic revenue—almost twice the amount it drew five years ago, when it was with Conference USA. The drain on university funds will likely take the form of slowdowns in hiring, heavier workloads for existing faculty, bigger classes, increases in students' fees, and increases in tuition. The story is a common one. During 2007-2008, only 25 of 119 Football Bowl Subdivision schools were in the black.[10] The financial burden is transferred to schools in ways that impact significantly the quality of education. What is strange is that no one, not even college presidents, seem to care about the drain on academic institutions as academies of learning. It is about visibility.

Marketing Violence

The money and popularity attending big-time pro and college sports in the twentieth century has had social effects. Competitive sport have become for many, if not most, boys and men in democratic societies a masculine, martial ideal. More than games, sports competition and spectatorship have become a rite of passage into manhood and a public demonstration of condoned, if not sanctioned, martial values like aggression, violence, and loyalty to authority.

One might expect that democratic societies—framed on equality of status and opportunity, committed to freedom of religion and speech, and dedicated to a plurality of kinds of work and play—would eschew violence in sport. Why, instead, are there so many violent sports—like the extreme fighting sports of UFC, Strikeforce, and WEC—and why are they so popular?

One suggestion is that, with their commitment to value-pluralism, democracies work on the assumption that competitive sport is part of the good life and, thus, they offer their citizens numerous outlets for sportive expression—some risky and violent; others risk-free and nonviolent. These societies also offer the freedom to make sport a way of life both for athletes and mavens. Such a wholesale investment in sport, however, encourages a martial approach in which losing is "not an option."

Another suggestion is that the free flow of ideas, the free choice of manner of living, the commitment to individualism and equality, and the toleration of diversity in democratic societies allow for technological advances and innovations in sport that are impossible in other societies. Technological advances and innovations allow for different approaches to competitive sport that make winning easier for innovative athletes and foster an anything-goes approach to competitive sport.

Still another suggestion is that commitment to value-pluralism and governmental noninterference limit what a state can do to interfere in the lives of its citizens. Athletes that choose risky, violent sports are knowingly and willingly assuming the dangers. States have a right to interfere only when sportive practice threatens public security or well-being.

A final suggestion is perhaps obvious. Competitive sport is valued because it is a microcosm of the cutthroat wrangling of free-market capitalism in free societies. Those persons accustomed to the martial approach to everyday living will prefer and pursue competitive and not recreational sport and a martial approach to competitiveness.

It is illuminating that within three of the great democratic countries—England, Australia, and the United States—sport is practiced with unmatched passion. In those countries, love of victory is embraced to a panagonist extreme. Aggressive, often violent sports and sportive behavior is condoned and often praised, but not without social consequences.

Hooliganism and European Soccer

The British have always been proud of their sporting heritage and its impact on the global community, and no sport has taken hold of the British like soccer. C.B. Fry wrote in 1895: "The great and widespread interest in football is a manifest fact. So much so that nowadays it is frequently urged that cricket can no longer be regarded as our 'national game', in the true sense of the word. Football, it is claimed, has now the first place in the popular heart."[11]

By the end of the nineteenth century, critics began to notice an alarming trend among followers of the sport: the organized fan brutality called "hooliganism." On May 29 of 1985, Liverpool played the Italian team Juventus in Belgium for the European finals and lost. Liverpool fans then killed 39 Juventus supporters and injured some 200 more. On April 15 of 1989, 96 people were crushed to death at the Hillsbrough stadium in Sheffield, England because of overcrowding and rowdy behavior in the stadium. The rampant violence in the 1980s forced the erection of fences at stadiums to keep fans from storming the field and attacking players. These fences, in turn, resulted in death to many fans that were crushed against them by onrushing enthusiasts at various games.[12]

Soccer hooliganism—now a problem in France, Germany, Scotland, and the Netherlands—began mostly in the mid-1960s. Patrick Murphy, John Williams, and Eric Dunning, experts on hooliganism in soccer, write of the connection between such violent behavior, masculinity, and war games:

> In England, especially since the mid-1960s, a certain kind of person has been attracted to football primarily because they see it as an attractive context in which to fight. In a football context, a ready-made group of opponents is available: the supporters of the opposing team. At a football match, too, given the large crowds, it is comparatively easy to act disruptively and escape detection and arrest. For such groups, football serves as a focus for a kind of "war game." They attack opposing supporters because they see them as "invaders," and they attack them in pubs, city centers and on public transport as well as in and around the football ground itself. Related to this is the fact that groups of this kind see travel to away matches as providing an opportunity for "invading" the territory of others and for attempting to establish control over it for a while.[13]

The main attraction of hooliganism is the opportunity to establish one's masculinity and local identity through fighting and demolition of property. Hooligans are usually between the ages of 15 and 25 and their targets are other groups of fans from opposing football teams. A study in the Netherlands on hooliganism sums a hooligan's mentality. He believes himself to be a true fan whose allegiance to his team is instrumental to its winning. Attending sporting events is an opportunity to antagonize rival fans in order to gain prestige and a masculine identity. Gerrit Valik sums, "The ability to fight, group solidarity and loyalty, plus the aggressive defence of culturally defined areas, are all elements of a satisfying masculine identity. Fighting at football is largely about young males testing out their own reputations for manliness against those of other similarly motivated young men."[14]

The "Warrior Ethos" in Australian Sports

After the United States, Australia is considered to be the second "great seeding bed of British sport,"[15] with cricket and rugby being sports that take pride of place.[16] From its importation, however, competitive sport in Australia has been overwhelmingly male in practice and attitude. In the late nineteenth century, for instance, Attorney-General of South Australia William Bundey maintained that sports leveled all social distinctions, though he endorsed only such "manly exercises" that by definition relegated females to nothing more than the role of spectator.[17] In part, the reason for the generation and continuation of this attitude is the connection between competitive sports and gambling, drinking, and violence.[18] The turn of the twentieth century saw women participating in a variety of non-competitive sports such as gymnastics, calisthenics, cycling, and skating. Yet even after World War II, rugby, combat sports, long-distance running, and some track-and-field events were closed to women. Though the opportunities for women today are ample, the Australian attitude towards female athletes remains somewhat mired in nineteenth-century bigotry.

Australian sport is still incorrigibly violent terrain in popular Australian culture. For example, young male children in Sydney can often be seen charging hard into each other in a strange ritual for rugby called "learning to tackle." According to one Australian sociologist, "It is the warrior drive and the warrior ethos that are resurrected in modern team football."[19] Additionally, boys are taught boxing or other defensive skills. In contrast, women who try their hand at rugby have traditionally been treated with derision and ridicule.[20] It is not uncommon for women who compete in "masculine" sports to have their sexuality questioned.

In general, neither sex takes female athleticism seriously.[21] Wrey Vamplew offers a plausible reason:

> The prime reason for this has been the attitudes not just of males but also of many females who share the predominant male view that high-exertion, highly competitive, physical contact sport is unfeminine. . . . The dominant masculine viewpoint of female sport has been nurtured and reinforced by the Australian media which, until recently, featured little serious discussion of women's sport and instead, when they deigned to offer any space, gave a largely discriminatory presentation of female athletes and their performances.[22]

Australian culture, on the one hand, has constrained the opportunities for female growth and expression through competitive sports by creating and maintaining the illusion that competition is exclusively or principally male province. On the other hand, sportive expression has had a tremendous role in shaping male character and cultivating sport-related skills in men. Writes Richard Cashman:

> The bonding of males through sport has been so strong that the culture of sport has excluded women. . . . While many female athletes participate both in female and in male sports cultures—following and attending male team-sports for instance—there are some others who 'hate' sport because they are defined as second-rate citizens within the male culture of sport. Women can be excluded from discussion about sport on the assumption that they don't know anything about it.[23]

Cashman concludes that Australian culture is overwhelmingly androcentric—so much that many would-be reformists see it as incapable of reform.[24] Women who wish to be taken seriously as athletes are pushed to conform to masculine ideals.

American Football as Rite of Passage

No sport consumes American males today like American football. Perhaps this is because, more than any other game, football preserves the historical connection of sport and militaristic values such as aggression and obedience to authority. Each head coach is a general who mobilizes his troops in readiness for battle. One team kicks off, while the other receives the kick-off. Plays, like battle plans, are scripted. At stake is subduing your adversary, encroaching upon their territory, gaining the upper hand, and winning. The means of accomplishing these goals is a curious admixture of skilled physical movements and physically aggressive force—sometimes referred to as "controlled aggression." For most enthusiasts, it is that aggressive element that endears them most toward football. That, they state, is what makes football better than other sports. As one coach stated, "Football is the closest thing to war you boys will ever experience. It's your chance to find out what manhood is really all about."[25]

Sociologists Donald Sabo and Joe Paneptino interviewed former players, who often described their coaches in language reminiscent of military commanders. Like a drill sergeant, a football coach is a tough disciplinarian who takes no guff, demands complete obedience, and whips players into shape willynilly. Humiliation, obedience, and indifference to and acceptance of pain seem to be significant elements in establishing the proper player-coach relationship.[26]

Former University-of-Pittsburgh athletic director Ed Bozik had this to say about the relationship between football and war games:

Football training is very much analogous to military training. In both cases young men are trained to do things they instinctively would not do. This has to condition your psyche, but the question is, can you convert that training and use its positive elements in normal life? In the military we have what we call 'war lovers,' the ones who can't turn it off. But everyone is constantly trained to act like gentlemen when not in a battle situation.[27]

Some sociologists who study the game argue that football is more than a war game for American youth. It is a rite of passage for boys into manhood. The "values" they learn from football are those every right-minded man needs to make it in American society. Anthropological studies of male initiation rites show that man-boy relationships, conformity and control, social isolation (especially from women), deference to male authority, and acceptance of pain are important factors in securing manhood. American football, it seems, has come to define American masculinity. It takes aggression (often violence), complete dedication, strength, suffering, and passion to play football, and these are the values of American masculinity.

Former NFL middle linebacker Chris Spielman was widely acknowledged to be one of the most intense competitors of the game. Football, he said in his days at Ohio State, is "controlled insanity" and "a life or death situation for me." For Spielman, the focus was on winning, not how one goes about winning.[28] Another tremendously intense former middle linebacker, Mike Singletary, said this about one of his punishing hits on an opponent: "I don't feel pain from a hit like that. What I feel is joy. Joy for the tackle. Joy for myself. Joy for the other man. You understand me; I understand you. It's football, it's middle-linebacking. It's just . . . good for everybody."[29] Former Oakland Raider Jack Tatum even published a book entitled *They Call Me Assassin* about his punishing hits, one of which permanently incapacitated an opponent Darryl Stingley. Astonishingly, Tatum, arguing that violence is part of the game, voiced no remorse in his book about the injury to Stingley.

Glorified aggression through American football was perhaps best exemplified by one of the most celebrated post-season "honors" given to the most macho players in the National Football League some years ago—the All-Madden-Team awards. Those awards were given generally to the biggest and most aggressive players in the league, and what seemed to be the sole criterion for inclusion was love of dishing out and receiving pain.

We must acknowledge, of course, some of the recent initiatives taken by the NFL to make the game safer for its players—e.g., the Brady rule for quarterbacks and the newly installed concussion rule. Still the rules have come to be because of the violence in the game. Protective equipment has improved over the years. Yet that leads to a paradox. When players, who get bigger each year, feel safer, they hit harder and with harder hitting, the potential for serious injuries is greater.

Violence in Women's Sports

The 20th century saw a massive increase in female sports participation, but instead of counterbalancing the win-at-all-costs attitude associated with masculinity, women's sports seem simply to have adopted it. We offer two instances: the Nancy Kerrigan/Tanya Harding incident in women's figure skating and the 2002 WNBA Championships.

On January 6 of 1994, while attempting to qualify for the U.S. figure-skating team at the upcoming Olympics, Nancy Kerrigan was clubbed on the knee by a blunt object at the U.S. trials in Detroit. This incident came just some eight months after tennis superstar Monica Seles was stabbed by a fan of Steffi Graff during a tennis match between the two superstars of women's tennis. Three men were linked to the Kerrigan incident, including Shawn Eric Eckardt, Tanya Harding's 350-pound bodyguard, who confessed to hiring two men to attack Kerrigan, presumably to clear the way for Harding to compete in the Olympics. Harding's lawyer flatly denied that his client played any role in the incident. She, however, did publicly admit to knowing of the attack days after it had occurred. "I had no prior knowledge of the planned assault on Nancy Kerrigan. I am responsible, however, for failing to report things I learned about the assault when I returned home from Nationals."

In the end Harding was allowed to compete along with Kerrigan at the Olympics. But she performed poorly and Kerrigan won the silver medal after all. On March 16, Harding would come clean on her involvement in the zany affair by agreeing to a plea bargain. In exchange for the pledge that she would not go to prison, she testified to obstruction of justice and willingly surrendered her membership in the U.S. Figure Skating Association. The same association would later strip Harding of her 1994 national championship and ban her for life. Harding declined to pursue an appeal, but her lawyer said, "She categorically denies the statements of Jeff Gillooly and others relied upon by the hearing panel that she had any prior knowledge of or participated in the assault on Nancy Kerrigan." The whole affair revealed a dark underside to the fairy-tale image of women's figure skating.

The second example of aggression and violence in women's sports, the 2003 WNBA Championship series between the Detroit Shock and the Los Angeles Sparks, is more subtle. A crowd of over 22,000, the largest crowd ever for a WNBA game, showed up for the third and final game to watch the Shock keep the Sparks from their third straight WNBA championship with a hard-fought, 83-78 win. The Shock, which had a league-record 23 losses a year ago and was on the brink of folding or moving, not only won the championship, they also led the league with 25 wins behind the slogan "From worst to first."

Los Angeles was led throughout the series by the gritty, assertive, and consistent play of their superstar, Lisa Leslie, who enabled them to fight their way back to leads in each of the last two games after having fallen behind considerably. In the third and deciding game, the timely heroics of series MVP Ruth Riley, who scored 27 points for Detroit, were countered by Mwadi Mabika's 29 points for Los Angeles. Though trailing most of the game, the Sparks rallied back to take a 73-70 lead with 3:40 left in the game, when an opportune basket by Riley and a critical three-pointer by Deanna Nolan, with under a minute to go, turned the game in Detroit's favor. It was an exciting series by two evenly matched teams that was perhaps decided by the home-court advantage that Detroit's best overall record awarded them.

Throughout the series, there were constant references to the NBA championship series between the Detroit Pistons and Los Angeles Lakers in 1989, where Detroit, in similar fashion, prevented Los Angeles from winning their third straight NBA championship. Both coaches of the women's teams, Detroit's Bill Laimbeer and Los Angeles' Michael Cooper, played in that series. Riley was frequently compared to Laimbeer as was Leslie to Cooper. At times the women played like the men—especially while ferociously fighting for rebounds under the basket. Bodies collided, arms were entangled, and elbows flailed. There were more than a few bloody lips in the series. At one point, when a Detroit player who had just taken an elbow to the mouth looked at the bench for some counsel or sympathy, Laimbeer shouted at her to get back into the game. Overall, far too few fouls were called in the paint.

There were two remarkable aspects of this WNBA championship. First, it was an extraordinary brutal competition and it is quite likely that the grittier, more physical, and less talented team won. Physicality, not talent, won the day. Moreover, since the grittier team won, one tends to forget certain beautiful episodes within the series. Leslie's graceful moves to the basket, for instance, now seem unremarkable and unmemorable. Others, such as Nolan's cool three-pointer, seem timeless—especially since, at the end of the day, Detroit won the battle and, more importantly, the war. Second, the play of women in this series was every bit as manly as that of the play of men in any NBA series. One has to be tough to endure and, though striving through adversity is admirable, the real measure of endurance is winning. This series was without question a hard-fought contest and, though Los Angeles showed considerable pluck and fought through much adversity, they still lost in the end. All in all, they were not brutal enough.

Our examples of sport in the twentieth century are illustrations of a model characterized by seriousness, individualism, commercialism, aggression, and often violence. Even women, to be accepted as full-fledged athletes, seem to have adopted these traditionally masculine characteristics, typical of what we call the Marial/Commercial model of sport. That is the subject of the second part of this undertaking.

Notes

1. Plunkett Research, "Sports Industry Overview," 2010, http://www.plunkett research.com/Industries/Sports/SportsStatistics/tabid/273/ Default.aspx.

2. Hoovers, Inc., "Professional Sports Teams and Organizations," 2011, http://www.hoovers.com/professional-sports-teams-and-organizations/--ID__315--/free-ind-fr-profile-basic.xhtml.

3. http://www.hoovers.com/professional-sports-teams-and-organizations/--ID__315--/free-ind-fr-profile-basic.xhtml.

4. D. Stanley Eitzen, "The Dark Side of Competition," *Philosophy of Sport: Critical Readings, Crucial Issues,* ed. M. Andrew Holowchak (Upper Saddle River: Prentice-Hall, 2002), 235-9.

5. http://www.hoovers.com/professional-sports-teams-and-organizations/--ID__315--/free-ind-fr-profile-basic.xhtml.

6. Torbjörn Tännsjö, "Is Our Admiration for Sports Heroes Fascistoid?" *Philosophy of Sport: Critical Readings, Crucial Issues,* ed. M. Andrew Holowchak (Upper Saddle River: Prentice-Hall, 2002), 347-58.

7. MaryJo Sylwester and Tom Witosky, "Athletic Spending Grows as Athletic Funds Dry Up," *USA Today*, 2/18/2004. http://www.usatoday.com/sports/college/2004-02-18-athletic-spending-cover_x.htm.

8. Jack Gillum, Jodi Upton, and Steve Berkowitz, "Amid Funding Crisis, College Athletics Soak Up Subsidies, Fees," *USA Today*, 15 Jan. 2010, http://www.usatoday.com/sports/college/2010-01-13-ncaa-athletics-funding-analysis_N.htm.

9. Jodi Upton, Steve Berkowitz, and Jack Gillum, "Big-Time College Athletics: Are They Worth the Big-Time Costs?," *USA Today*, 15 Jan. 2010, http://www.usatoday.com/sports/college/2010-01-13-ncaa-athletics-subsidies_N.htm.

10 Micheal Marot, "College Sports: studies Show Most Athletic Departments Lose Money," *The Seattle Times*, 20 Oct. 2009, http://seattletimes.nwsource.com/html/collegesports/2010103078_ncaa21.html

11. James Walvin, *Football and the Decline of Britain* (London: The Macmillan Press Ltd., 1986), 1.

12. John H. Kerr, *Understanding Soccer Hooliganism* (Open University Press, 1994), viii-ix.

13. Patrick Murphy, John Williams, and Eric Dunning, *Football on Trial: Spectator Violence and Development in the Football World* (New York: Routledge, 1990), 11.

14. Gerrit Valk, "Football Hooliganism," September 11, 2000, http://stars.coe.fr/doc/doc99/edoc8553.htm, 4.

15. Roger Hutchinson, *Empire Games: The British Invention of Twentieth-Century Sport* (London: Mainstream Publishing, 1996), 53.

16. John A. Daly, "A New Britannia in the Antipodes: Sport, Class and Community in Colonial South Australia," *Pleasure, Profit, Proselytism: British Culture and Sport at Home and Abroad 1700-1914,* ed. J. A. Mangan (London: Frank Cass, 1988), 170-171.

17. Wray Vamplew, "Australians and Sport," *Sport in Australia: A Social History,* eds. Vamplew and Stoddart (Cambridge: Cambridge University Press, 1994), 14.

18. Richard Cashman, *Paradise of Sport: The Rise of Organized Sport in Australia* (New York: Oxford University Press, 1995), 73.

19. Barbara Humberstone, "Warriors or Wimps? Creating Alternative Forms of Physical Education," *Sport, Men, and the Gender Order: Critical Feminist Perspectives,* Eds. Messner and Sabo (Champaign, IL: Human Kinetics Books, 1990), 202.

20. Rob Hess, "Women and Australian Rules Football in Colonial Melbourne," *The International Journal of the History of Sport*, Vol. 13, No. 3 (London: Frank Cass, 1996), 367.

21. Lois Bryson, "Challenges to Male Hegemony in Sport." *Sport, Men, and the Gender Order: Critical Feminist Perspectives,* eds. Messner and Sabo (Champaign, IL: Human Kinetics Books, 1990), 175, 179.

22. Vamplew, "Australians and Sport," 15-16.

23. Cashman, *Paradise of Sport*, 72-73.

24. Cashman, *Paradise of Sport*, 90.

25. Donald Sabo, "Psychosocial Impacts of Athletic Participation on American Women: Facts and Fables," *Sport in Contemporary Society: An Anthology*, 5th ed., ed. D. Stanley Eitzen (New York: St. Martin's Press, 1996), 124.

26. Sabo, "Psychosocial Impacts of Athletic Participation," 121-126.

27. Rick Telander, "Football and Violence," *Sport in Contemporary Society: An Anthology,* ed. D. Stanley Eitzen (New York: St. Martin's Press, 1996), 178.

28. Telander, "Football and Violence," 177.

29. Telander, "Football and Violence," 173.

PART II
What's Wrong With Sports Today?

Chapter 6
The Martial/Commercial Model

"Why do I put up with this life? I guess it comes down to this: *Because it feels so good when you win.*" Bill Parcels, former NFL coach

WHAT IS WRONG WITH SPORTS TODAY? The question probably has a thousand different answers. Some might say drugs, others the emphasis on winning, still others violence or blatant commercialism. We believe that the root of the problem is an attitude rather than any particular issue. It is an attitude that views sport as serious business—a form of war or commerce rather than recreation or even education. That attitude has deep historical roots.

The brief historical sketch in the first part of this book revealed that competitive sport has always retained some link with war. With the democratization of sport in the latter part of the twentieth century, competitive sport also became a marketable product, and eventually big business. The predominant model for competitive sport today, we maintain, is an admixture of these martial and commercial elements—what we call the "Martial/Commercial Model" of sport (hereafter, the MC model).

The MC model, as its title indicates, is both militaristic and commercial. Athletes are viewed well-disciplined soldiers that undergo rigorous training under the watchful eye of drill-sergeant coaches for the sake of unblemished performance during competition. Promoters market competitive sport in its martial guise and the victories and losses of athletes and teams are the victories and losses the fanatic mavens, whose consumer dollars fuel the industry.

The military and commercial aspects of the attitude are marked generally by the seriousness with which they take their goal. Competition, viewed as battle, is believed to prepare people for the rough-and-tumble free market by cultivating toughness through instilling aggressive, military values. Military metaphors are used abundantly in men's sports—especially basketball, football, and wrestling. Messner, Hunt, and Dunbar elaborate:

On an average of nearly five times per hour of sports commentary, announcers describe action using terms such as "battle," "kill," "ammunition," "weapons," "professional sniper," "taking aim," "fighting," "shot in his arsenal," "reloading," "detonate," "squeeze the trigger," "exploded," "attack mode," "firing blanks," "blast," "explosion," "blitz," "point of attack," "lance through the heart," "gunning it," "battle lines are drawn," and "shotgun."[1]

The notion that competition is battle has more than terminological implications. It has sociological and ethical implications. If competition is essentially battle, then competitive sport itself is inescapably aggressive and violent, and therefore more the province of males than females.[2] That, of course, has implications for our tolerance of aggression and sexism in sport as well as the outside of sport. One could argue that sport seems to be manufactured precisely to enforce the idea that male aggression and superiority are natural and inevitable.

MC sport is characterized by the following general features: it focuses on external goods, pursues victory at all costs, affirms rather than challenges existing beliefs, emphasizes the individual over the group, and prioritizes the commercial. We discuss each of those in turn.

External Goods

First, the goods sought in MC sport are wholly external. Like war and commerce, competitive sport is not undertaken for its own sake, but rather for the sake of goods beyond the game—such as praise, glory, school or national pride, and, most commonly, money and celebrity.

Not only are those goods external to sport, they are also, in a certain sense, external to athletes. Athletes are not expected to be improved as persons by engaging in MC sport and they do not value personal benefits such as improved physical and psychological health. Rather, they use sport as a means to gain benefits that are external to their competitive actions. Sport, on the MC model, then is *instrumental*—a tool for achieving other things.

Using athletes and sport neglects the welfare of both. Athletes are asked to sacrifice themselves in various ways. They are expected to endure endless hours of training. They are asked to risk injury for the sake of victory. There is a culture in MC sport of insensitivity to pain. Sociologist Don Sabo writes:

> Sports are just one of the many areas in our culture where pain is more important than pleasure. Boys are taught that to endure pain is courageous, to survive pain is manly. The principle that pain is good and pleasure is bad is plainly evident in the aphorism, "No pain, no gain."[3]

The phenomenon is not limited to males. Even so-called feminine sports like aerobics and gymnastics have embraced the "toughness" ideal. Jane Fonda's iconic exercise videos were famous for the slogan "feel the burn." Gymnast Kerri Strugg was lauded for landing a vault on an injured leg in the 1996 Olympic Games.

The disrespect inherent in this instrumentalist attitude extends beyond individual athletes and impacts sport itself, but it is thought to be justified by its link to success. As Mike Messner states, "the more 'success oriented' a man is, the more 'instrumental' his personality will tend to be...."[4] Bruce Kidd adds, "Because sports elevate external goals over intrinsic ones, sports have encouraged athletes to treat their bodies instrumentally, to undergo physical and psychological injury, and to inflict it upon others."[5]

Players who taunt others to humiliate them and gain a psychological edge are examples of MC sports' instrumentalism. In the more violent sports, like soccer or American football, injuring opponents can even be part of a game plan. Writes Gilda Berger:

> While competing, some athletes tend to think of the opposing team members as not merely opponents who are human beings just like themselves but as enemies. This reduces their sense of responsibility; it releases them from the usual demands of morality. Hurting the "enemy" to get him out of the game or using intimidation to interfere with his performance becomes acceptable behavior. In any other area of life, those same athletes would consider such acts as immoral. But in sports, they feel, anything goes—as long as it helps to win the game or to come in first in the race.[6]

Finally, sport itself is abused in the pursuit of external goals. The rules that make sport possible in the first place are viewed as just obstacles to be overcome. The mentality is, "It's not cheating if you don't get caught." Safety-inspired bans on doping, rough play, or intentional injury are exploited coolly according to a strategic cost/benefit analysis. Disrespect for rules amounts to disrespect for sport, but sport itself is not valued on the MC model, it is merely a means to external goods.

"Just Win, Baby!"

Because external goods depend on victory, winning is the express goal of MC sport. "Winning is the only thing," the saying goes, because "To the victor go the spoils." In contrast to the Olympic Games, where competing itself is esteemed and the excellence of the first three places is acknowledged by medals, for MC sport, coming in first is everything. It is more disgraceful to place second on a continual basis than it is to finish recurrently in last place. Joan Hundley nicely captures this defect of MC sport.

> [S]port cannot be reduced to numbers on a score board, and . . . the winning-is-everything perception of sport undermines the meaning and objectives of sport. Sport ought to be regarded as an activity in which the will to win is a means to the end of attaining physical excellence, not one in which human excellence is regarded as a means to the end of winning. The latter idea undermines sport because you can "win" without physical excellence, e.g., by "psyching out" opponents.[7]

The MC model expressly identifies winning as the only acceptable outcome in sports. Winning is pounded into athletes' heads through platitudes such as Vince Lombardi's "Winning is not everything. It is the only thing" or former Washington Redskins' football coach George Allen's "Losing is worse than death. You have to live with losing." Former football coach Bill Parcels has stated, quite astonishingly, that winning was his reason for living. "Why do I put up with this life? I guess it comes down to this: *Because it feels so good when you win*."[8]

The focus on winning—i.e., coming in first—is certainly an essential part of the culture of free-market capitalism. It is not unfair to say that Americans have become obsessed with winning, so much so that athletes and teams that fail to win are categorized as "losers"—especially those who have often come close to winning it all, but have failed to do so, like football's Buffalo Bills. An excellent performance is considered worthless if it fails to secure victory—even if that failure was caused by factors outside the athletes' or their coach's control.

A recent example is the gold-medal hockey game in the 2010 Olympics in Vancouver. Canada was facing the United States. It was a tight, evenly played game. Canada had a 2-1 lead late into the third period, when the United States tied the game with 24 seconds left. So evenly contested was the match that it seemed that justice had been served by the tie. Canada eventually won the game in overtime and the gold medal. When the players met at center ice to receive their medals, the U.S. players, to a man, were noticeably disconsolate. Heads limply leaning forward and frowns on their faces, each U.S. player had a silver medal placed around his neck. The scenario was otherwise with the jubilant Canadian players.

When two teams play a game so evenly for three periods—and the statistics bore that out—it is generally arbitrary who wins and a matter of luck, not effort or talent, that one team gets silver and the other gold. So, there was no reason for any U.S. player to be discontented. They had beaten Canada earlier in the Olympics and were as good as Canada on the day they earned their silver medals. The U.S. players were discontented only because they had been taught, in MC fashion, that winning is everything and coming in second means nothing.

The effect of the exclusive emphasis on winning reaches far beyond athletes' reactions to results. It motivates a kind of arms-race to secure any possible edge over an opponent. Huge sums of money are invested to develop training technologies, clothing, equipment, even psychological techniques. Moreover, the obsession with outcome effectively reduces the number of athletes that can afford to compete. It deprives them and opponents of the benefits of close competition—all in the name of easier, more efficient, and more secure victory.

Belief-Affirmation

Of course the athletic superiority of individuals and teams that can afford the latest training and equipment technologies conveniently reinforces the assumption that their privilege is justified by their inherent superiority. MC sport is belief-affirming in this sense: It tends to corroborate assumptions rather than seek knowledge. Even though the structure of sport resembles such knowledge-seeking practices as court trials and scientific experiments,[9] MC sport is marketed in such a way as to thwart that function.

An excellent historical example of that is the history of race and sport in the United States. It is currently acknowledged by nearly all persons that blacks are at least athletically equivalent to whites in competitive sports.[10] Decades ago, however, whites were believed to be athletically superior to blacks and that was the reason why blacks were excluded from professional sports leagues and segregated into their own poorly funded "negro leagues," where they appeared to perform below the level of whites. Eventually sports were racially integrated and the perception of black athletic inferiority was disavowed. It was not sport itself that was racist, but rather the people who marketed it.

The presumption today affirmed by the administration of sport is male superiority. The segregation of males and females is thought justified by biology, and perhaps it is.[11] Still we should be wary of how the MC model's belief-affirming tendencies affect the administration of sports. In any case, athletic superiority does not equate with social superiority and it is certainly not a case for moral superiority.[12]

Furthermore, the qualities that contribute to sporting success may not have social value. The MC model of sport tends to stress strength, speed, and aggression. Those features devalue or disallow sports, like bowling or synchronized swimming, which emphasize different features. What is more, the emphasis on strength, speed, and aggression seems to give males a ready-made advantage, while marginalizing most females as well as smaller, weaker males.

M.J. Kane and L.J. Disch write, "The most glorified sports in this society are those that emphasize physical domination and subjugation. In these sports, men's bodies, particularly as weapons of physical violence, become sites of power."[13] Joan Hudley agrees:

> Male-dominated sports are regarded as instruments which are employed to perpetuate male supremacy because they reinforce what I will refer to as the ideal of physical dominance, aggression, and violence. By this I mean quite simply the ideal that supports the antiquated notion that stronger and more aggressive individuals or nations have the right to dominate weaker, less aggressive individuals or nations.[14]

Former world-class powerlifter, Fred Hatfield attests to the perceived superiority of big, strong men:

> To feel strong, to walk among humans with a tremendous feeling of confidence and superiority is not at all wrong. The sense of superiority in bodily strength is borne out by the long history of mankind paying homage in folklore, song, and poetry to strong men. You will sense it; you will be awed by it; and your fellow man will indeed, as he has done for thousands of years, pay you homage.[15]

The question must be asked whether such homage is really justified—especially in a world where brute human strength has become unnecessary. MC sport, however, does not ask questions; it reinforces existing beliefs. Just as soldiers are trained not to question their superiors and not to second-guess orders, MC competitors indulge in sports without second-guessing both the merit of their activities and whether those activities tend to social betterment or deterioration.

Elitism

Another characteristic of MC sport is its emphasis on elitism—often at the expense of teammates and always at the expense of opponents and everyone else that cannot compete at the highest levels. Spending on elite sports greatly outpaces efforts to encourage mass participation. That is true worldwide, as well as in the American college and university system, where the schools with the most recognizable athletic programs often have the lowest levels of sport participation among the student body. They are filling their stadiums, but not their gymnasiums.

Elitism even dominates team sports—e.g., soccer, American football, basketball, and hockey—which are lauded for their ability to teach selflessness and cooperation. Big-time college athletes, focused on the external goal of a professional contract, are evaluated atomically and almost exclusively through the quantifiable analysis of certain skills they possess. Consider the skills competition that is now held every year for willing college football players that are entering the National Football League draft—the NFL Scouting Combine. Athletes—evaluated by leaping ability, speed, strength, throwing accuracy, throwing length, ability to overcome obstacles, etc.—are reduced to numbers that give scouts no idea of how well a ballplayer can play on a team. Such methods of evaluation encourage individuation and selfish play, which are ways individuals can "win" even if their teams do not function so well.

Indeed the entire modern obsession with statistical measurement of athletic performance artificially removes athletes from the context of their team and reduces the conception of athletic excellence to quantifiable physical feats. If excellence cultivated through athletics is to have social value beyond sport, excellence must be understood as something more than athletic performance and athletes must be understood not as individuals but as parts of communities.

The link between elite athletic excellence and the qualities that justify leadership and admiration is as old as sport itself. The ancient conception of excellence (*aretē*) always focused on individuals' roles within and benefit to their community. Both sport and athletes have become increasingly removed from the community context however. The MC model markets competitive athletes in a manner that fosters elitism. It is as if they inhabit a parallel world, set apart from the expectations and criticism of the "real world," except insofar as it provides revenue and entertainment. That seems true even at universities, where athletics were originally considered to be part of the educational program.

Commercialism

The elitist individualism that infects MC sport are the result of its overriding commercialism. Multimillion-dollar salaries and endorsement contracts have motivated individuals to market their skills and themselves as individuals, not as members of a team or participants of a particular sport. Playing for a team is important, but increasingly players strive to make themselves visible in team sports through exceptional play that is not team-oriented, showboating, and even taunting and fighting opponents, managers, or teammates. Former defensive standout "Neon" Deion Sanders (a.k.a., "Prime Time") and wide receiver Terrell Owens are noteworthy examples of exceptionally talented players who have gotten much mileage out of ego-puffing: showboating, self-promotion, and perhaps even belittling others (see chapter 11).

The focus on external goals, identified as the first characteristic of MC sport, reaches its apogee in a completely commercialistic attitude within which profit is an accepted justification for almost any tactic or behavior. Modern sports fans can witness professional athletes trading victory for under-the-table payoffs from criminals who bet against them. Such behavior is criticized, when exposed, not so much because athletes have sacrificed sport for money, but because the practice has threatened to undermine the lucrative sports-betting industry. Moreover, they were dumb enough to get caught.

Even at amateur and scholastic levels, MC sport is dominated by a commercial paradigm. Little leaguers are used to promote local businesses. High schools recruit star basketball players to attract tuition-paying students. Universities justify huge athletic expenditures by alumni donations attracted by winning programs and television exposure.

We have no objection to professional sport or commercial sponsorship in general. The problem with MC sport is that it threatens to become nothing more than a business. We, for instance, are paid to teach and write philosophy, but we certainly do not do philosophy merely for the money—it is not a typical get-rich-quick occupation—and we certainly would not compromise the way we philosophize to please consumers—though some students would be thrilled to pay for good grades without having to earn them. Indeed, we might call such an act "unprofessional." It is commercialism, not professionalism, which is the danger in MC sport.

The remaining chapters of this part examine more closely some of the more salient aspects of MC sport: performance enhancement through drugs and other aids, aggression and gender discrimination, the love affair with statistical data in competitive sports, and the commercial encouragement of sensationalism and ego-puffing. In the third part of the book, we consider an alternative to MC sport—the Aesthetic/Recreational model—in an effort to highlight the defects of the MC model. The final part is an attempt to reconcile the defects of MC and AR sports by proposing medial resolution through a new model—Aretism.

Notes

1. Michael Messner, Darnel Hunt, and Michele Dunbar, "Boys to Men: Sports Media Messages about Masculinity," http://www.childrennow.org, 1999, 4.

2. True competitors, however, are said to know how to leave competitive aggression on the practice or playing field. For a refutation of that thesis, see M. Andrew Holowchak, "Aggression, Gender, and Sport: Reflections on Sport as a Means of Moral Education," *Philosophy of Sport: Critical Readings, Crucial Issues*, ed. M. Andrew Holowchak (Upper Saddle River, NJ: Prentice-Hall, 2002), 466-75.

3. Michael Messner and Donald Sabo, *Sex, Violence, & Power in Sports: Rethinking Masculinity* (Freedom, CA: The Crossing Press, 1994), 86.

4. Michael Messner, "The Meaning of Success: The Athletic Experience and the Development of Male Identity," *Sport in Contemporary Society: An Anthology,* ed. D. Stanley Eitzen (New York: St. Martin's Press, 1996), 383.

5. Bruce Kidd, "The Men's Cultural Centre: Sports and the Dynamic of Women's Oppression/Men's Repression," *Sport, Men, and the Gender Order: Critical Feminist Perspectives,* eds. Messner and Sabo (Champaign, IL: Human Kinetics Books, 1990), 40.

6. David Whitson, "Sport Promotes Negative Male Values," *Sports in America: Opposing Viewpoints* (San Diego: Greenhaven Press, 1994), 175.

7. Joan Hundley, "The Overemphasis on Winning: A Philosophical Outlook," *Philosophy of Sport: Critical Readings, Crucial Issues* (Upper Saddle River, NJ: Prentice-Hall, 2002), 207.

8. Bill Parcells and Jeff Coplon, *Finding a Way to Win: The Principles of Leadership, Teamwork, and Motivation* (New York: Doubleday, 1995), 4.

9. Heather L. Reid, "Sport, Philosophy, and the Quest for Knowledge," *Journal of the Philosophy of Sport* 36:1 (2009), 40.

10. There is incontestable evidence that West-African runners dominate sprinting competitions and East-African runners dominate marathon events. See Amby Burfoot, "White Men Can't Run," *Philosophy of Sport: Critical Readings, Crucial Issues*, ed. M. Andrew Holowchak (Upper Saddle River, NJ: Prentice-Hall, 2002), 428-36.

11. Biological explanations also justified the exclusion of women from higher education, but once granted access to the academy, females seemed to thrive there.

12. See Heather L. Reid, *The Philosophical Athlete* (Durhan, NC: Carolina Academic Press, 2002) 237-239.

13. Mary Jo Kane and Lisa J. Disch, "Sexual Violence and the Reproduction of Male Power in the Locker Room," *Sociology of Sport,* 10, 1993, 347.

14. Joan Hundley, "The Overemphasis on Winning: A Philosophical Look." *Women, Philosophy, and Sport: A Collection of New Essays,* ed. Betsy Postow (Metuchen, NJ: The Scarecrow Press, Inc., 1983), 191.

15. Hatfield, *Powerlifting,* 2-3.

Chapter 7
Drugs and Competitive Sport

"I know that you can't put something in your body to make you hit a fastball, changeup or curveball. . . . But, at that age (40), you have to ask: Did [Barry Bonds] accomplish all of this by rejuvenating his strength from day to day with those substances? I know that when you reach a certain age, you just don't bounce back as quickly as you think you can when you're playing all of those games. . . . Let me say this. Any way you look at it, it's wrong." Henry Aaron

NE OF THE GREAT FAILINGS of the Martial/Commercial (MC) model is that it uses competitive sport as a means to extrinsic goods like fame and wealth while disregarding intrinsic goods, such as worthwhile challenge and the pursuit of virtue. Competitors today will do whatever it takes to attain goods like fame and wealth—even if that means cheating or subjecting themselves to inordinate harm. The most visible problem caused by this focus on extrinsic goods is the use of performance drugs like steroids. In MC sport, the money and glory associated with victory seem to justify the taking of considerable risks. Worse, the practice of doping threatens those intrinsic goods, such as worthwhile challenge and the cultivation of excellence,[1] which make sport valuable in the first place. The focus on extrinsic rather than intrinsic goods in sport accounts for widespread doping in sports like baseball, cycling, and track and field.

Steroids in Track and Baseball

On December 4 of 2004, United States Senator John McCain, for a second time, demanded that major league baseball do something about the rampant use of steroids in baseball. In an interview during the Army-Navy football game, McCain said, "I warned them a long time ago that we needed to fix this problem. It's time for them to sit down together and act. And that's what they should do. If not, clearly, we have to act legislatively, which we don't want to do." McCain was responding to the grand-jury testimony by Jason Giambi, Gary Sheffield, and Barry Bonds that revealed each superstar had been using performance-enhancing drugs. McCain was motivated by concern for the nation's youth. He said, "I don't care about Mr. Bonds or Mr. Sheffield or anybody else. What I care about are high school athletes who are tempted to use steroids because they think that's the only way they can make it in the major leagues."[2]

McCain's comments came on the heels of a television interview on ABC's "20/20," where Victor Conte, head of the Bay Area Laboratory Co-Operative (BALCO), talked openly and candidly about the use of steroids in baseball and track and field. Among other things, Conte stated that he sat right next to track superstar Marion Jones, when she injected herself with HGH (human growth hormone) one day prior to a meet in California. "She pulled the spandex of her bicycle shorts above her right thigh," wrote Conte in *ESPN: The Magazine*. "She dialed up a dose of four-and-a-half units of growth hormone and injected it into her quadriceps." He continued, "I started providing her with insulin, growth hormone, EPO and 'The Clear', as well as nutritional supplements." Jones responded to the Associated Press that, "Victor Conte's allegations about me are not true, and the truth will come out in the appropriate forum."[3] She then repeated the lies to two grand juries. In October of 2007, she finally admitted to taking steroids and lying to the grand juries and was stripped of all awards dating back to September 1 of 2000 and sentenced to six months in jail.

To most people, however, the real BALCO bombshell was the testimony of baseball superstar Barry Bonds. Bonds admitted that he had been taking a clear substance and a cream, which, he said he believed to be flaxseed oil and a rubbing balm for his arthritis, but later learned were performance-enhancing agents. The slugger already holds the single-season home-run record with 73 in 2001 and currently has 762 career home runs, which is more than Babe Ruth (714) and Henry Aaron (755). On November 15 of 2007, Bonds was indicted of four counts of perjury and one count of obstruction of justice. The issue has yet to be resolved.

There were other incidents. In 1998, Mark McGwire shattered Roger Maris' major league single-season home-run record of 61 round trippers with 70 of his own. In the same season, McGwire admitted to taking a legal anabolic steroid, androstenedoine, along with creatine. He said, "Everything I've done is natural. Everybody that I know in the game of baseball uses the same stuff that I use. . . . It's legal." Moreover, the National League's Most Valuable Player in 1996, Ken Caminiti, who has since passed away, admitted to having used steroids that year and throughout the rest of his career.

Like McGwire, Caminiti showed no regrets about his own use of supplemental drugs. "I've made a ton of mistakes. I don't think using steroids is one of them." Retired slugger Jose Canseco has also stated that he took steroids and that 85 percent of all players take them. Finally, pitching great Roger Clemens is mentioned 82 times in the government-commissioned Mitchell Report on steroid use in baseball. New York Yankees trainer Brian McNamee testified to injecting Clemens with drugs on several occasions. Clemens has consistently denied all allegations, though there are inconsistencies in his testimonies and there is substantial evidence to suggest he has used performance drugs.

As expected, critics and fans have expressed dismay that a sport such as baseball, which seems to place dexterity and intelligence before power, could be tainted by the use of performance drugs. The once-sacred 50-home-run mark was commonly achieved by sluggers between 1997 and 2007. Within that span, three players hit over 60 home runs, and two of those players hit 70 or more round trippers. Why were balls flying out ballparks so frequently? There was speculation on loaded bats and loaded balls, but few persons imagined that the answer was loaded players.[4]

Is there really anything wrong with loaded players? The players themselves did not seem to think so; they seemed to regard doping as something that had to be done to reach their goals. Why, then, is there such public fury?

Performance Drugs and Autonomy

Those who hold the MC view of sport are likely to regard the problem as legal rather than moral—i.e., doping is wrong because it is illegal. Yet one moral issue concerns the paternalistic bans that make doping illegal.

Paternalism is the view that we are sometimes warranted in interfering with the liberties of others when there is evidence that their actions will result in harm to them. Philosopher John Stuart Mill has forcefully argued that regard for an individual's autonomy—especially in areas of social, political, religious, and moral concerns where there is no consensus regarding truth—must reign supreme over paternalistic influence.[5] In other words, interfering in others' activities is only justified when the harm of agents' actions extends to others, unless it can be demonstrated that agents are mentally incompetent or acting under coercion. A mentally competent and uncoerced agent, if he so chooses, may act in such a way as to bring harm to himself—e.g., through smoking, drinking, or taking steroids—and force is never warranted as long as no one else is harmed. That has come to be known as Mill's "principle of harm."

Over the years, the issue of paternalism in competitive sport has become weighty. Many argue simply that informed athletes ought to able to do what they want with their own bodies, whatever the risk to themselves, in order to gain an advantage over competitors. In the MC culture, with its focus on extrinsic goods, such risks are thought to be acceptable parts of athletic competition. Any attempt by one person to prohibit another from some action—including taking steroids—is merely an attempt by the former to fob off her own namby-pamby conception of what is good on to the other person. That itself is considered unjust and, perhaps, immoral. On the MC model of sport, it might be viewed similarly to disarming soldiers or interfering with free markets. Yet is all really fair in sport and war?

Performance Drugs and Fairness

A telling hypocrisy of the MC attitude is athletes' persistent public denial of doping, even when it seems obvious. Two of baseball's greatest sluggers, Barry Bonds and Sammy Sosa, have consistently denied using steroids, yet both added substantial muscle mass to their frames, beginning in their thirties. Bonds has only come clean in the last few years—and only somewhat clean.

In his days with the Pirates, Bonds was a strong but slender player whose overall talent for the game exceeded that of almost all others. At Pittsburgh, Bonds was listed at 6'1" and 185 pounds. By his forties, Bonds had packed over 40 pounds of muscle mass onto this relatively slight frame and had become the game's most powerful hitter. At the age of 37, he surpassed McGwire's single-season mark of 70 homers, with 73 of his own—an astonishing feat for someone who should have been thinking about retirement. Before his grand-jury testimony late in 2004, Bonds admitted only to using creatine, amino acids, and other supplements, but never anabolic steroids. The extraordinary gain of strength, he maintained, had come only through exceptional maintenance to a rugged workout schedule and, perhaps, a little broccoli! It is more likely that Bonds could not face the prospect of losing his dominance and the fame and fortune that went with it, so he sought out drugs as a means to preserve it.

In 2002, *Sports Illustrated* columnist Rick Reilly turned up the heat, so to speak, on the issue of steroids in baseball, by challenging Cubs slugger Sammy Sosa to voluntarily submit himself to testing for steroids at a local clinic. The idea was to quiet speculation that his astonishing home-run numbers had been enhanced pharmacologically.[6] Sosa himself had previously pledged to be "first in line," should the player's association and baseball agree to test for steroids. In response to Reilly's pressure to get tested, however, the Cubs superstar finally snapped, "This interview is over! Over mother fucker!"[7]

Sosa's anger was probably provoked by the threat to expose the dirty little secret that had become baseball's cash cow. Fans and sponsors revelled in the homerun races, refusing to speculate on the source of players' newfound power. Penn State professor, Charles E. Yesalis, a renowned expert on steroids, had this to say about their deliberate blissful ignorance, "When you see mature men who have already strength-trained for years, and all of a sudden they gain 30 pounds of lean mass, I am tremendously suspicious because that doesn't happen naturally. You don't need to be a steroid scientist to know that is incomprehensible."[8]

Insofar as baseball is regarded as a business and since both players and teams were profiting from drug use, few considered such secrecy unethical. Asking baseball to expose steroid use was like asking Coca-Cola to divulge their formula. Nevertheless, Detroit Free Press sports writer Drew Sharp, who wrote about McGwire's chase of Maris' record in 1998, called into question the first baseman's ethics in taking performance drugs. He said, "sports' governing bodies have long understood that the unfair physical advantages that anabolic steroids provide ultimately cheapens the accomplishments of those using the substances."[9] McGwire's use of drugs is unethical, according to Sharp, because it gave him an unfair advantage that other players did not have.

Yesalis, too, echoes Sharp's sentiment and frustration, "I'm bothered by the fact that these chemically enhanced athletes are breaking records of my idol, Mickey Mantle, where my strong belief is these clowns couldn't carry Mantle's jockstrap." Yet he continues: "But the important question is, "Mr. and Mrs. Fan, are you bothered enough to turn off your television? Or not pay $200 for an evening at Camden Yards?" I think we know fans are not bothered much. If anything, given the fans' love of watching the ball go over the wall, steroids have been very, very good for baseball.[10] On the MC model of sport, it seems that drug use is acceptable because it entertains fans and therefore brings in revenue—sports' ultimate extrinsic good.

Despite Yesalis and Sharp's concerns unfair advantage is not the main issue with doping because it is easily solved by legalization.

Unfairness Debunked

Following philosophers in the liberalist tradition such as John Stuart Mill and John Rawls, W. Miller Brown has argued for legalizing drugs in sport on the basis that athletes' risks are their own—i.e., risk-taking is a private, not public, affair. In "Paternalism, Drugs, and the Nature of Sports," he writes:

> We can indeed forbid the use of drugs in athletics in general, just as we do in the case of children. But ironically, in adopting such a paternalistic stance of insisting that we know better than the athletes themselves how to achieve some more *general good* which they myopically ignore, we must deny in them the very attributes we claim to value: self-reliance, personal achievement, and autonomy.[11]

In short, the "good" at which we aim in forbidding athletes the use of performance-enhancing substances is almost always outweighed by the damage done through paternalism—insisting we know better what is good for another. That, of course, is just Mill's thesis in his monograph *On Liberty*.

The paternalist objection is strong, but not decisive. It turns out that the harm done by promoting performance drugs is not merely personal; doping also harms other competitors and society at large putting extrinsic rewards ahead of athletes' well-being in sport. Legalization of doping or even tacit toleration by lax enforcement of anti-doping rules pressures athletes to take additional, unnecessary risks in order to reap the extrinsic rewards of athletic competition.

It is no mystery why athletes engage in doping despite the risk. In most sports, those competitors that take performance-enhancing substances clearly outperform those competitors that do not. Pitcher Kenny Rogers says, "Basically, steroids can jump you a level or two. The average player can become a star, and the star player can become a superstar. And the superstar? Forget it. He can do things we've never seen before."[12]

In powerlifting, a sport that Holowchak has been involved with for over 30 years, performance drugs can add over 15 percent to one's strength. A lifter pressing 400 pounds, by taking performance drugs, becomes a lifter pressing 460 to 480 pounds. Holowchak himself took anabolic steroids in the early 1980s and can testify that the gains are not a result of the placebo effect.

In Reid's sport, cycling, doping has been a problem almost from the start. In multi-day races such as the Tour de France, pharmacological aids to performance and recovery are both effective and difficult to detect. Although Reid never took drugs herself, she witnessed their effects on her competitors and was often frustrated by officials' inability to control the problem.[13] Because they distorted the results of her competitions and may have prevented her from achieving her athletic goals, Reid considers herself harmed by drugs in sport, even though she never took them.

Direct harm to drug users only makes the situation worse. Though there is much we have yet to learn about the long-term use of anabolic substances, they do have side effects that can be very harmful, even lethal—especially if used immoderately or for long periods of time. Caminiti, for instance, ended up with a testosterone level that was 80 percent below normal. He died on October 10 of 2004 due to heart failure—presumably linked to problems with cocaine, pain killers, and alcohol. Steroids were likely a contributing factor.

Although some risks are necessary for the intrinsic goods of sport—e.g., figure skating without the risk of falling would hardly be a sport—the additional unnecessary risks posed by performance-enhancing drugs is accepted by athletes, whose focus lies beyond the game at extrinsic rewards like money and fame, or by athletes that judge such risks necessary to reap the intrinsic goods that depend on close competition.

The performance-enhancement benefit provided by doping coerces all serious athletes, at some point, to ask themselves: Should I attempt to improve my performance significantly at the risk of my physical health? The rewards for an affirmative answer seem large. In baseball, an average *minor*-league player could become an average *major*-league player through taking steroids. Since the average major-league salary is over $2,000,000, the lure here is great. Moreover, a financially secure but mediocre major-league player could rise to the level of superstar. In every such case, it seems, there is a dilemma: An athlete either concerns herself with only intrinsic goods and forgets about competing with those who use performance-enhancing drugs, or she takes the drugs and risks moral and physical harm.

The lure and immediacy of the potential anabolic payoff is generally too great a temptation. One former baseball trainer had this to say, "Steroids and the confidence that comes with them can be the difference between working at Wal-Mart and being among the richest people in the world. When you're a teenager, the long-term risks don't seem real, but the money and fame does."[14] Holowchak too, when taking steroids, felt the same way.

On the MC model of sport, questions of moral integrity and fairness take a back seat to performance concerns. Fairness issues are easily addressed by legalizing performance-enhancing drugs and making them readily available to all athletes who want them. Yet there remains the issue of harm—i.e., the unnecessary risks posed by pharmacological supplements. The legalization of drugs adds no goods to sport, it only increases the risk that athletes must take in order to achieve those goods.

Choice and Coercion

Some may still object that athletes should be free to accept the risks caused by doping just as they freely accept any other risk that comes along with sports participation. The suggestion that steroids and other risky drugs should be banned because, if legalized, many athletes would be forced to use them and unwillingly exposed to undue health-related risks, they say, fails to acknowledge that participation is a matter of choice in the first place.

We agree with those who say that risk of harm to individuals who freely choose to take steroids does not, by itself, justify paternalism, especially in light of the other possible risks—e.g., torn ligaments—that these very same athletes already knowingly accept. Regard for autonomy requires that we allow others the opportunity to decide for themselves what is right for them, even if it ultimately results in great personal harm. We deny, however, that doping harms only the user.

The more interesting scenario concerns harm done to others by those, like Giambi and Bonds, who "freely" choose to take performance enhancing drugs. Even those persons that insist athletes have a right to do with their bodies what they so choose limit that right at the boundary of its impact on others. The question is this: Does the taking of performance-enhancing drugs by some athletes put coercive pressures on others to likewise risk their health? Justifying intervention in such cases depends upon whether or not we actually have examples of coercion. After all, information concerning the risks involved with steroids is widely available to all athletes and, thus, the taking or not taking of such drugs would seem to be a matter of deliberate and free choice, not coercion.

The issue, we suggest, is not as cut-and-dried as critics have traditionally made it out to be. On the one hand, it is clear and trivially true that athletes always have a choice: They can choose to take performance drugs or they can refuse. On the other hand, athletes who are inclined not to take such drugs face tremendous external pressures to take them in order to remain competitive with those who do. Since many of sport's intrinsic goods depend on close competition—as it is hard to cultivate virtues like courage, or achieve peak experiences like "the zone" in lopsided competition—the complete freedom to choose is rendered illusory. By choosing not to take steroids, most athletes must also choose to give up not only the extrinsic rewards available at the highest levels of their sport of victory, but also the intrinsic benefits derived from close competition. Meanwhile other athletes risk great harm to their bodies so that they may compete with dopers, when this need not be the case. Is that free choice or coercion?

Philosopher Robert Simon disagrees. The doping issue is not one of harm to others through coercion. What is the difference, he asks, between the coercion generated by use of steroids and that, say, generated by training heavily with weights? After all, a heavy routine with weights may be more dangerous to some athletes than steroids. He sums up:

> Arguably, the charge that drug users create unfair pressures on other competitors begs the very question at issue. That is, it presupposes that such pressures are morally suspect in ways that other competitive pressures are not, when the very point at issue is whether that is the case. What is needed is some principled basis for asserting that certain competitive pressures—those generated by the use of performance enhancing drugs—are illegitimately imposed while other competitive pressures—such as those generated by hard training—are legitimate and proper. It will not do to point out that the former pressures are generated by drug use. What is needed is an explanation of why the use of performance-enhancing drugs should be prohibited in the first place.[15]

The "principled basis" that Simon seeks is legitimate, and Holowchak has suggested a principled answer: Performance drugs should be banned because, given what we know, they are dangerous to the athletes who take them.[16]

Steroids and other risky aids show greater regard for athletic performance than for the improvement and well being of athletes themselves, and performance aids that do just that do not properly belong in sport. There is no such reasonable suspicion concerning weight training. Athletes do get hurt while training with heavy weights, but, done cautiously, such training is more helpful than hurtful. In fact, lifting weights reduces the risk of injury in sports like football or wrestling. Steroids provide no such physical benefit. Furthermore, whereas weight training can promote such virtues as self-discipline and patience, steroid use seems to promote only vices such as cheating and chemical dependency.

We agree with Simon, however, when he says that risk is a very large part of the fabric of sport and the goal of sport is not necessarily to reduce risk in it.[17] Yet it does not follow from that that sports become better when the risks are increased or that all risks are equal. As Bernard Suits so eloquently stated, sports are characterized by rules that "prohibit more efficient in favor of less efficient means."[18] It is the prohibition of efficiencies, such as completing a marathon course by motorcycle, which gives sport its ability to render goods like challenge and cultivation of virtue. Doping, even if it were not harmful, is a justly prohibited efficiency because it does not promote and may even threaten the excellence and overall well-being of athletes.

Are Steroids Harmful?

Doubt might remain, of course, about whether steroids are really dangerous. The issue is now empirical. Research has linked performance drugs to cosmetic defects, heart disease, liver toxicity and tumors, as well as reproductive problems. Steroids are also strongly suspected to be causally linked to pulmonary (and related) problems such as blood-cholesterol increase (because steroids affect how sugars and fats are handled), increased blood pressure, hypertension, and, consequently, stroke, and heart attack. There are definite causal relationships between use of steroids and decrease in the production of testosterone, shrinking of testes, low-sperm counts, and infertility in males as well as masculinization, enlargement of the clitoris, and irregular menstruation in females—most of which lead to impaired reproductive ability. Many athletes these days prefer human growth hormone (HGH)—a polypeptide hormone produced by the pituitary gland. But HGH may cause hepatitis, antibody formation directed against the hormone, hyperglycemia, diabetes, and acromegaly.[19]

The problem with gleaning conclusive evidence that steroids are dangerous is that their illegality makes those who take them shy away experiments involving their long-term effects. Moreover, studies in laboratories cannot mimic the extreme doses that athletes consumed by the MC attitude toward sport are known to take.[20] No such studies are ethically permissible today in American laboratories, due to public hostility about the perceived dangers.[21]

Obviously, it can be argued that many athletes take steroids in reasonably low amounts and the likelihood of injury is, thus, minimal. Their use for such a trivial benefit as athletic enhancement, however, must be justified in terms of benefit to athletes as human beings, not merely in terms of sports performance, victory, or their attendant rewards.

Nonetheless, there are many celebrated examples of death or serious harm linked with steroids: Steve Courson's heart disease at age 32, bodybuilder Steve Valley's heart attack in a Phoenix gym and subsequent death at age 21, World's Strongest Man competitors O.D. Wilson, Jon Paul Sigmarsson, and U.S. weight-lifting coach, Dr. John Zeigler, who was responsible for the development of the steroid dianabol—the steroid Holowchak used to take. Zeigler himself used steroids and died in 1983. Before his death, Zeigler warned others in a taped

message: "I wish I had never heard the word 'steroid.' . . . All these young kids .
. . don't realize the terrible price they are going to pay."[22]

Given the serious dangers involved in taking anabolic steroids, it would be
incautious, unwise, and immoral to advocate their use in competitive sport. Legalizing steroids to accommodate those persons that want to take them, in spite
of the great risks to their health, would coerce many other serious athletes to
take them, who otherwise would not, in order to compete at the highest levels.
That, quite clearly, is injurious to these others by interfering with their autonomy
and, more importantly, their pursuit of excellence through sport.

If fairness dictates a level playing field, common sense dictates that we level it by maintaining the current ban on steroids. Philosopher Warren Fraleigh
agrees:

> Under current historical conditions of sport, why, morally speaking, should a
> highly competent athlete be forced either to lower his/her expectancies or dis-
> continue sport involvement because he/she cannot compete with drug users?
> Why should the effective coercive force not be in the opposite direction against
> drug users? The effect of more people harmed by coerced drug use . . . amounts
> to tacit social approval of coerced self-harm of athletes. To me the forced
> choice of either coerced self-harm or of dropping out or lowering one's expec-
> tations is a morally unconscionable choice.[23]

The dilemma athletes face under the MC model of sport is real and acute.[24]
Athletes, like Reid, that competed without the assistance of performance drugs
will never really know if indeed they were as good as or even better than athletes that competed with such drugs. In that sense, doping harms all competitors,
not just those who take the drugs.[25] Overall, those few that are willing to sacrifice their moral and physical well being in the headlong pursuit of victory impose their dangerous standards on the majority that would rather compete without such risks. Harm, through coercion, dictates that performance drugs ought to
be banned from socially sanctioned competitions. Harm notwithstanding, performance drugs are a justifiably excluded efficiency since they interfere with
rather than enhances sport's ability to produce goods through challenge. The
doping ban preserves rather than destroys human integrity and autonomy.

Notes

1. Excellence (*aretē*), strictly speaking, is not a good intrinsic to sport the way that
challenge and the joy of competition are. It is, however, a good internal to athletes,
whereas the money and glory associated with athletic victory are extrinsic both to the
game and to athletes.

2. William C. Mann, "Fight Steroid Use or Face Legislation," *The Morning Call,*
December 5, 2004, A5.

3. Steve Wilstein, "Steroids in Sports," *The Morning Call,* December 4, 2004, A3.

4. Statistics began to tail off in 2008. The American League leader had 37 homers; the National League leader had 48. In 2009, the AL leader had 39 homers; the NL leader had 47 homers.

5. John Stuart Mill, *On Liberty* (Indianapolis: Hackett Publishing Company, Inc., 1985).

6. He had broken the 60 home-run mark three times since 1998 and was noted for his tape-measure drives.

7. M. Andrew Holowchak, "Baseball, Hotdogs, Apple Pie, and Steroids: Coming Clean about Cleaning Up Baseball," *Sensibilities*, Vol. 6, No. 1, 2003, 8.

8. http://sportingnews.com/voices/dave_kindred/20020812.html, 2.

9. http://sportingnews.com/voices/dave_kindred/20020812.html, 3.

10. http://sportingnews.com/voices/dave_kindred/20020812.html, 3.

11. W. Miller Brown, "Paternalism, Drugs, and the Nature of Sports," *Journal of the Philosophy of Sport*, XI, 14-22, 1985, 21.

12. Holowchak, "Baseball, Hot Dogs, Apple Pie, and Steroids," 9.

13. Heather L. Reid, "My Life as a Two-Wheeled Philosopher," *Cycling and Philosophy*. Eds. Mike Austin and Jesus Ilundain. Malden, MA: Blackwell, 2010, 151-161.

14. Holowchak, "Baseball, Hot Dogs, Apple Pie, and Steroids," 9.

15. Robert Simon, "Good Competition and Drug-Enhanced Performance," *Journal of the Philosophy of Sport,* Vol. 12, 6-13, 1985, 9.

16. M. Andrew Holowchak, "'Aretism' and Pharmacological Ergogenic Aids in Sport: Taking a Shot at Steroids," *Philosophy of Sport: Critical Readings, Crucial Issues,* M. Andrew Holowchak (Upper Saddle River, NJ: Prentice-Hall, Inc., 2002), 307-22.

17. Simon, "Good Competition," 10.

18. Bernard Suits, *The Grasshopper: Games, Life, and Utopia* (Ontario: Broadview Press, 2005), 49.

19. Some athletes take dosages of more than 100 times their body's own level. See Michael Colgan, *Ultimate Sports Nutrition: Your Competitive Edge* (Ronkonkoma, NY: Advanced Research Press, 1993, 395-418) and Charles E. Yesalis and James Wright, *Anabolic Steroids in Sport and Exercise* (Champaign, IL: Human Kinetics Publishers, Inc., 1993) 108-111.

20. Charles Yesalis and M. Bahrke, "Current Comment from the American College of Sports Medicine: Anabolic Steroids," April, 1999 (Official position statement of the ACSM), 98.

21. Such experiments are conducted in Europe, though these focus on changes in athletic performance or lean body-mass, instead of long-term effects to health.

22. Colgan, *Ultimate Sports Nutrition,* 395-401.

23. Warren Fraleigh, "Performance-Enhancing Drugs in Sport: The Ethical Issue," *Journal of the Philosophy of Sport*, XI, 23-29, 1985, 28.

24. Breivik argues cleverly that the coercive element plays itself out in the form of a prisoner's dilemma, where rational self-interest winds up self-defeating. G. Breivik, "The Doping Dilemma: Some Game Theoretical and Philosophical Considerations," *Sportwissenshaft*, XVII.1, 1987, 83-94.

25. Reid argues that doping threatens self-respect, respect for others, and respect for the sport. Heather L. Reid, *The Philosophical Athlete* (Durham, NC: Carolina Academic Press, 2002), 139-143.

Chapter 8
Problems of Performance Enhancement

"Where it was possible to consider the goods to be achieved by sports practices as agent-independent, little headway seemed possible even in a society where it could be assumed that the basic goods of life were distributed in a just manner. The problem is that although risk appraisal is a statistical matter, risk taking is a personal one. Risk taking is not agent-independent, but, rather, relative to the overall circumstances and goals of individuals," W. Miller Brown

DRUG-ENHANCED PERFORMANCE, THE TOPIC of the last chapter, is a hot issue among critics of sport today. Yet we hope to show in this chapter that performance-enhancement through drugs conceals a deeper issue in competitive sport today—performance-enhancement itself. MC sport, with its commitment to winning at all costs, also encourages performance enhancement through all sorts of performance-enhancing aids: some legal, some not. To what extent should competitive sport embrace such practices?

This question is meaty for two reasons. First, commitment to performance enhancement at all costs, part of the panagonistic element of MC sport, is itself commitment to a certain philosophical approach to sport. Second, performance-enhancement often comes by innovation that increases risks and threatens the internal goods of sport. Thus, the question of performance enhancement cannot be answered without first saying something about risk-taking and innovation in sport.

What are Ergogenic Aids?

With the volume of papers on performance-enhancing drugs by philosophers, sociologists, and others, it is strange that the larger issues of performance-enhancement (i.e., ergogenicity) and performance-enhancing aids (i.e., ergogenic aids) have been mostly ignored. Perhaps the thinking is that competitive sport, if it is about anything, is about performance enhancement and to argue the obvious is vain. Yet since so much emphasis in competitive sport is placed on winning, especially from the MC perspective that predominates today, the investment in performance enhancement is great. When, from a moral perspective, is the cost too exorbitant?

Ergogenic aids are substances, techniques, or materials that improve performance. They may be grouped into five kinds: pharmacological, mechanical, psychological, physiological, and nutritional. Passing over pharmacological aids, covered fully in the previous chapter, let us look at the other four ergogenic aids in turn.

Mechanical ergogenic aids are materials and physical techniques used to enhance performance. For example, in baseball, on the material side, batters often use lighter, streamlined bats to increase bat speed, while fielders often have gloves tailored to their respective position on the diamond. On the physical side, some batters use novel swinging techniques to improve bat contact, while pitchers might add a new pitch—such as a slider, curve, or screwball—to their arsenal to improve deceptiveness and effectiveness. Equipment-intensive sports like cycling and skiing place such great value on mechanical advantages that efforts have to be taken to preserve the primacy of the "human factor" in contest results.

Psychological ergogenic aids are mental techniques that have proven effective in enhancing performance. Athletes learn techniques like pre-performance visualization or distraction control during performance. Coaches give motivational speeches prior to athletes to improve their concentration or level of arousal. Specialized video games have been developed for car and motorcycle racers to help them learn track layouts, increase concentration skills, and reduce reaction times.

Physiological ergogenic aids, meanwhile, are those techniques that directly improve physical performance. Altitude training by runners and cyclists stimulates the production of red-blood cells in response to oxygen-depleted conditions and that enhances their performance in normal conditions. Keeping body-fat low also gives athletes a physiological edge. Having greater muscle mass means having more contractile tissue and less non-contractile tissue, and that generally translates into improved performance.

Last, nutritional ergogenic aids are dietary enhancements such as protein or carbohydrate supplements, vitamins and minerals, sport-specific bars, gels, and energy drinks, caffeine, and baking soda. Even water, which has no calories, can be considered a nutritional ergogenic, at least indirectly, in that athletes that replace fluids with regularity have a decided performance advantage over those that do not.

There is no doubt that ergogenic aids are an integral part of competitive sport. Is there a point at which their use becomes problematic, even unethical?

Are Ergogenic Aids Unnatural?

Perhaps the most intuitive objection to certain ergogenic aids is that they are unnatural. Expressed baldly, the argument runs: We are morally obliged to ban unnatural aids from competitive sport, since unnatural aids are "unclean" and unclean things have no place in sport.

On the one hand that reasoning seems too loose. Human growth hormone (HGH), for instance, is a substance that is manufactured in each person's body,[1] so, how can taking HGH be unnatural? One might concede that, however, but add that what is unnatural is injecting additional HGH into a body that produces it naturally. Here, what is unnatural is the amount of the hormone. The objection, however, makes the criterion seem too strict, since the same argument can be used against dietary supplements like vitamins, minerals, or protein powder. They too might seem unnatural for the same reason, but few people, would object to their use.

Moreover, one can enhance performance substantially through the use of effective training, active recovery, intelligent coaching, and psychological techniques. Are any of those natural? Indeed there is little about sport at the highest levels of competition that is natural.[2]

Perhaps the problem centers on just what we mean by "natural," Attempts to distinguish between "natural" and "unnatural" aids usually assume that it is completely understood what those terms mean when applied to sport, but it seems that the opposite is true. Presumably, when we call something "natural," what we mean is something like "having its source or origin in and not outside of an athlete." Roger Gardner writes:

> [O]ne might want to argue that the psychologist, biomechanist, diet, and so on are simply bringing out the best in the athlete, and the athlete (qua human) is still ultimately responsible for the performance and any gained advantage. The resulting capability is not external to the athlete . . . but inherent within the athlete. The enhancement allowed for through the scientist or diet simply permits the athlete to overcome some "undesired inhibitor" to better performance. . ., and thereby reach his or her full potential. Yet, it would seem that the same argument could be made with respect to the use of substances such as amphetamines or steroids. . . . If the limiting condition is to be humanness, then the objectionable enhancement must be shown to be nonhuman.[3]

If we should buy into that internal sense of "natural," we would then do away with a large number of ergogenic aids that do not seem to be morally objectionable. In powerlifting, for instance, denim benching shirts, denim squatting suits, thick leather lifting belts, knee wraps, wrist wraps, and chalk substantially improve an athlete's capacity to lift massive weights—often by hundreds of pounds. But those aids are just the mechanical ergogenic aids, called "advances" in sports technology.

From our aretic perspective, "unnaturalness" is not the issue, but rather how the ergogenic aid affects goods internal to athletes and to their sport.

Ergogenic Aids and Unfairness

One way that ergogenic aids may be said to harm sport is by offering some athletes an unfair advantage over others. Even if an aid is legal and theoretically available to all, it might be argued that some athletes have privileged access to them, while others do not. Access to the best coaches is an example. Access to world-class equipment and facilities is another.

Let us keep in mind here that it is not the ergogenic aids that are at issue, but their accessibility, and a large part of accessibility boils down to money. A wealthy athlete will have access to the latest and best-designed equipment, coaching, psychological counseling, nutritional supplements, and other such ergogenic aids. How then does an equally ambitious, poorer athlete compete? She cannot.

From the perspective of an MC model of sport, economic advantage may seem to be part of the game. Amateur athletes and even National Olympic Committees may regard their ability to buy expensive equipment as a completely legitimate means for gaining an edge. "I deserve the advantage I get from my bike," an amateur cyclist once told Reid, "because I worked to earn the money to pay for it."

Nevertheless, athletic contests should not be designed so that they can be won at the cash-register. The economic exclusion of worthy competitors harms both sport and athletes that seek to cultivate excellence through it. Sports federations, therefore, should do what they can to limit the sporting advantages gained by wealth. In cycling, there is a minimum weight for the bicycle and some types of expensive equipment are banned. The organization called Olympic Solidarity, meanwhile, distributes a portion of Olympic television revenue to underprivileged athletes and National Olympic Committees.

Ultimately, however, economic disparity is an unfortunate fact of life. Third-world nations, with limited resources, can have little concern for high-level sport while civil strife, drought, unemployment, and hunger plague their people. In countries where clean water and air are luxuries, sparkling sports facilities are appropriately absent. In addition, climate or resources can limit one's options. A young man who lives in Egypt would find it frustrating to have a passion for skiing. The same could be said for someone in northern Siberia who loves beach volleyball. Part of the magic of the human competitive spirit in sport is that some persons or teams can overcome specific disadvantages and still prevail through sheer determination, moxie, and pluck.

Ergogenic Aids, Risk, and Harm

What about the issue of harm? Can we object, as we did in the previous chapter, to certain ergogenic aids that are proven or even suspected of being harmful? Over the years, W. Miller Brown has repeatedly argued that harm is a personal, not a public, issue.[4] Risk is a part of sport and a part of life, he maintains. For example, in "Practices and Prudence," he writes:

> Where it was possible to consider the goods to be achieved by sports practices as agent-independent, little headway seemed possible even in a society where it could be assumed that the basic goods of life were distributed in a just manner. The problem is that although risk appraisal is a statistical matter, risk taking is a personal one. Risk taking is not agent-independent, but, rather, relative to the overall circumstances and goals of individuals.[5]

Of course, some sports are riskier than other sports and often it is the risk factor that makes one sport more appealing and rewarding than another to a competitor. In "As American as Gatorade and Apple Pie: Performance Drugs and Sports," Brown adds:

> In many sports, the activities of the sports themselves are far more dangerous than the use of any of the performance drugs that have even a bare chance of being effective. Deaths and injuries due to the use of performance drugs are rare. . . . But deaths and serious injuries due to the sports themselves number in the hundreds in sports like football, boxing, mountain climbing, hockey, cycling, and skiing.[6]

Against Brown, we assert that harm caused by performance enhancers in sport is not exclusive to individuals and thus not just a matter of personal choice. Sport is a social institution that not only reflects social values, but also contributes to the moral degeneration or betterment of individuals and communities. Excessive risks in competitive sports transform them from tests of excellence to thrilling spectacles that sacrifice the wellbeing of its competitors for the entertainment of its audience. We return then to the gladiatorial games. Societies that embrace such spectacles theatricalize sport at the expense of athletes and their cultivation of excellence.[7]

Accordingly, ergogenic aids that promote risk at the expense of excellence should not be a part of sport and competitions that unduly weigh risk at the expense of athletes' wellbeing should not be socially sanctioned. What holds for performance-enhancing drugs holds also for other ergogenic aids.

Undue risk is often a matter of quantity rather than quality—a consideration especially important in the MC model's tendency toward excess. Many otherwise benign supplements have significant ergogenic capacities when taken in large amounts that can prove harmful, even fatal, to an athlete over time. Research shows that increased protein intake improves muscle mass and strength. In one study, world-class Bulgarian weightlifters increased protein intake to over 300 grams per person and there was a corresponding 5% increase in body mass and 6% increase in strength. Many athletes have a daily protein intake of over 200 grams. Studies show, however, that protein that is not utilized is converted, in part, to ammonia, which is highly toxic. When more ammonia is generated than can be excreted, the kidneys become overloaded and the blood is literally poisoned.[8]

Also, many athletes use rigorous plyometric techniques to improve explosive-muscle firing in many sports. Olympic weightlifters sometimes jump down from the top of a high platform, such as a staircase, and catch themselves below in a squatting position to improve ballistic strength out of that position. Such plyometric techniques are very dangerous to tendons and ligaments—especially those around the knee. Is that sufficient harm to warrant a ban on such training techniques?

Those examples are troubling, but they seem beyond our control. Do we want agencies, such as the World Anti-Doping Agency (WADA), to regulate protein intake and training techniques of athletes in addition to all of the things they already monitor? How much political power should we allow such governing agencies to have? When does governance become intrusive and paternalistic?

As philosopher John Stuart Mill recognized, the problem must first be addressed on the individual level. In *On Liberty* he states, "Each is the proper guardian of his own health, whether bodily or mental and spiritual. Mankind are greater gainers by suffering each other to live as seems good to themselves than by compelling each to live as seems good to the rest."[9] Mill acknowledges that we each must suffer a little "for the sake of the greater good of human freedom."[10] In other words, there must be some degree of harm that each is willing to accept so that humans can flourish through personal freedom. So, though risk-taking is not just a personal matter, some degree of risk taking is important in competitive sport in free societies.

How does an athlete know when and where to limit risk and how do governing bodies know when paternalistic intervention should be invoked?

Innovation, Social Justice, and Sport

The first thing to observe is that increased athletic performance, by itself, does not justify an ergogenic aid's acceptance—there must be some other benefit from it. Perhaps the mere fact of innovation is benefit enough. Arguments proposing to allow certain types of ergogenic aids in sports, like golf clubs that compensate somewhat for mechanically bad swings, amount to a methodological innovation in sport itself. Yet is innovation really a benefit? Here we are not arguing about innovation within any particular sport. There have been several instances of that. Here we are arguing about innovation in sport generally.

Michael Burke has argued that our moral condemnation of ergogenic aids like drugs in sport is a result of a confusion resulting when an oral culture of sport gets fixed into a "written culture of constancy" that is inconsistent with human nature. Sport is dynamic and flowing, and this dynamism and flow are responsible for innovation in and redefinition of sport. He writes:

> Drug users test the latitude of the rules in a way that is not as far removed from the change that Dick Fosbury produced with his new technique as we would like to think. New knowledge, technical innovation, training methods, new materials, and stronger, faster athletes all create redefinitions of games. . . . All testing of the latitude involves egocentric attempts by players to shape the practice. No one attempt is more morally condemnable than any other. All attempts, whether successful or not, involve the production of beneficiaries and victims. The drug user in modern times is a victim, much as the exponents of the scissors method of high jumping were also victims. Both are victims of aesthetic sensibilities of the community.[11]

The definition and redefinition of "sport," Burke believes, is found in the actual practice of sport and not in any written culture, for the latter crushes autonomy in order to preserve sameness in practice.

Burke asks whether the drug ban attempts to "impose an essentialist and written logic on the freedom of the athletes?" His answer is "yes," There is a conspiracy, it seems, to keep "game conditions as constant as possible," and this conspiracy is rooted in the false notion that the proposition, "Drugs are, by nature, evil," is capable of rational demonstration.[12] Those persons responsible for the ban on drugs in sport are the very conspirators, presumably, that would have competitors keep the rules of all sports fixed for all times.

Yet nothing of the sort follows. We agree that there is nothing inherently wicked about drugs, but we are also sure that there is no underlying conspiracy by those that support their ban to do away with creativity and innovation in competitive sport. Ergogenic aids, like steroids, are wrong, because they place athletic performance and victory ahead of the well-being of athletes and society. It is, after all, their contribution to personal and social wellbeing that gives sports value in the first place. The Fosbury Flop in high jumping, just like the split-finger fastball, was a technical innovation that harmed neither athletes nor society.

W. Miller Brown takes a different approach. He states that sports and their goods, being predominantly expressions of individual character, invite an exploration of human differences that pave the path for "new ways of being human." The worthwhile price for that, he thinks, is that sport will reflect, though not solve, problems of social justice.[13]

What Brown fails to mention is that some of the new ways of being human do more to harm than to help communities or societies—i.e., they neither reflect, nor solve, but create grand problems for social justice. The indiscriminate use of ergogenic aids is one such instance.

The normative view of sport that we defend, "Aretism," puts no stranglehold on human expression. It merely invites us to temper our exploration of our own humanity through sport by sensible and appropriate moral guidelines. It acknowledges that sport transcends individual expression and has clear social implications. Thus, sport can be a vehicle of creative human expression within the confines of one's communal obligations. Though it might be too much to ask that sport, through its practice, must aim to solve problems of social injustice, sport, as a social institution, cannot be wholly indifferent to such problems. Sport must at least strive to steer clear of social injustice.

A rational and relatively fixed notion of "sport" is philosophically highly desirable and does not rule out innovation, change, novelty, and autonomy. It merely challenges us to come up with a view of sport that reflects timeless values, such as respect for self and others, through the exercise of competitive challenge.

Ergogenic Aids and Excellence

Let us return to the issue of unfairness. It is not so much the fairness or unfairness of using legal ergogenic aids that is questionable, but rather the manner in which the advantage is gained. What is objectionable about certain types of ergogenic innovations in sport is that they improve performance without promoting excellence; athletes' results are improved but athletes themselves are not.

We can go some ways toward distinguishing between acceptable and unacceptable ergogenic aids by examining their effect upon the development and well-being of athletes.[14] Ergogenic aids that present no unnecessary risk of harm may be permitted at the discretion of individual athletes, the governing bodies of particular sports, or larger units that govern many sports like the NCAA or the IOC. Only ergogenic aids that also promote athletic excellence, however, should be actively encouraged.

How does that apply to cases such as performance-enhancing swimsuits? Does a better suit promote athlete excellence? It certainly does not seem to do so, yet that alone may not seem to be a good reason for banning it. On the other hand, the high cost of the suits may reduce the number of competitors able to challenge those that are wealthy enough to buy them and that could indirectly militate against development of excellence—insofar as close competition promotes excellence. Swimmers who use such suits wind up improving their times without any meaningful benefits to themselves and, at the same time, they reduce the number of close competitors, thereby arguably harming their sport.

Some ergogenic aids, however, could promote athlete excellence by encouraging close competition, virtuous skills, or by reducing risk of injury. The introduction of the fiberglass vaulting pole, for example, made that sport safer and opened it up to females and smaller athletes. Good nutrition and hydration, meanwhile, promote self-discipline. Slide-resistant ski suits reduce the harmful consequences of crashes and encourage skilled risk-taking even while they promote safety. In general, when an ergogenic aid promotes athletes' excellence, its use should be encouraged.

Aretism and Ergogenicity

It is unquestionable that ergogenicity is a part of sport. Certain ergogenic aids, like visualization or distraction-control techniques, are unobjectionable. Others, such as use of potentially harmful supplements, seem morally objectionable. Still other ergogenic aids, like golf clubs that forgive bad swings or swimsuits that improve speed without promoting excellence, invite rigorous debate. Just where do we draw a line?

We think the most compelling argument for imposing limits on ergogenic aids is based on aretic considerations: Ergogenic aids that improve competition and promote athlete excellence (*aretē*) should be embraced. Aretism demands, unlike the MC model, respect for human limitations. It acknowledges that victory in sport has no intrinsic value and that competitive sport is a good insofar as it is a means to human improvement.

Of course, one can argue that there is nothing about the nature of sport that necessarily invites aretic considerations. We agree. Our argument has nothing to do with the "nature" of sport. Our argument all along has been normative. Sport, as a social institution and normatively understood, is a quest for excellence through integration, and that has social implications. Despite the importance placed on winning in the MC model, the aretic is, and must be a part of sport. Athletes, institutions, and contests that fail to cultivate any aretic dimension, like professional wrestling, have no claim to legitimacy and should not be socially sanctioned. Performance and winning are important parts of sport, but sport itself derives its value from internal goods such as challenge and the cultivation of excellence, which are not endemic to sport. Ergogenic aids that promote per-formance without improving challenge or excellence have no defensible value.

Notes

1. This is called somatotropin, which is secreted by the anterior pituitary gland.

2. See Michael Lavin, "Sports and Drugs: Are the Current Bans Justified?" *Ethics in Sport*, eds. William J. Morgan, Klaus V. Meier, and Angela J. Schneider (Champaign, IL: Human Kinetics, 2001), 173.

3. Roger Gardner, "On Performance-Enhancing Substances and the Unfair Advantage Argument," *Journal of the Philosophy of Sport*, VI, 59-73, 2001, 304.

4. Brown and Holowchak debated the issue of performance-enhancing drugs at Ohio University on January 19, 2001.

5. W. M. Brown, "Practices and Prudence," *Philosophy of Sport: Critical Readings, Crucial Issues*, M. Andrew Holowchak (Upper Saddle River, NJ: Prentice-Hall, Inc., 2002), 246.

6. W. Miller Brown, "As American As Gatorade and Apple Pie: Performance Drugs and Sports," *Ethics in Sport*, eds. William J. Morgan, Klaus V. Meier, and Angela J. Schneider (Champaign, IL: Human Kinetics, 142-168, 2001), 146.

7. Rome's *ludi* are often given as an example of this, although Reid argues that gladiators could nevertheless cultivate *aretē*, see H. Reid, "Was the Roman Gladiator an Athlete?" *Journal of the Philosophy of Sport* 33:1 (2006): 37-49. Reid also argues that modern American college football resembles Rome in its exploitation of athletes. See H. Reid, "Heroes of the Coliseum." *Football and Philosophy*, ed. Mike Austin (Lexington, KY: University Press of Kentucky, 2008), 128-140.

8. Michael Colgan, *Optimum Sports Nutrition: Your Competitive Edge* (New York: Advanced Research Press, 1993), 153.

9. John Stuart Mill, *On Liberty* (New York: Penguin Books, 1985), 72.

10. Mill, *On Liberty*, 149.

11. Michael Burke, "Drugs in Sport: Have They Practiced Too Hard? A Response to Schneider and Butcher," *Journal of the Philosophy of Sport*, XXIV, 1997, 60.

12. Burke, "Drugs in Sport," 60.

13. W. Miller Brown, "Practices and Prudence," 246.

14. See M. Andrew Holowchak, "Ergogenic Aids and the Limits of Human Performance in Sport: Ethical Issues, Aesthetic Considerations," *Journal of the Philosophy of Sport*, Vol. 29, No. 2, 74-86.

Chapter 9
Gender, Aggression and Violence

"Modern biology describes a world with limited resources and a practically unlimited ability on the part of life to reproduce far beyond those resources. Malthusian catastrophes look inevitable in nature. We may expect human society to be gentler and to contrive to live within its resources. But in doing this it will have abandoned the natural for the artificial." Daeshik Kim and Allan Back

T HE FIRST PART OF THE BOOK SHOWS that episodes of aggression and violence have been a part of competitive sport since it began. The link between violence and sport is so intimate that we have labeled the current panagonistic model of competitive sport the Martial/Commercial model. The marginalization and exclusion of females is also a persistent feature of that model. Many believe that the two are connected: sport's essential aggressiveness explains why females are inferior athletes.

We must not forget, however, that competitive sport is a human construction. If it rewards violence and aggression, that is because we have constructed it that way. If it marginalizes or excludes females, that is because we allow it to. Furthermore, if sport is to continue promoting violence and the marginalization females, we need some social justification for those choices.

The MC model's response is characteristically belief-affirming. It assumes, without questioning, that human beings are naturally aggressive and that males are naturally superior. Competitive sport, conducted in its martial manner, is then seen as confirming those beliefs. Can sport's traditional violence and androcentrism be defended?

The Lessons of Ancient Greece

It is tempting to locate the origins of athletic aggression and androcentrism in ancient Greece. Sport appears there as a form of training for war and the competitive sprit permeates nearly in all facets of masculine public life—including poetry, entertainment, business, industry, education, music, public service, and even politics.[1] Antony Raubtischek writes:

> The [Greek] "agonistic" attitude was from the very beginning not confined to
> athletic exercises but it constituted a code of conduct, the striving for excel-
> lence (*aretē*) and for its recognition in the form of honor (*timē*). Both Achilles
> and Odysseus strive to be the best, and the honor and glory and recognition
> they seek are caused by ambition and the love of honor (*philotimia*) and not by
> the avoidance of "shame." . . . Here lies the root of the Greek spirit of competi-
> tion which permeates Greek culture and which is present in the world today.[2]

It is tempting to imagine Greek athletics as militaristic—there were races in armor and brutal combat events. Wrestling had no weight classes, boxing had no
rounds, and *pancratium*, a kind of fighting that banned little more than eye-
gouging, often resulted in blood, injury, and sometimes even death. Yet Greek
athletics were distinctive precisely because they were *not* war.

The Pythian, Isthmian, Nemean, and Olympic festivals we mentioned in
Chapter 1 were primarily religious. Athletes competed in honor of a god, and to
bring pride, honor, and divine blessings to themselves, their families, and their
city states.[3] Consider the Theban poet Pindar's encomium of Aristocleides of
Aegina, the winner of the *pancratium* in 475 B.C.

> A burst of song [by youths] speaks to the triumph of Aristocleides, who linked
> this island with glorious praise, and the holy Theoric temple[4] of the Pythian god
> [Apollo] with bright ambitions. For it is trial that makes manifest the prime of
> those virtues, in which anyone will have proved himself preeminent, whether as
> a boy among boys, a man among men, or . . . as an elder among elders, accord-
> ing to the several portions of life which we, the race of men, possess.[5]

The Pan-Hellenic festivals transcended daily affairs, even war, so much that
they commanded a sacred truce (*ekecheiria*) that extended for weeks before and
after the games and that protecting pilgrims traveling to and from the site. No
persons with arms were allowed into the sanctuary and no death penalties were
carried out for one month. Not only was killing thought to be inconsistent with
the sacredness of the games, but also the honor due Zeus demanded the full attention of Greeks everywhere.[6]

It is otherwise with MC sport, which values excellence, but only as a means
to external ends. Because competitive sport has become a marketable commodity, it focuses on entertainment and revenue. Spectators enjoy viewing athletic
excellence, but they are also thrilled by risk-taking, violence, and even theatri-
cality. Much of the excitement of auto-racing comes through knowing that there
is always the possibility of a serious crash and loss of life. Moreover, the great
popularity of Ultimate Fighting Championship derives from its brutality, which
perhaps provokes some measure of catharsis for mavens. Finally, the extraordinary popularity of World Wrestling Entertainment (formerly World Wrestling
Federation) over the years shows that audiences can be abundantly entertained
by athleticism as staged violence and flam.

In what follows, we first examine the extent to which violent behavior is biologically rooted in human beings and then examine sport's potential as means of social change. Our view is that profitability is no justification for violence in competitive sport.

MC Sport and Conflict-Resolution

Recall from chapter 5 Jim Parry's statement that competitive sports are "laboratories for value experiments."[7] We agree with Parry that competitive sport does seem to be, in some sense, large-scale experiments. To assess the relationship between sport and violence, we need first to understand the various models of aggression.

In a prior publication, Holowchak distinguished among three models of aggression: strong-disposition models, culture-pattern models, and weak-disposition models.[8] Strong dispositionalism posits that aggression is instinctive or inherited and that the tendency to aggress is inevitable, because aggression is hard-wired in humans. If this view of aggression is correct, there is little humans can do to overcome aggression, other than releasing aggressive impulses or deciding on strategies to deflect it in relatively harmless ways. Sport may be seen as cathartic on this view, a healthy vent for the natural buildup of aggression.[9]

Though data are not unambiguous, current research indicates strongly that exposure to aggression leads not to catharsis, but rather to heightened aggression. Yet catharsis is still popular in the minds of lay people and investigators who fail to undertake a careful review of the current literature on it. Psychologists Brad Bushman, Roy Baumeister, and Angela Stack write:

> The scientific community has largely disconfirmed and abandoned catharsis theory and, if anything, is looking to understand why the opposite effect occurs (i.e., venting anger leads to higher subsequent aggression). Meanwhile, the popular mass media continue to suggest that catharsis theory is true and has scientific support, so the message reaching the general public is that catharsis is an effective, desirable way of handling angry impulses.[10]

In stark contrast to strong-disposition models are culture-pattern models of aggression. According to such models, aggression is predominantly learned behavior. Exposure to aggressive play tends to make people more, not less, aggressive. If the culture-pattern view is right, then aggressive sports have socially deleterious consequences that can be avoided.[11] The main problem with these models is that in explaining human aggression as essentially learned behavior, they mostly dismiss or ignore current physiological research, which shows key bio-physiological links to aggression.

A third, conciliatory path has been forged by those who posit that aggression is a biological disposition that can be inflamed or held in check through learning. Within the last fifty years, it has become apparent cultural and environmental factors are inseparable. Biological factors predispose individuals to react to particular circumstances in certain ways, but upbringing and other environmental factors have an impact on aggression[12] and even affect physiology itself.[13] Studies indicate that attempts to isolate the precise roles of biology and learning are futile. As Gene Bylinsky states:

> The most recent research suggests that the biological and environmental causes of violence are so closely intertwined as to require a less fragmented search for remedies. The research is showing, among other things, that the environment itself can leave a physical imprint on a developing brain. The wrong kind of upbringing can make a young animal, and probably a child too, more inclined to violent behavior as an adolescent or an adult. The hopeful augury of this research is that such behavior can be prevented if steps are taken to assure that young brains develop properly.[14]

It follows that the correct approach to an understanding of aggression must be a weak-disposition model of some sort that allows for biology and learning to factor importantly into explanation. This conclusion has consequences not just for violence in sport, but also for gender and sex.

Sex, Aggression, and Culture

Whatever type of weak-disposition model of human aggression is true, what strikes even the most casual observer is the predominance of aggression in males and its lack in females.[15] As E.L. Thorndike wrote nearly 100 years ago:

> The most striking differences in instinctive equipment consist in the strength of the fighting instinct in the male and of the nursing instinct in the female. . . . The out-and-out physical fighting for the sake of combat is pre-eminently a male instinct, and the resentment at mastery, the zeal to surpass, and the general joy at activity in mental as well as physical matters seem to be closely correlated with it.[16]

How is that explained? What does it mean for sport?

Some contemporary culture-pattern approaches want to explain away all sexual differences in behavior as social constructions or learning. For example, M. Ann Hall, in her work *Feminism and Sporting Bodies*, defines differences of sex in such a way that excludes the possibility of natural or biological factors.[17] Hall then goes on to point out that "biology itself provides no clear justification for a dichotomous view of gender" and that the wide variety of genetic types and hormonal conditions make any such dichotomy impossible. She sums up, "Biological sex . . . is a vast, infinitely malleable continuum that defies categorization." The two-sex system, she asserts boldly, is in "defiance of nature."[18]

Jennifer Hargreaves, too, argues that differences of aggression and competitiveness are satisfactorily explained by socialization:

> The commonplace claim that men are *naturally* more aggressive, more competitive and, therefore, better at sports than women suggests that these are inherent conditions and hence unchangeable. But it is illogical and inaccurate to argue that because relatively more men than women display aggressive and competitive behaviour, these characteristics are exclusive to the male sex. This is not to deny that there are essential differences between the sexes, but to resist the strong tendency *to treat as natural everything that is customary* [our italics]. . . . Differences between the sexes in displays of aggression and competitiveness can be explained as a result of social and cultural experiences—part of a process which starts at birth.[19]

Hargreaves literally dismisses biological differences by claiming flatly that behaviors like aggression are customary, not biological.

Both Hall and Hargreaves, however, fall prey to the fallacy of argument from ignorance. They insist that lack of clear-cut biological evidence for a sexual dichotomy is proof positive that no such dichotomy exists. All *relevant* causation, they maintain, occurs at the socio-cultural level. Nigel Edley and Margaret Wetherell elaborate eloquently on the flaw of this line of thought. "[I]t is . . . wrong to take the absence of clear cross-cultural patterns in sex-related behaviour as meaning that there are no biological forces at play, for there is no logical reason why biological factors need always find expression. Instead, they may be "masked" or overridden by social or cultural influences operating in a different "direction." One has only to consider the celibate person or the hunger-striker. Both are generally acknowledged to be acting against natural instincts.[20] Therefore, given the evidence available, an explanation that accounts only for social is improbable.

Overall, a layman's tendency to explain the difference in aggressive behavior between males and females in terms of biochemistry reduction is neither appalling nor completely wrong. Still the equation is not as simple as "testosterone equals aggression." That testosterone and aggression are correlated is undeniable: during puberty, when testosterone levels peak, so does male aggression. Athletes who take in many times their body's normal levels of testosterone anabolic performance drugs are also much more aggressive than other males. Former football players Lyle Alzado and Bill Romanowski immediately come to mind. Moreover, experiments with countless different species of animal show that castration leads to substantially reduced levels of aggression.[21] Nevertheless this relationship does not suggest a simple causal link—that aggression is caused by testosterone and nothing but testosterone.[22] In all, except in cases of extremes of excess and defect, amount of testosterone does little by itself to predict aggression in individuals. Another biological possibility concerns the different types of sexual hormones in males and females. Many studies show marked differences both in the anatomy of mature male and female brains and in the development of the brains of each sex. The problem with this line of research comes in showing that these differences are causally linked to behavioral variations, such as aggression in males and nurturing in females.[23] Still, one thing is factual: Males are born with many more brain cells that specialize in aggressive behavior than are females.[24]

Overall, the historically observed prevalence of male dominance and aggression is good enough evidence for there being some biological component to the observed sex differences in aggressive behavior.[25] Specifying that biological component is the task of future reward. Our current task is to assess sport's reaction to these differences, and our observation is that sport has exploited them to promote a false idea of male superiority.

Androcentric Measures of Athletic Success

It is reasonable to conclude that aggression, much more evident in males than in females, is a result of both socialization and biology. Allowing for equality of opportunity in sports, it follows that men will tend toward and dominate in those sports that reinforce aggressive behavior. In addition, other physical differences—greater on-average size and muscle mass and less body fat in males—will ensure male superiority in sports emphasizing strength and speed, many of which are violent sports.

Yet we ought to exercise caution here. B.C. Postow writes:

> Now sports constitute a socially valued activity. Men's genuine physiological superiority to women in their capacity for achievement in sports can therefore confer a higher social value on men, thereby helping to perpetuate the image of female inferiority. People who perceive this and whose image of female inferiority is reinforced by it are not simply committing the error in inferring that because women are inferior in sports, they are also inferior intellectually or morally.[26]

In short, superiority in sport must not be taken as an argument for superiority of gender. There is a harmful equivocation here. To say men are superior in sport is to say something like men, on average, can physically outperform women in most sports, which is a descriptive claim. To say, quite baldly, men are superior to women, however, could easily be taken as a normative claim that implies men are morally better than women. Yet that does not follow from the empirical literature.

Even speaking exclusively of physical superiority of males in competitive sport is problematic. Katheryne Pyne Addelson says:

> To rank men over women in sports because the best statistics in record books belong to males is to take those top-ranking males as champions who symboli-

cally win the battle for all males. . . . It ignores the fact that sports excellence is judged for individual and team performance, and that in some leagues, women have outperformed men. It ignores the fact, that is, that competition in sports ranks individuals and teams, not ideologies or nations or sexes. The meritocracy includes all the women who do well, *and* all the men who do well, even though women and men alike might not come up to the top male record in some sports.[27]

Postow's argument does not go far enough. The measures of athletic excellence have always been those sports that tend to feature martial skills that favor males, such as speed and strength.[28] What, for instance, if grace and balance were the measures? That illustrates something wholly unremarkable: The very structure and language of sport is in origin androcentric.

The ancient Olympic Games excluded female competitors and at least unmarried female spectators. There was a footrace for girls on the Olympic track, but it was held at a different time, honored a different god (Hera), and covered a shorter distance. A reasonable conclusion is that the Greeks assumed females to be athletically inferior so they affirmed that belief by denying female competitors at the main festival, reducing the lengths of their events at the festival for Hera, and granting more prestige to events that favored male strengths.[29] The situation is not so different today. Our contemporary MC model of sport still assumes male superiority and manages sport in a way that confirms that belief.

Why do we allow sport to continue excluding and marginalizing females? Whether differences between men and women are biological or cultural, they do not justify unequal treatment in sport.[30]

Is Reform of MC Sport Possible?

Let us return to Parry's suggestion that competitive sport may be a large-scale experiment involving human aggression and violence.

The greatest obstacle to reform of MC sport has been and continues to be the dogged insistence by numerous critics—scholars, athletes, and fans—that aggression has a cathartic effect. We cite two examples. Roger Horrocks, in *Male Myths and Icons: Masculinity in Popular Culture*, writes: "Football [soccer] provides an arena, where one's view of life can be acted out, theatricalized, and contained. The containment is crucial: here one can go through hatred and love and loyalty and despair. Then the game is over, and the crowds slowly disperse. The catharsis is complete. . . ."[31] Jeffrey Segrave states that the metaphors of violence in "sportspeak" attest to a ritualized and controlled release of aggression. He writes:

Certainly, both war and sport contain an element of dire struggle as well as the need for supreme organization, but sport is a sublimation of war, a ritualized form of violence that emerges, like religion and art, from the freedom from necessity. . . . In other words, sport is controlled violence; or to put it another way, sport is a ritualized form of self-control. . . .

The value of violence in sport, then, lies not in its expression but in its control; it is in fact only by controlling violence that sport sustains our interest and enlivens our attention. Sport detoxifies emotions and instincts that left unchecked would otherwise serve to our destruction, not our edification. Sport in this sense may well be one of our most important civilizing agents.[32]

The cathartic thesis is refuted by evidence. Exposure to aggressive behavior leads to heightened aggression or increased frequency of aggression, not catharsis. Therefore, we need to re-evaluate seriously our love and patronage of sports such as Ultimate Fighting Championship, Strikeforce, Mixed Martial Arts, professional boxing, American football, rugby, and North American hockey. By condoning aggression in sport, we contribute to aggression and violence in society.

There is no evidence to show that humans are predestined to aggress. Sociologist Mike Messner argues that people merely need a more humane ethic and more egalitarian economic system and that competitive sport can lead the way.

If many of the problems faced by all men (not just athletes) today are to be dealt with, class, ethnic, and sexual preference divisions must be confronted. This would necessarily involve the development of a more cooperative and nurturant ethic among men, as well as a more egalitarian and democratically organized economic system. And since the sports world is an important cultural process that serves partly to socialize boys and young men to hierarchical, competitive, and aggressive values, the sporting arena is an important context in which to begin to confront the need for a humanization of men.[33]

Reform of the martial element in MC sport is not only possible, but desirable. Our notion of reform comes through proposing a model centered on (male and female) excellence in competitive sport, not violence.

Notes

1. Antony E. Raubitschek, "The Agonistic Spirit in Greek Culture," *The Ancient World: Athletics in Antiquity*, Vol. VII, nos. 1 & 2, 1983, 7.

2. Raubitschek, "The Agonistic Spirit in Greek Culture," 7.

3. Ancient athletes often became wealthy from patrons and prizes at less prestigious money games. The intangible rewards of Pan-Hellenic victory, however, were prized more greatly. See David C. Young, *The Olympic Myth of Greek Amateur Athletics* (Chicago: Ares Publishers, Inc., 1985), 115-27.

4. Temple of the sacred envoys, who were often sent from Aegina to the festivals of Delphi.

5. Pindar, *The Odes of Pindar,* trans. Sir John Sandys (Cambridge: Harvard University Press, 1989), Nemean Ode III. We have altered Sandys' translation, first published in 1915, to make it more accessible to modern readers.

6. For more on the significance of the truce see Heather L. Reid "Olympic Sport and Its Lessons for Peace." *Journal of the Philosophy of Sport* 33:2 (2006), 207-209.

7. Aggression he defines as assertive behavior that need not be violent, and violence as behavior that aims at harming another. Jim Parry, "Violence and Aggression in Contemporary Sport," *Philosophy of Sport: Critical Readings, Crucial Issues,* ed. M. Andrew Holowchak (Upper Saddle River, NJ: Prentice-Hall, Inc., 2002), 263.

8. M. Andrew Holowchak, "Aggression, Gender, and Sport: Reflections on Sport as a Means to Moral Education," *Philosophy of Sport: Critical Readings, Crucial Issues,* ed. M. Andrew Holowchak (Upper Saddle River, NJ: Prentice-Hall, Inc., 2002), 466-75.

9. According to cathartic models, aggression is an impulse that builds up within each person and requires periodic release, otherwise it is debilitating. Periodic release allows for catharsis—a purging of aggression. Examples of cathartic models of aggression include Freud's thanatic model, Lorenz's hydraulic model, and the frustration-aggression model.

10. Brad J. Bushman, Roy F. Baumeister, and Angela D. Stack, "Catharsis, Aggression, and Persuasive Influence: Self-Fulfilling or Self-Defeating Porphecies?" http://www.apa.org/journals/psp/psp763367.html, 1999. Of course, this certainly does not mean that catharsis cannot enter into the overall explanation in *some* capacity. If it does, however, it is likely a small part of the overall picture.

11. Examples of culture-pattern models include social-learning theory and culture-learning theory.

12. In his work on rhesus monkeys, Psychologist Harry Harlow showed decades ago that lack of early nurture was a strong predictor of aggressive behavior in later life. His observations show that contingencies of reinforcement during early childhood are responsible for dispositions toward aggressive behavior in later life. Harry F. Harlow and Stephen J. Suomi, "Social Recovery by Isolation-Reared Monkeys," *Proceedings of the National Academy of Science of the United States of America* 68(7), 1971,1534-1538.

13. Neurophysiologist James W. Prescott, one of the pioneers on the effect of environmental circumstances on physiology, has argued convincingly that violent upbringing changes the very structure of the brain. Repeated hippocampal stimulation predisposes individuals to aggress. Moreover, lack of nurturant behavior toward infants results in underdeveloped or abnormally developed brains, as somatosensory deprivation causes impairment of the central nervous systems. See Dorothy Lewis, "From Abuse to Violence: Psychophysiological Consequences of Maltreatment," http://www.org/wgbh/pages/frontline/shows/little/readings/, 2000, 4.

14. Gene Bylinsky, "New Clues to the Causes of Violence," *Fortune*, January, 1973, 135. See also Johan M. G. van der Dennen, "Problems in the Concepts and Definitions of Aggression, Violence, and Some Related Terms." http://rint.rechten.tug.nl/rth/dennen/problem1.htm, 2000, 22.

15. Nigel Edley and Margaret Wetherell, *Men in Perspective: Practice, Power and Identity* (New York: Prentice Hall, 1995), 21.

16. Edward L. Thorndike, *Educational Psychology: Briefer Course,* (New York: Teacher's College, Columbia University, 1914), 350-351.

17. She writes: "Biological determinism forces thinking that is both reductionistic and categoric. Reductionism attempts to explain the properties of complex wholes in terms of the units that compose the whole. . . . Therefore, in the case of sex differences, genes are said to play a causal role in determining male/female differences by being expressed through the sex hormones, which in turn act on the brain (referred to some as "brain sex"). Reductionism also spawns thinking in terms of dichotomous categories: male versus female, male sex hormone versus female sex hormone, black versus white, and so forth. A dichotomy forces a polarization and ignores overlaps; differences are seen as more interesting than similarities, and there is a tendency to see these differences as absolute." M. Ann Hall, *Feminism and Sporting Bodies: Essays on the Theory and Practice* (Champaign, IL: Human Kinetics, 1996), 14.

18. Hall, *Feminism and Sporting Bodies*, 15-17.

19. Jennifer Hargreaves, *Sporting Females: Critical Issues in the History and Sociology of Women's Sports* (New York: Routledge, 1994), 146-147.

20. Edley et al., *Men in Perspective*, 23-24.

21. Dorothy Lewis, "From Abuse to Violence: Psychophysical Consequences of Maltreatment," http:/www.org/wgbh/pages/frontline/shows/little/readings/.

22. If we reduce testosterone to 20 percent of the normal amount or increase it by 100 percent, there is no appreciable diminution or elevation of aggression. Observance of highly aggressive behavior in individuals without high levels of testosterone shows that testosterone is not exclusively responsible for aggression. Chemical imbalances—diminished levels of brain serotonin or magnesium deficiency—can also result in aggressive behavior. In many instances, social conditioning seems to make up for the absence of the hormone. Ned H. Kalin, "Primate Models to Understand Human Aggression," *Journal of Clinical Psychiatry*, 60, 1999, 30. In addition, physiological data suggest that testosterone is not by itself causally responsible for exciting aggressive behavior. Researchers are coming to discover that testosterone merely functions to heighten the excitation of neural pathways between the amygdala (the part of the brain believed responsible for aggression) and the hypothalamus (the part of the brain that regulates aggression and that is responsible for emotive activity) that have already been excited. Robert Sapolesky, "Testosterone Rules," *Discover* 18.3, 1997, 45-50 and Gene Bylinsky, "New Clues to Violence," 135.

23. Edley et al., *Men in Perspective*, 32-33.

24. Bylinsky, "New Clues to Violence," 136.

25. See Steven Goldberg, *Why Men Rule: A Theory of Male Dominance* (Chicago: Open Court, 1993).

26. B.C. Postow, "Masculine Sports Revisited," *Journal of the Philosophy of Sport* VIII (Champaign, IL: Human Kinetics Publishers, 1981), 60.

27. Kathryn Pyne Addelson, "Equality and Competition: Can Sports Make a Woman of a Girl?" *Women, Philosophy, and Sport: A Collection of New Essays* (Metuchen, NJ: The Scarecrow Press, Inc., 1983), 148.

28. Postow, "Masculine Sports Revisited," 61.

29. This is also the observation of Mark Golden, *Sport and Society in Ancient Greece* (Cambridge, UK: Cambridge University Press, 1998) 131.

30. Reid, *The Philosophical Athlete,* 260-264 argues that gender segregation in sport must not be abused as a way to deny females access to sports' goods.

31. Roger Horrocks, *Male Myths and Icons: Masculinity in Popular Culture* (New York: St. Martin's Press, 1995), 167.

32. Jeffrey Segrave, "A Matter of Life and Death: Some Thoughts on the Language of Sport," *Journal of Sport & Social Issues*, Volume 21, No. 2 (Sage Publications, Inc., 1997), 214-215.

33. Mike Messner, "The Meaning of Success: The Athletic Experience and the Development of Male Identity," *Sport in Contemporary Society: An Anthology*, ed. D. Stanley Eitzen (New York: St. Martin's Press, 1996), 386.

Chapter 10
Sport by the Numbers

"The virus that infected professional baseball in the 1990s, the use of statistics to find new and better ways to value players and strategies, has found its way into every major sport. Not just basketball and football, but also soccer and cricket and rugby and, for all I know, snooker and darts—each one now supports a subculture of smart people who view it not just as a game to be played but as a problem to be solved." Dan Winters

ICHIGAN AND TEXAS PLAYED A THRILLING GAME in the 2005 Rose Bowl. Fraught with numerous lead shifts and reversals of fortune, the game came down to a single play in which Texas kicker, Dusty Magnum, booted a 37-yard field goal and Texas beat Michigan, 38-37. Some of the more noteworthy statistics follow:

- Texas quarterback Vince Young was responsible for five touchdowns (four rushing, one passing; ties record)
- Young also rushed for 192 yards and four touchdowns (new record, quarterback)
- Michigan receiver and kick returner Steve Breaston had 315 all-purpose yards (new record)
- Breaston also had 221 kickoff return yards (a record for all bowl games)
- Michigan quarterback Chad Henne passed for four touchdown passes (ties record)
- Michigan All-American receiver Braylon Edwards caught three touchdown passes (new record)

In short, what the after-the-game statistical analysis revealed about the 2005 Rose Bowl was that there were numerous individual contests within the game and even losing players could claim their share of victories. Henne, Breaston, and Edwards, in a losing effort, did what they did in front of a national audience and a multitude of National Football League scouts. Their great individual performances also became part of college-football history. The Wolverines may have lost the war, but individual players won a good number of statistical battles along the way.

Of course, numbers related to competition are themselves neither good nor bad. Some numbers seem interesting for their own sake. Michigan and Texas were deserving of their Rose Bowl match-up, among other things, because they are two of the winning-most programs in college football with 842 and 787 wins at the time. This shows that both schools have football programs, steeped in tradition, with commitments toward winning football games. Other numbers, like Michigan tying the record for most points scored in a losing effort, seem insipid.

Nonetheless, the numbers chosen make the 2005 Rose Bowl an illustration of one thing: an emphasis upon quantified individual performance in the MC model of sport that is in gross disproportion to the value of competitive sport in democratic societies.

Greek Agonism

The first problem with statistical elitism is that it attempts to quantify something inherently unquantifiable—excellence (*aretē*). The ancient Greek and Roman Stoic philosophers, who understood *aretē* in its psychical sense—i.e., virtue—to be the only goal in life, also understood the path to virtue to be inordinately difficult. A person progressing toward *aretē* could make daily advances, but was still considered wholly vicious in that he lacked virtue and was, in that regard, no better than any other person lacking virtue. A person 10 feet outside the Acropolis is still outside the Acropolis just the same as one 1,000 miles outside. The achievement of *aretē*, however, was a qualitative change and separated the virtuous from the non-virtuous. Each virtuous person was the equal of every other virtuous person and all virtuous actions were equally virtuous.

The point we wish to make does not concern the veridicality of the Stoic view of progress toward virtue and the paradoxes it entails, though this is, in key respects, a book about virtue. Instead we wish to show that virtue (*aretē* or *virtus*) or moral excellence for Stoics was not something that could be quantified. To quantify it was to misapprehend it. In key respects, we think the same mistake is being made in MC sport.

To illustrate, let us return to Greek sporting practices, for textual and archeological evidence gives substantial evidence that Greeks esteemed athletes and athletic excellence as much as we today do. Circa 400 B.C., Hippias of Elis created a list of Olympic victors based on records found in an archive at Olympia. The veridicality of the list is dubious, as names of early victors are sham. Hippias filled them out using mythological lore, family tradition, and perhaps ingenuity. Hippias' list, however, was preserved and revised by Aristotle and Erotosthenes in the third century B.C. and Eusebius (fl. early fourth century A.D.) in Book 1 of his *Chronology*. The list consists of the victor, event contested, city of the victor, and year. There is neither mention of evenness or lopsidedness of a contest, nor mention of statistics (e.g., time in which the stade was run, distance of a javelin or discus throw, or number of blows thrown or sustained in a boxing match).[1] The idea was to honor and remember *persons* who demonstrated excellence, not to quantify their deeds and thereby reduce them to their athletic performances. In that regard, the Ancient Greek view, though agonistic,[2] was radically unlike the panagonistic MC view that holds sway today.

Why, then, are statistics such a critical component of evaluating athletes in competitive sports today? Quantifying sport, in the minds of many, is a means of legitimizing sport. Bero Rigauer writes:

> Athletic achievements now take place in the "objective framework" of the c-g-s (centimeter, gram, second) system or in point scores which rely either upon objectively measurable achievements (as in the pentathlon and decathlon) or in referees' calls and subjective judgments (as in team games, gymnastics, boxing, etc.). The application of a socially sanctioned system of measurements allows the objective comparison of all athletic achievements—exactly like the achievements of labor productivity. They are all rationalized into universally understandable measurements of value. With such quantified, abstract forms, it is possible to compete even against opponents who are not present. One may race, for example, against a world record.[3]

In quantifying their performances, however, we have reduced them from persons to athletes, and we have reduced their excellence from a holistic ideal like *aretē* to an infinitely measurable and comparable set of numbers.

Let us illustrate through the sport of baseball, which is perhaps the paradigmatic statistical American sport. For all players, there are offensive and defensive statistics and, except for pitchers, offensive statistical data are prominent determinants of a player's worth. There are offensive data of or related to a player's batting average, on-base percentage, slugging percentage, singles, doubles, triples, and homers, times hit by pitch, walks, strikeouts, runs batted in, runs, stolen bases, double plays hit into, and sacrifices. There are defensive data of or related to assists, double plays, caught stealing, errors, games played, outfield assists, passed balls, pickoffs, putouts, stolen bases allowed, total chances, and triple plays. For pitchers, there are data of or related to a pitcher's wins, losses, strikeouts, walks, singles, doubles, triples, and homers allowed, fly outs, grounds outs, shutouts, earned runs, complete games, hit batters, intentional walks, innings pitched, base-runners per nine innings, innings per start, opponent's batting average, plate appearances, runs allowed, shutouts, saves, total bases allowed, and wild pitches. In addition, there are formulae for combining data in an effort to assess a player's total contribution to a team—as if that contribution could somehow be made in isolation from the other players.

For the ancient Greeks, religio-sporting festivals were special occasions, not a way of life. Though serious athletes trained all the time to compete at the various festivals, mavens did not view competitions on a daily basis as they can today. For instance, the Olympic Games were held ever fourth year and the Isthmian Games of Corinth were held every second year. Though there were other festivals, spectatorship was often a luxury. One would have to leave one's affairs in limbo, for festivals occurred over several days and required much travel time. Spectators made those efforts because they regarded sport not as a product to be consumed, but as a cultural event in which to participate. The crowned Olympic champions represented the humanity's physical best, which were offered symbolically to the gods in thanks for their benefits to humans and in hope of receiving more benefits.[4] Athletic *aretē* in that context was much more than individual performance; it was a form of community service.

With the democratization and commodification of modern sport, however, competitive sport has become a way of life not only for athletes, but also for mavens. Fans that live in a large city can go to numerous types of sporting events throughout the year. Some can go to an event nearly every day or even more than one event on the same day. More than that, there is round-the-clock televised sport through ESPN, Versus, and the many local cable networks that cater to local venues. Hockey fans, for example, can purchase a viewing plan to watch as many games as they want during the hockey season. The constant exposure to sport, especially through television packages, talk shows, and the endless statistics on the Internet allows for a sort of fanaticism in which fans consider themselves experts and imagine themselves as part of the team.

Moreover, availability of statistical data creates an endless number of the sorts of time-killing questions one can pursue. Was Babe Didrikson a better athlete than was Jim Thorpe? Is the 2010 University of Connecticut women's basketball team the greatest sports team of all-time? Would Cassius Clay have beaten Rocky Marciano had the two fought? Are the New York Yankees a more dominant sports franchise than the Montreal Canadiens? Is American football a better game than European football? On the one hand, each of the questions is in some sense intriguing. On the other hand, it seems a fitting question to ask anyone that spends the lion's share of his time mulling over such questions whether he has anything better to do. In such discussions, individuals and even teams are artificially extracted from context and reduced to disembodied numbers—their connections with each other, their communities, and society at large is ignored. It is no wonder that many moderns are skeptical about the transferability of athletic *aretē* beyond sport, as we rarely ever think of athletes as having lives outside of sport.

In recent years, there has emerged a new way to consume competitive sport exclusively through use of statistical data—fantasy sports. Fantasy sports are essentially computer games that allow users to imagine themselves the owner of a professional sports team. Fantasy owners build their own team by selecting players from real team sports, such as the NFL or NBA. They then compete against other "owners" and other teams by comparing statistics. Weekly data from individual players on various pro teams during the season of their sport generates the raw data that is combined into the fantasy team statistics upon which the weekly competitions are based. In the main, owners with players that tend to over-perform on a weekly basis—and over-performance is based on evaluation of current performances as they relate to past player performances—

will have teams that do well. It is the opposite for owners with players that tend to underperform. Thus, performance is translated into points that compiled and totaled. Disgruntled owners can sign new players and trade or cut old ones. Teams here are literally just collections of individuals, in the rawest sense.

Do fantasy sports work—i.e., does the point system on which it is based give "owners" a good feel for what presumably would really happen, were each owner to have a team of such players? It certainly seems implausible that if you extracted each athlete from his actual team and game and somehow reinserted him into a completely different context that he would do more or less the same things. Removing an athletes' statistics, their competitive context is as artificial as removing athletes from social communities. Because they isolate players from communities, statistics fail to capture true athletic excellence—especially in team sports.

Individualizing Statistics and Team Sports

At the end of the 2008 season, the Detroit Pistons were 59-23 and the Denver Nuggets were 50-32. In 2009, after trading Chauncey Billups to Denver and getting Allen Iverson, Detroit dropped to 39-43, while Denver improved to 54-28. As of this writing, Detroit is 23-53 and Denver is 50-27. Was the loss of Billups responsible for Detroit's meteoric fall and Denver's improvement? Can one player make such a difference?

In basketball, the answer is certainly yes. With only five persons on the court at any given time and no need to shift persons frequently on and off the court, as there is in ice hockey, one person makes a considerable difference. The Cleveland Cavaliers' have been contenders ever since signing LeBron James. That is perhaps why the NBA and the WNBA market their superstars.

Nonetheless, Billups is often recognized as an all-star player, but seldom as a superstar like James, Kobe Bryant, or Maurice Wade. He just does not score enough. Yet does that mean he does not deserve the same status—that he is not as excellent?

Scoring many points each game certainly would seem to warrant superstar status, but let us look at the issue more closely. Allen Iverson for years was among the league's premier scorers and most intense players, yet his presence and absence on the court seemed to matter little in terms of winning and losing for many of the teams on which he played. When Billups was added to Denver and Iverson was added to Detroit, Denver improved and Detroit fell apart.[5] After trading Billups, Detroit immediately fell from contention.

Is Billups that good? Examination of his career statistics shows that he is no LeBron James. Over his 14-year career, Billups has averaged 32 minutes per game, 15.1 points per game, 2.2 rebounds per game, and 5.6 assists per game. Let us compare that to LeBron James. Over his six-year career with Cleveland, James has averaged 41 minutes per game, 27.5 points per game, 7 rebounds per game, and 6.7 assists per game. There seems statistically to be no comparison. James easily wins the battle of statistics. Yet Detroit's play with and without Billups suggests that he was every much as important to Detroit's success as is James to Cleveland's. How can that be?

According to *New York Times* writer Dan Winters, the story is the same with Houston Rockets' guard Shane Battier. Battier averages 40 minutes per game, 10 points per game, 4.8 rebounds per game, and 1.9 assists per game. He is, by the statistical measure of superstars, a dud. Still he is said by Houston's general manager Daryl Morey to be one of the league's fiercest defensive competitors and one of its best and most cerebral players. The Grizzlies, who were 23-59 in Battier's rookie season, were 50-32 in his third year. He was traded to Houston in 2006-2007. Houston went from 34-48 that season to 52-30 and 55-27 the next two seasons with Battier. Writes Winters, "Here we have a basketball mystery: a player is widely regarded inside the N.B.A. as, at best, a replaceable cog in a machine driven by superstars. And yet every team he has ever played on has acquired some magical ability to win,"[6]

Morey, a whiz at statistical data, was hired to make Houston competitive without superstars so that they could play with the best without having to pay with the best. Morey, like other innovative thinkers on statistics, noticed the tendency for traditional data to discount team play. He began sorting through ways of distinguishing between traditional statistics and a player's actual contribution to the team. Winters says:

> The five players on any basketball team are far more than the sum of their parts; the Rockets devote a lot of energy to untangling subtle interactions among the team's elements. To get at this they need something that basketball hasn't historically supplied: meaningful statistics. For most of its history basketball has measured not so much what is important as what is easy to measure—points, rebounds, assists, steals, blocked shots—and these measurements have warped perceptions of the game. . . . How many points a player scores, for example, is no true indication of how much he has helped his team. Another example: if you want to know a player's value as a rebounder, you need to know not whether he got a rebound but the likelihood of the *team* getting the rebound when a missed shot enters that player's zone.[7]

Morey traded for Battier—a slow, poor-dribbling, and physically awkward player. Battier seems to make up for lack of physical skills with a cerebral presence that few players in basketball have ever had. He is given and collects a wealth of data, which he uses to improve his play in innovative ways that cannot be measured by traditional statistics. By the measure of traditional statistics, he is an impoverished player. By the measure of his team's record when he plays or fails to play, he is a superstar or, as Morey calls him, the "most abnormally unselfish basketball player."[8]

Morey has instituted a plus-minus stat for basketball—much the same way that the National Hockey League has a plus-minus stat. The NHL plus-minus stat, which began in 1968, measures a team's goal differential when a specific player is on the ice. If Alexander Ovechkin is on the ice when his team scores an even-strength or shorthanded goal, he is given a +1 rating; a -1 rating, every time his team gives up an even-strength or shorthanded goal. Goals scored by a team on a power play do not impact the rating. Empty-net scenarios at a game's end, when neither team has a penalty, are relevant plus-minus scenarios. Morey thinks that the plus-minus stat will be for basketball what it is for hockey—an importantly relevant statistical measure of a player's real worth.

Winter's sums:

> The virus that infected professional baseball in the 1990s, the use of statistics to find new and better ways to value players and strategies, has found its way into every major sport. Not just basketball and football, but also soccer and cricket and rugby and, for all I know, snooker and darts—each one now supports a subculture of smart people who view it not just as a game to be played but as a problem to be solved. Outcomes that seem, after the fact, all but inevitable of course LeBron James hit that buzzer beater, of course the Pittsburgh Steelers won the Super Bowl—are instead treated as a set of probabilities, even after the fact. The games are games of odds. Like professional card counters, the modern thinkers want to play the odds as efficiently as they can; but of course to play the odds efficiently they must first know the odds. Hence the new statistics, and the quest to acquire new data, and the intense interest in measuring the impact of every little thing a player does on his team's chances of winning. In its spirit of inquiry, this subculture inside professional basketball is no different from the subculture inside baseball or football or darts. The difference in basketball is that it happens to be the sport that is most like life.[9]

Morey's insight and innovation reveals traditional statistics' tendency to individualize athletic performance in a way most unrepresentative of worth, especially in teams sports. It does not solve the greater problem caused by trying to quantify excellence, however.

Quantification and *Aretē*

Improvements in the accuracy and relevance of sport statistics are likely to harm sports more than to improve them. As we have observed, statistics tend to dehumanize athletes and excellence, reducing them to quantifiable performance.

We may imagine a time, say 500 years hence, where the human capacity to garner relevant information from biological systems is so greatly enhanced that sports results become completely predictable. Sophisticated supercomputers process hordes of information about each player's physical state, competitive tendencies, psychological condition, and historical data. They even take into consideration details such as weather fluctuations and crowd behavior. So efficiently do such computers process information prior to each match that they know in advance the winner, final score, and all the minutiae of the game, prior to its occurrence. Human curiosity being what it is, most sportspersons might prefer to watch a computer-generated version of the game, made available the night before it actually happens, that is an exact replica of it. Before long, the contests themselves with real athletes would become redundant.[10]

If the meaning of sport and the nature of excellence really is reducible to quantifiable and predictable athletic performances, its demise may not be much of a loss. If sport is to have real social value—as opposed to mere entertainment, commercial, or recreational value—we must remain conscious of its potential effect on persons understood as members of communities, not atoms. The MC model's obsessive tweaking of numbers supplants full appreciation of the excellence of athletes, the drama of contests, and the beauty of sport more generally—especially when statistical data are collected and used in the frantic service of extolling individuals in an essentially community-based activity.

That is something that running-back great Barry Sanders understood. In the final game of the 1989 season, Atlanta was hosting Sanders' Lions in a meaningless game. So meaningless was the event that not even 8,000 spectators showed for it. The sole drama was whether Sanders would lead the league in rushing yardage. The Lions, leading 31-24 with roughly a minute left in the game, got back the ball. Sanders had 158 yards already and needed 10 more to lead the league. Detroit coach Wayne Fontes called over Sanders and asked, "You're 10 yards from leading the league in rushing. Do you want to go in?" Sanders replied unworriedly, "Coach, give the ball to [fullback] Tony [Paige]. Let's win it and go home." When asked later about his refusal to go into the game and try for the rushing title, Sanders said, "When everyone is out for statistics—you know, individual fulfillment—that's when trouble starts. I don't want to ever fall victim to that." He remained out of the game and Kansas City Chiefs' running back Christian Okoyé of the Kansas City Chiefs won the rushing title.[11] Unfortunately, athletes like Sanders, who understand that excellence is not a statistic, are rare.

"There is no 'I' in 'Team'"

The point of all this chapter is not to denigrate statistics but rather to exalt sport—its complexity, its unpredictability, its alchemy. Furthermore, it is to point out that sport is about communities and not individuals. Even so-called individual sports are practiced by a community of competitors that strive together toward excellence.

Outstanding individuals that put up impressive numbers, often do so in less than impressive contests. The numbers derived from the greatest athletic contests, by contrast, are characterized by evenness. The gold-medal game between Canada and the United States at the 2010 Vancouver Olympics is a good example. The game was tied 2-2 after three periods. So too were the shots at 32 apiece. Canada had a two-minute power-play advantage going to overtime, but that was evened when they took a penalty in overtime. Even the faceoff wins were tied late into the third period. The statistics bore out what was apparent to most observers even before the overtime period: Each team played with equal grit and heart and neither deserved to lose. It was great game between great teams that did not exalt any single individual.

Because the ancient Olympic Games excluded team sports and recognized only the winner (not the runners up) in each event, they are often criticized as elitist and individualistic in a way that modern team sports are not. We have been arguing, in contrast, that modern team sports are defectively individualistic because they use statistics to remove players from their teams, and promote a quantifiable conception of excellence that removes them from their communities. As we will show in section three, however, *Aretism* is an essentially communal concept that focuses on the integration of athletes with their communities. Individuals remain important and their excellence is rewarded, but only in the context of the larger community.

Notes

1. For a recent discussion of the dating of the Games at 776 B.C., see Paul Christensen, *Olympic Victor Lists and Ancient Greek History* (New York: Cambridge University Press, 2007).

2. Golden wisely advises caution in urging that agonism was a uniquely Greek view. See Mark Golden, *Sport and Society in Ancient Greece* (New York: Cambridge University Press, 1998), 28-33.

3. Bero Rigauer, *Sport and Work,* trans. Allan Guttmann (New York: Columbia University Press, 1984), 57-58.

4. Heather Reid, "Of Sport, Service, and Sacrifice: Rethinking the Religious Heritage of the Olympic Games." *Cultural Imperialism in Action: Critiques in the Global Olympic Trust.* Eds. N. Crowther, R. Barney, M. Heine (London, Ontario: ICOS, 2006) 32-40.

5. On April 3 of 2009, Detroit's coach Michael Curry decided that Iverson would no longer be a starter. That was unacceptable to Iverson, who was then deactivated. On September 10 of 2009, he was traded to the Memphis Grizzlies, but again relegated to a secondary role, which he again found unacceptable. His contract was terminated two months later. Shortly thereafter, he signed a contract with his old team, Philadelphia, but was deactivated for the season.

6. Dan Winters, "The No-Stats All-Star," *New York Times,* Feb. 15, 2009, http://www.nytimes.com/2009/02/15/magazine/15Battier-t.html.

7. Winters, "The No-Stats All-Star," Feb. 15, 2009.

8. Winters, "The No-Stats All-Star," Feb. 15, 2009.

9. Winters, "The No-Stats All-Star," Feb. 15, 2009.

10. This scenario is based on assumption of a deterministic universe, at least at the macro-level. It is possible that the universe, at the macro-level, is a deterministic system—i.e., that the uncertainty of the micro-level is swamped over or wiped out at the macro-level. If so, refinement of relevant statistical data would allow for increasing precision in predicting scenarios in which an indefinitely large number of variables are in

volved. That, at least, is the direction in which savvy users of statistical data for sporting competitions are going. A key question here is this: What would happen if a player should watch her performance the day before it occurs? Would that change her play?

11. Austin Murphy, "A Lamb among Lions," *Sports Illustrated,* 10 Sept. 1990, http://sportsillustrated.cnn.com/features/1999/year_in_review/flashbacks/retire_sanders9 0/.

Chapter 11
Sensationalism and Ego-Puffing

"It helps you, if you help them beat themselves." Ty Cobb

𝕬 FTER SCORING WHAT TURNED OUT to be the game-winning touchdown in a National Football League game against Seattle in 2002,[1] former San Francisco wide receiver Terrell Owens pulled out a pen from his sock and autographed the football. After the game, Owens said, "I just tried to be creative. I was just having fun." Seattle's coach, Mike Holmgren, who did not see the incident, responded later, "I think it's shameful. There's no place for anything like that in our game. It's too great of a game." Holmgren then added that one of his ballplayers should have confronted Owens. "I think certain times players cross the line, and you've got to take care of business." The NFL later issued a warning against similar displays, because of the danger of carrying around a pen during play, not because of any denigration of character or show-boating.

At first glance, Owens' end-zone autograph session seems harmless. It was not hateful or malicious. He did not set out to cause anyone bodily harm. Many fans were supremely entertained and Owens' "brand" as a player received tremendous media-exposure, even though his deed had nothing to do with the game. Owens' deed might even be seen as masterful self-promotion. Were Owens' antics just a creative way of having fun or was it, as Holmgrem said, crossing the line?

In the last chapter, we looked at how statistics promote a kind of dangerous individualism in sport. In this chapter, we observe the way that commercialism exacerbates and reinforces that problem.

Numbers Don't Lie

One of the greatest matches in National Football League history games was a 1982 playoff game between the Miami Dolphins and the San Diego Chargers.[2] The game was played with much pluck by both teams and was punctuated by numerous reversals of fortune. By game's end, San Diego won on Ralph Benirschke's field goal, 13:52 into overtime. Along the way, playoff records for most points in a playoff game (79), most total yards (1,036), and most passing yards (809) were broken. What the players were most interested in, though, were their personal statistics.

- Quarterback Don Strock (Miami) came off the bench and completed 29 of 43 passes for 403yards and four touchdowns, all personal bests.
- Receiver Duriel Harris (Miami) caught six passes for 106 yards of offense.
- Running back Tony Nathan (Miami) rushed for 48 yards, caught nine passes for 114 yards, and scored two touchdowns.
- Tight end Bruce Hardy (Miami) caught five passes for 89 yards and a touchdown.
- Quarterback Dan Fouts (San Diego) completed 33 of 53 passes (postseason records) for 433 yards (franchise and postseason records) and three touchdowns.
- Receiver Charlie Joiner (San Diego) caught seven passes for 108 yards.
- Running back Chuck Muncie rushed for 124 yards and a touchdown.
- Receiver Wes Chandler (San Diego) caught six passes for 106 yards and returned a punt 56 yards for a touchdown.
- Running back James Brooks (San Diego) had 19 rushing yards, 31 receiving yards, 85 kickoff-return yards, eight punt-return yards for 143 all-purpose yards as well as two touchdown catches.
- Tight end Kellen Winslow (San Diego) blocked a game-winning field goal and had 13 receptions for 166 yards and a touchdown.

Why do players care about such numbers—sometimes more than the ones that represent the outcome of the game? It is because they are evaluated and ultimately paid according to them.

As we saw in the last chapter, however, such statistical data that pulls them outside the framework of the team or the sport they play. Poor numbers can mask the excellence and reduce the salary of an inspiring team leader, while good numbers result in lucrative contracts even for players who act as poison to their team. Certain players, usually the most insecure ones, become ego-puffed by the numbers that "prove" their superiority. Ego-puffed players feed off numerical analysis to the extent that they care more for their own numbers than for their team or sport. To them, the numbers prove their worth, which they understand primarily in financial terms.

One of the most notorious examples of greed-driven ego-puffing was "Neon" Deion Sanders (a.k.a., "Prime Time").[3] As one of the most talented defensive backs ever to play in the NFL, Sanders was also one of the showiest. As a senior at Florida State, he arrived at FSU's stadium for a game against Florida in a limousine and dressed in a tuxedo. Exiting the limousine, he said, "How do you think defensive backs get attention? They don't pay nobody to be humble." As a college player, he wasn't supposed to be paid at all. That ostentation turned out to be more marketable in the NFL, where Sanders had unquestioned success as a defensive back and kick- and punt-returner. He also made millions as a corporate pitch-man and commanded a second lucrative salary playing Major League Baseball.

If sport, on the MC model, is about getting rich, Sanders was among its greatest success stories. Success in life, however, is more complicated. Over time, the flashy jewelry and clothes, fine cars, and other byproducts of his competitive successes took a toll on Sanders. Despite Super Bowl victories with Dallas and San Francisco, difficulties in his personal life led him to attempt suicide in 1997. He then found meaning, as he tells the story, by turning away from Deion toward Christ. "I'll have to be honest. I never liked Deion Sanders. Too much of a showboat for me. Now I'm going to spend eternity with him because he is trusting in Christ."[4]

Why do coaches, owners, players, and fans tolerate such money-driven arrogance? Within the confines of MC sport, answers are straightforward. First, one has merely to look as Sanders' numbers over his career as a defensive back and punt- and kick-returner. Those numbers, it seems, justify the self-absorption. Second, self-centered antics lead to exposure in newspapers and magazines as well as on television and radio sports shows, and sports news and exposure is especially helpful for helping marginally talented players appear to be better athletes than they are and, thereby, landing more lucrative contracts and paid commercial endorsements.

Indeed the fans who consume sports seem especially enchanted by players like Kobe Bryant—one of the most talented scorers in the NBA—who selfishly elevate themselves above their teams and even basic standards of civility. After the LA Lakers put together what was supposed to be the "greatest team of all time" in 2003-2004 and then got trounced by the Detroit Pistons in the NBA finals, four games to one, many believe that Bryant went to work behind the scenes to get his coach, Phil Jackson, fired and to bring about the trade of teammate Shaquille O'Neal, whose feud with Bryant was long-running and public.

The day after O'Neal was traded to Miami, Bryant signed a seven-year, 136.4-million-dollar contract with the Lakers. When asked whether he had anything to do with the superstar coach and center moving on, Bryant replied like a businessman, "They did what they had to do. That had nothing to do with me."

What allows Bryant to have such an impact on the personnel of the Lakers? The answer seems clear. Professional basketball is a business and the fans, as sports-media sources show plainly through their headlines, are more interested in the individual efforts of players like Bryant and James than they are in exceptional team play of the sort exhibited by San Antonio, Phoenix, and Dallas over the years. The league markets its point scorers, not its teams. Writes Dan Winters of the *New York Times*:

> There is a tension, peculiar to basketball, between the interests of the team and
> the interests of the individual. The game continually tempts the people who
> play it to do things that are not in the interest of the group. . . . In football the
> coach has so much control over who gets the ball that selfishness winds up being self-defeating. The players most famous for being selfish—the Dallas
> Cowboys' wide receiver Terrell Owens [now with Buffalo], for instance—are
> usually not so much selfish as attention seeking. Their sins tend to occur off the
> field.
>   It is in basketball where the problems are most likely to be in the game—
> where the player . . . faces choices between maximizing his own perceived self-interest and winning. The choices are sufficiently complex that there is a fair
> chance he doesn't fully grasp that he is making them.[5]

Ego-Puffing: Cobbian vs. Ruthian

The narcissistic antics of self-absorbed athletes exist not only because fans tolerate them, but because fans encourage them. Fans of competitive sport show their enthusiasm for ego-puffed athletes by how they spend money. They follow teams that feature such players, they buy expensive replica jerseys with the players' names emblazoned on the back, and they consume the products that these players endorse. It is a game almost as old as professional sport itself.

The history of modern sport is replete with self-promoters. In baseball's early history, Ty Cobb and Babe Ruth immediately come to mind. The two are significant because they had importantly different approaches to baseball, even life. For Cobb, baseball was a tough and dirty sport, where players would do what they could to secure any advantage. To excel, one had to be tougher and smarter than others. For Ruth, baseball was a relatively simple sport that came easily to him, whether he pitched or hit. Throw hard; swing hard; play hard. Through it all, have fun.

Their different approaches to the game were manifest in different approaches to ego-puffing. Ruth was a straightforward self-promoter. In contrast, Cobb's self-promotion came in large part at the expense of others. "It helps you," he wrote of opponents, "if you help them beat themselves."[6]

A classic example of Cobb's back-door ego-puffing is the batting race of 1911 between Cobb and Shoeless Joe Jackson. Cobb writes of the race in his own memoirs. Toward the end of the year, Jackson had a nine-point lead over Cobb when Cobb's Tigers went to Cleveland for six games in four days with Jackson's Indians and Cobb saw this series as an opportunity to turn around things. Though Cobb and Jackson, both southerners, were friendly toward each other, Cobb did everything that he could to throw off Jackson during the series through mind games. For instance, he would ignore Jackson's greetings or snap at him for no reason when their paths crossed. "My mind was centered on just one thing: getting all the base hits I could muster. Joe Jackson's mind was on many other things. He went hitless in the first three games of the series, while I fattened up. By the sixth game, I'd passed him in the averages."[7] Apparently, the mind games worked. Jackson's average fell to .408 by season's end, while Cobb led the league with a .420 average.

Overall, Cobb's approach to baseball was situational and cerebral. If circumstances dictated that a bunt would move a runner into scoring position, he would bunt. If he could secure advantage by getting under a pitcher's skin, he would find a way to get under his skin. He was baseball's most notorious win-at-any-cost player. Of his putative dirty play, Cobb had this to say:

> If any player took unfair advantage of me, my one thought was to strike back as quickly and effectively as I could and put the fear of God into him. Let the other fellow fire the first shot, and he needed to be on the *qui vive* from then on. For I went looking for him. And when I found him, he usually regretted his act—and rarely repeated it. I commend this procedure to all young players who are of the aggressive type. The results are most satisfactory.
>
> Along with the counsel of my father, I fell back on Polonius, when in *Hamlet* he advises Laertes: "Beware of entrance to a quarrel; but being in, bear't, that the opposed may beware of thee."

In stark contrast to the indirect self-promotion that Cobb practiced—puff yourself up by deflating your opponents—Ruth was in-your-face about baseball and life. He was a bon vivant, who loved the pageantry and excitement that baseball had to offer. Whereas Cobb, looking to gain advantage, analyzed every aspect of every situation of a game, Ruth would simply swing for the fences in everything he did. "How to hit home runs: I swing as hard as I can, and I try to swing right through the ball. . . . The harder you grip the bat, the more you can swing it through the ball, and the farther the ball will go. I swing big, with everything I've got. I hit big or I miss big. I like to live as big as I can."[8]

Unlike that of Cobb, Ruth's approach to baseball was neither cerebral nor situational. For him, baseball was a simple game. It was about hitting the ball out of the park, when batting, or striking out batters, when pitching. "If I'd tried for them dinky singles I could've batted around six hundred," Ruth once boasted.[9]

Ruth was never shy about his talent and accomplishments. In response to a reporter's objection that the salary he asked for was five thousand dollars more than that of the president of the United States ($80,000 to $75,000), Ruth replied, "I know, but I had a better year than Hoover." Said former Boston teammate Harry Hooper of Ruth:

> Sometimes I still can't believe what I saw. This 19-year-old kid, crude, poorly educated, only lightly brushed by the social veneer we call civilization, gradu-

ally transformed into the idol of American youth and the symbol of baseball the
world over—a man loved by more people and with an intensity of feeling that
perhaps has never been equaled before or since. I saw a man transformed into
something pretty close to a god.

Ruth was, of course, full of himself. Yet he was, as Hooper admitted, larger than
life and his gloating and self-indulgence can almost be forgiven, because his on-
the-field deeds were so outstanding that they transformed the game of baseball.

Sensationalism in Sport Today

What of Terrell Owens[10]—perhaps today's most celebrated ego-puffed athlete
not only in football, but in American sports? Of the two approaches, Owens'
type of ego-puffing is clearly Ruthian—seemingly, the least harmful of the two.
Like Ruth, Owens seems to love the game he plays and his showy displays suggest that he has a certain amount of fun competing. Yet Ruthian ego-puffing is
reprehensible for at least two reasons.

First, market-motivated self-promotion makes light of the efforts of
teammates. Writes East Penn Press's Paul Willistein of Owens' celebrity:
"While we enjoy Terrell Owens athletic acumen, do we really need post-game
analysis of his sideline [antics] and "Desperate Housewives" TV commercial
antics? Based on the amount of newspaper ink and commentators' air time,
Owens symbolizes the triumph of team member over team."[11] Owens'
"triumph" is difficult to swallow, since he, though a talented player, has not
done for football what Ruth has done for baseball or Ali has done for boxing.

Second, self-promotion makes light of the efforts of opponents. One has
only to consider the 2002 episode of Owens' autographing the ball after a
touchdown and Seattle's Coach Holmgren's virulent response. It is virtually
impossible to puff yourself up without deflating opponents. As mentioned
earlier, athletic competition is inherently cooperative and community-oriented:
Even the greatest athlete needs the cooperation of an opponent if she is to
develop and display her excellence. Disrespect for opponents reflects a
fundamental disregard for the nature of sport itself.

Why do sports fans, coaches, players, and owners not only tolerate, but
encourage self-promotion in athletes? Part of the answer is sensationalism in
competitive sport and sensationalism in life. On the MC model, sport is a
business and sensationalism sells.

Humans tend, as philosopher John Dewey has stated, toward a
sensationalistic attitude toward events. A sensationalist attitude, for Dewey, is
oversimplified and anti-intellectual—one that takes episodes out of their proper
context and fails to see them in relation to other things.

One effect [of sensationalism] . . . has been to create in a large number of persons an appetite for the momentary "thrills" caused by impacts that stimulate nerve endings but whose connections with cerebral functions are broken. Then stimulation and excitation are not so ordered that intelligence is produced. At the same time the habit of using judgment is weakened by the habit of depending on external stimuli. Upon the whole, it is probably a tribute to the powers of endurance of human nature that the consequences are not more serious than they are.[12]

The problem with sensationalism is the abandonment of what Dewey calls an intellectual approach to events—here, competitive sporting events—for cultivation of a momentary, thrill-seeking approach to them. Consumers prefer the sudden jolt of episodic thrills that sporting events offer—being unexpectedly blown away by a spectacular home run, a hockey player brawl, or a basketball slam-dunk—to a fuller and richer grasp of athletic competitions, within the larger context of other events. We are more moved by Owens' ego-puffed signing of the football after his touchdown than by the concerted effort of his team that allowed the catch to happen—the strong play by the defense that enabled the offense to get the ball, the solid blocking by the offensive line, the quarterback's precise throw, the other receivers who acted as decoys, etc.. Ego-puffing is the wicked bastard child of sensationalism—wicked because it promotes further sensationalism at the expense of a fuller grasp of just what is going on in a contest. With a commercially motivated sensationalist approach to competitive sport, much of what is great about sport is lost.

After Owens was released from the Eagles at the end of the 2005-2006 season, former teammate N.D. Kalu had this to say:

What did I learn from it? That the chemistry thing is real. I never was one to believe in chemistry, but you had to notice that we'd always brought in the same kind of guys, guys who didn't care about the spotlight or about stats, guys that just wanted to win. You bring in one guy who doesn't feed into that thinking and it disrupts the whole team.[13]

Kalu is right. Competitive sport is about chemistry—the chemistry between players on a team, the chemistry between players within a particular sport, and the chemistry between players' competitive and private lives, each of which is inescapably social.

Notes

1. 14 Oct. 2002.
2. 2 Jan. 1982.
3. Sanders often notes with pomp that he gave himself both nicknames.

4. "Where Sanders Goes, Teams Win," ESPN.com, http://espn.go.com/sportscentury /features/00016459.htm, January 10, 2008.

5. Dan Winters, "The No-Stats All-Star," *New York Times*, Feb. 15, 2009, http:// www.nytimes.com/2009/02/15/magazine/15Battier-t.html.

6. Ty Cobb, *Memoirs of Twenty Years in Baseball*, ed. Ron Cobb (William R. Cobb, 2002), 177.

7. Cobb, *Memoirs of Twenty Years in Baseball*, 176.

8. http://en.wikiquote.org/wiki/Babe_Ruth.

9. Here is what Mickey Mantle said about a very Cobb-like player, Pete Rose: "If I had played my career hitting singles like Pete, I'd wear a dress." Baseball Almanac, http://www.baseball-almanac.com/recbooks/rb_html, January 19,2011.

10. Owens was released in 2006 from the Philadelphia Eagles after a series of episodes that were deemed not conducive to team play. He played two years with the Dallas Cowboys and was released from them in March of 2009, because he had a divisive impact on the team. He plays now for the Buffalo Bills.

11. Paul Willstein, "'Basketbrawl' Epitomizes Pro Sports' 'Slam Dunk' Nonteam-Player Mentality," *East Penn Press*, December 8, 2004, 18.

12. John Dewey, *Freedom and Culture* (Amherst, NY: Prometheus Books), 39-40.

13. Dana Pennett O'Neil, "At Season's End, Several Eagles Come Clean about Terrell Owens," *Philadelphia Daily News*, Jan. 5, 2005.

PART III
Why Can't We Just Enjoy Sports?

Chapter 12
The Aesthetic/Recreational Model

"Act in such a way that you always treat humanity, whether in your own person or in the person of any other, never simply as a means, but always at the same time as an end." Immanuel Kant

E HAVE LOOKED AT THE MARTIAL/COMMERCIAL model in the previous part of this book and focused on what we took to be the limits and demerits of that model. MC sport views athletes and athletic competitions narrowly as goods to be peddled to a consuming public. Its perceived value lies in its capacity to generate extrinsic goods such as entertainment and revenue. It also lauds myopic individualism, aggression, violence, and sexism. We identified many, if not most, of the problems in sport today with the excesses of the MC model.

In Part III of this undertaking, we consider a natural counterpart to the MC model—namely the idea that sport is "just for fun." As a subset of play, which is by nature autotelic (i.e. an end in itself), the goods valued on this form of sport are intrinsic to the practice. Competition, if it is tolerated at all, takes a back seat to pleasure, enjoyment, and the experience of beauty. These goods are community-oriented—i.e., they are experienced by all and not merely victorious individuals. This is an aesthetic approach to sport that seeks no practical justification beyond recreation, for that reason we call it the Aesthetic/Recreational or AR model. Let us survey the features of the AR model.

Intrinsic Goods

First, the goods sought in AR sport are intrinsic to the activity. Sport is undertaken for its own sake, as a means of self-expression through creativity and spontaneity, which aims not at profit or glory but simply the pleasurable experience of beauty. Although this approach is more often associated with child's play or dance, it is also applicable to sport.

J.W. Keating, in an important early paper in philosophy of sport, makes a distinction between "sport" and "athletics." "Sport" he defines roughly as "a kind of diversion which has for its direct and immediate end fun, pleasure and delight and which is dominated by a spirit of moderation and generosity." "Athletics," in contrast, "is essentially a competitive activity, which has for its end victory in the contest and which is marked by a spirit of dedication, sacrifice and intensity."[1]

AR sport is "sport" as Keating defines the term. AR sport has for its end enjoyment, which is for all intents and purposes to say that it is done for its own sake, not the sake of some other end. It is not undertaken for fitness, refinement of physical skills, or any of the extrinsic perks mentioned in the MC model. Participants assume the attitude, as it were, of curious children in a relatively new environment. Even professional athletes in championship games are capable of assuming an AR approach toward sport.

We cannot help but call to mind the attitude of the former Cincinnati baseball player Pete Rose in the sixth game of the 1975 World Series against Boston. Cincinnati had a 6-3 lead going into the eighth inning. Bernie Carbo tied the game with a three-run dinger in the bottom of the eighth. The game went into extra innings and, when Rose came to bat in the bottom of the tenth inning, he turned to Boston catcher Carlton Fisk and said rhetorically, "This is some kind of game, isn't it?" Whatever Rose's failings were as a player and perhaps as a human being, one can forgive him much for a comment such as that. Rose was a tough competitor, but there was a part of him that always *played* baseball for its intrinsic goods.

Non-Agonism

Second, AR sport tolerates competition only insofar as it encourages enjoyable, spirited play. To the AR athlete and sports fan, winning is irrelevant and cooperative and enthusiastic participation is key. The outcome of the contest always takes a back seat to the aesthetic value or personal enjoyment of a well-played game. There is no desire to establish rank or quantify performance. The aim, in contrast, is to involve as many persons as possible in play, insofar as their talents and abilities allow them to participate, all in the name of fun.

This focus on fun inspires a friendly attitude not only toward opponents but also the rules. In AR sport, rules are recognized as guidelines that make the game possible. Rules are respected but not inviolable. Since spontaneity and free expression of creativity are essential to AR, rules which inhibit them are changed or ignored. In a driveway game of basketball, for example, a novice player may be given open shots at the basket to make the game more enjoyable. The AR approach to rules is flexible and pragmatic, in an effort to maximize the pleasure of competitors.

Just as rules are not viewed as obstacles to winning in AR sport, neither are competitors. Whereas MC sport focused on domination, AR sport focuses on cooperation. That is, in part, the thesis defended by philosopher Robert Simon, who seeks to justify the practice of competitive sport in spite of many seemingly objectionable features of it.

> [C]ompetition in sports should be regarded and engaged in not as a zero-sum game but as a mutually acceptable quest for excellence through challenge. Underlying the good sports contest, in effect, is an implicit social contract under which both competitors accept the obligation to provide a challenge for opponents according to the rules of the sport. Competition in sports is ethically defensible, in this view, when it is engaged in voluntarily as part of a mutual quest for excellence.[2]

Adopting this cooperative attitude toward competition gives all participants access to its intrinsic goods. Simon's thesis is engaging, sober, and similar, in many key respects, to our aretic thesis.

AR sport, however, is more about play than contest, and it attempts to eliminate the painful consequences of losing.[3] Scoring or winning is relevant only insofar as it contributes to enjoyment. A game or competitive event that does not have a winner or an end is of little consequence. What is important is that athletes immerse themselves in creative play in a cooperative manner.

Knowledge-Indifference

Third, AR sport is knowledge-indifferent. Unlike MC sport, which seeks to affirm the very things that are assumed true at the outset, AR sportive expression is open-minded. It neither challenges nor affirms the status quo beyond sport, and critically questions itself only in terms of its ability to generate beauty and pleasure.

In one sense, the AR model's emphasis on beauty and creative expression seems to indirectly challenge the MC status quo by promoting so-called "feminine" sports such as figure skating and gymnastics. It is worth observing, however, that practice of those sports at the highest levels—by women as well as men—still privileges strength and speed. Indeed figure exercise that privileged balance and precision—and even gave figure skating its name—has been eliminated from top-level competition. Scoring now privileges acrobatic jumps over creative expression.

Overemphasis on strength and speed in MC sport has real social consequences. As Eleanor Metheny observes, MC style sport features (1) an attempt to subdue physically an opponent through bodily contact, (2) direct application of bodily force to some heavy object, (3) an attempt to project one's body through space over long distances, and (4) cooperative, face-to-face opposition where bodily contact often occurs. Those features, she adds, are masculine, even "supermasculine," traits imposed on sport.[4] Following Metheny's lead, B.C. Postow argues that women might have a moral reason not to participate in such sports because men, for biological reasons, will tend to dominate and domination might provide grounds for sexual discrimination against female athletes.[5]

So even though the AR model of sport values traditionally feminine characteristics such as grace and durability, it seems powerless to promote them at a meaningful level. It is not that such feminine characteristics are irrelevant to competitive sport. Consider former Detroit Lions running back great Barry Sanders, who carried himself low to the ground and seemed impossible to tackle, because he was elusive, slippery, and graceful. San Francisco 49ers receiver Jerry Rice even studied ballet to improve his results on the gridiron. The examples of Sanders and Rice may challenge MC sports rejection of feminine characteristics, but AR sport is indifferent.

Unity

Fourth, AR sport emphasizes equality and social unity. Unlike MC sport, where competition functions to individualize, quantify, and rank competitors, AR sport, as a means of self-expression and self-understanding, rejects such practices as a threat to the communally enjoyed beauty of play. Competition is endorsed only as long as it promotes unity rather than division, as in the case of team play. The commitment to team play, for AR sport, is not a commitment to agonism, in contrast to the panagonism of MC sport, it is merely a commitment to others—an affirmation of Aristotle's statement that humans are "political animals"[6] and the good life, the best possible human life, is one in which joys and sorrows are shared with other persons.

D. Stanley Eitzen in "The Dark Side of Competition" mentions a 200-meter race between three 12-year-olds at a Special Olympics competition. When the three were some 25 yards away from the finish line, one runner fell. The other two stopped, helped up their fallen competitor, held hands, and jogged together to the finish line. The message, Eitzen says, would likely not be grasped by Americans, because they are so focused on winning. He sums: "[S]uccessful life involved the pursuit of excellence, a fundamental respect for others, even one's competitors, and enjoyment in the process. Competition as structured in our society with its emphasis on the outcome undermines these goals."[7]

AR sport is team-oriented, not individualistic, because play is best enjoyed when it is shared. Of course, the tension between individual and community interests must be addressed in sport. In AR sport, as the example showed, individual interests are sacrificed to maximize the overall happiness of the group. It might also be argued, however, that individual interests might be pursued in such a way that they benefit the entire group. This is the case with *aretē*, as we shall see in the final section. If sports benefits are restricted to intrinsic goods such as enjoyment, however, the group must always take precedent.

Pleasure and Beauty

Finally, the overriding values in AR sport are pleasure and beauty. Whereas commercialism dictates the direction of MC sport, AR sport is dedicated to fun, leisure, diversion, enjoyment. This shift in focus obviates the culture of drug abuse and insensitivity to pain. AR "competitors" do not use their bodies as a means to the end of winning, rather they take pleasure in sport through cultivating spontaneity of movement and creative imagination. AR sport seeks to engage natural bodily rhythms and respect bodily limits. It finds beauty in efficiency. Writes E.F. Kaelin:

> At the most basic level, [aesthetic] significance is achieved merely by ordering our bodily existence in accordance with the ends imposed upon it by the natural environment and dominated by biological necessity. . . . At this level of experience the possibilities of aesthetic perception are already multiple: we may abstract from the necessity to achieve a particular goal and focus on the movement pattern employed in its achievement, thereby developing "natural" grace. This is recognized as much for its maximum efficiency—the greatest among of result for the least effort—as for the "beauty" of its execution. The feeling of being at one with nature, using it to fulfill our own aims with consummate ease, is a direct aesthetic response of the mover to his motion.[8]

This aesthetic economy of motion stands in stark contrast to the MC model's unlimited commercial economy. The extreme amounts of money involved in MC sport are repeatedly used to justify the extreme behavior of those competitors involved. The AR model, by contrast, values constraint. It may seem, at first glance, that one can never have too much pleasure. But as the Epicurean philosophers showed, much of what we call pleasure is simply relief from unnecessary pain—most often the pain of desire caused by irrational indulgence in luxuries.

Sport, too, should be characterized by moderation. The obsessive pursuit of records encourages the drug abuse and wasteful spending on ergogenic aids. Human beings are by nature limited and sport should be practiced in a way that respects these limitations. The AR model embraces restraint because it knows beauty is not a matter of quantity or excess. At the same time sport need not be regarded as a merely frivolous pursuit. There is pleasure in excellence and not just indulgence.

Ends and Means

The MC and AR models of sport differ in their approach to ends and means. In evaluating them philosophically, we must take account of both. It is not enough to simply condemn the final goals of profit or pleasure. It is not meaningful to declare practices like doping or non-competitive games as wrong. A holistic approach is needed and we aim to adopt a holistic approach in our construction of Aretism. There is one principle regarding ends and means, however, which should be universally adopted. It is the principle of treating persons as ends rather than means—the principle of respect for human dignity. Using others as means even to noble ends violates that principle.

Former baseball player José Canseco, was interviewed by Mike Wallace on *60 Minutes* just prior to the publication of his tell-all book *Juiced: Wild Times, Rampant 'Roids, Smash Hits & How Baseball Got Big.* "I don't recommend steroids for everyone and I don't recommend growth hormones for everyone. But for certain individuals, I truly believe, because I've experimented with it for so many years, that it can make an average athlete a super athlete. It can make a super athlete incredible. Just legendary."[9]

With the publication of his book, Canseco has been hailed both as a "beacon of truth in the dishonest world of baseball" and as a "slimy opportunist" for sensationalizing facts for personal profit. Writes Pat Lackey:

> [T]he characterization of Canseco as some kind of angel of truth is misguided. He saw that a book full of the names [of baseball players that have used steroids] would be profitable, so he wrote it. When it became clear that much of what he wrote would be publicly corroborated and that playing the role of whistleblower would be lucrative, Canseco shifted gears towards that role instead.[10]

If Lackey's assessment is correct, then Canseco's "moral" allegations à propos of indicted fellow baseball players are mere cant and, thereby, morally suspect.

Philosopher Immanuel Kant insists proper moral action requires that no person be treated as an instrument to further some end. "Act in such a way," he writes, "that you always treat humanity, whether in your own person or in the person of any other, never simply as a means, but always at the same time as an end."[11] What Kant means, as it relates to the practice of competitive sport, is that sport must be conducted in such a manner that fellow competitors, whether teammates or opponents, must be treated always with dignity and respect. That leaves no room for trash-talking, psychological tactics, intent to harm, lying or dissembling, or deception of any sort.

For Kant, persons are duty-bound to treat others as ends. Actions with regard for morally binding duty are, thus, not necessarily actions done from rational recognition of morally binding duty—i.e., right actions. Canseco's actions might have been right, but, if done for the wrong reasons, they are for Kant morally faulty actions. We agree. Canseco, in his avowed quest for justice, seems to have little regard for the persons he incriminated in his book. If so, his actions are morally condemnable.

The AR model, with its focus on cooperation and intrinsic goods, demonstrates Kant's principle of ends and requires that sport, played competitively or otherwise, is played in such a manner that all persons involved are treated with full respect. This principle is perhaps the AR model's greatest insight about ethics in sport, but it does not, by itself, entail wholesale rejection of the values of MC sport.

In the rest of this section we will examine the limitations and consequences of the AR model of sport. This will break ground for our construction, in the final part, of a medial model of sport called Aretism. We propose Aretism as a solution to the defects of MC sport that allows for some expression of some AR sport features in a manner that grants inclusion of competitive sport as an important human good.

Notes

1. J.W. Keating, "The Ethics of Competition and its Relation to Some Moral Problems in Athletics," *The Philosophy of Sport*, ed. R.G. Osterhoudt (Springfield, IL: Charles C. Thomas, 1973), 265.

2. Robert Simon, *Fair Play: The Ethics of Sport*, 2nd ed. (Boulder, CO: Westview Press, 2004), 27.

3. We think the painful consequences of losing have educative value.

4. Eleanor Metheny, "Symbolic Forms of Movement: The Feminine Image in Sports," *Connotations of Movement in Sport and Dance* (Dubuque, IA: Wm. C. Brown Publishing Co., 1965), 49.

5. B.C. Postow, "Women in Masculine Sports," *Philosophy of Sport: Critical Readings, Crucial Issues*, ed. M. Andrew Holowchak (Upper Saddle River, NJ: Prentice-Hall, 2002), 389-92.

6. They are "political" insofar as they are essentially polis-dwelling or social creatures. Aristotle, *Nicomachean Ethics*, trans. Terrence Irwin (Indianapolis: Hackett Publishing Company, Inc., 1999), 1097b9.

7. D. Stanley Eitzen, "The Dark Side of Competition," *Philosophy of Sport: Critical Readings, Crucial Issues*, ed. M. Andrew Holowchak (Upper Saddle River, NJ: Prentice-Hall, 2002), 240.

8. E.F. Kaelin, "The Well-Played Game: Notes toward an Aesthetics of Sport," *Philosophy of Sport: Critical Readings, Crucial Issues*, ed. M. Andrew Holowchak (Upper Saddle River, NJ: Prentice-Hall, 2002), 106.

9. Hal Bodley and Mel Antonen, "Canseco: Steroids Made Baseball Career Possible," *USA Today*, 13 Feb. 2005, http://www.usatoday.com/sports/baseball/2005-02-13-canseco-60minutes_x.htm.

10. Pat Lackey, "From the Windup: Jose Canseco, Steroid Era Hero or Slimy Opportunist?" 19 Feb. 2009, http://mlb.fanhouse.com/2009/02/19/from-the-windup-jose-canseco-steroid-era-hero-or-slimy-opportu/.

11. Immanuel Kant, *Grounding for a Metaphysics of Morals* trans. James W. Ellington (Indianapolis: Hackett Publishing Company, Inc., 1993), §429.

Chapter 13
Aesthetic Spectacle

"I made such an incredible start, and it was such fun, to put it mildly."
Annika Sorrenstam

ONE OF THE GREATEST FAILINGS of the Martial/Commercial model of
sport, as section II suggests, is its focus on extrinsic goals like fame
and fortune—a focus that encourages sensationalism and reduces
sportive participation and enjoyment to episodic thrill-seeking. What
is lost is a broader grasp of the significance of competitive sport in free societies; a grasp that derives from questions that ask for some exercise of reason
like, "Just what contribution does competitive sport make to the good life?" or
"What is the true significance of this particular contest?" Such questions become
meaningless when sport is regarded as an entertainment business that caters to
human passions, which are unstable, insatiable, and ever-changing.

It may seem that the Aesthetic/Recreational model of sport, with its overriding emphasis on pleasure, endorses sensationalism in the athletic spectacles. But
the AR model derives enjoyment from sport's intrinsic goods and employs rationality in its appreciation of them. It might be unfashionable for anyone, even
philosophers, to talk about rationality—especially in sport, which is understood
merely as a test of physical skill. But rationality enhances the aesthetic value of
sport—its challenge, its drama, its capacity to amaze. The first lesson the AR
model teaches us about sport is that we must understand and appreciate what
sport is, if we are to derive maximum pleasure from it.

This chapter is about aesthetic spectacle in competitive sport. Aesthetic
spectacle is reason-driven, not sensationalist, and it has both momentary and
historical dimensions. Historical spectacle is a matter of the drama of particular
competitive sporting events, considered within their historical context. Momentary spectacle concerns isolated moments within competitions that are so overwhelming, when one grasps their significance, they seem to transcend time itself. In both cases, both athletes and spectators must grasp the full significance
of these otherwise mundane events, in order to appreciate their beauty.

We begin with an illustration of a historical spectacle—a look the 2003
American League Championship Series in baseball. We then turn to two exam-

ples of momentary spectacle—one "fun" day in former golfing superstar Annika Sorenstam's life and one extraordinary event in the 1980 World's Strongest Man Contest.

Baseball's 2003 ALCS

Of competitive sports that are driven largely by spectator-appeal, aesthetic expression manifests itself sometimes subtly and often openly to the spectator through drama. The drama of competitive sport is, as it were, the theatrical display and the emotional gamut that competitors and spectators experience as a competition unfolds in its historical context. Through the contingencies of any contest—such as reversals of fortune (e.g., the lead changes in the 2005 Rose Bowl)—drama showcases competitors' and teams' talents, creativity, and mettle in a temporal setting. How players and teams handle these contingencies leads to enhanced or diminished drama.

Major League Baseball's 2003 American League Championship Series was one such dramatic event. It pitted perennial favorites, the New York Yankees, against their archrivals, the Boston Red Sox. Boston featured an unrivalled hitting machine, featuring eight players with 85 or more RBIs and six players with 25 or more home runs. The Yankees—a brilliantly coached team[1] that seemed to do what it had to do year after year to win their division and make a move to win the World Series—were, of course, the Yankees and therefore undaunted by Boston's vaunted offense.

The first two games were in New York. Behind the accomplished knuckleball pitching of Tim Wakefield, Boston took the lead in the ALCS with a 5-2 win in New York. The Yankees responded coolly by winning the next game, 6-2, to tie the series. The third game, in Boston, unfortunately featured a bench-clearing brawl, in which, among other things, 72-year-old Yankees bench coach Don Zimmer lunged at Red Sox pitcher Pedro Martinez, who quickly shoved Zimmer to the ground. In the ninth inning, two New York pitchers were involved in an altercation with members of Boston's grounds crew. New York eventually won this game, 4-3. Boston bounced right back with a hard-fought, thrilling 3-2 win to even the series. With New York winning game five, 4-2, and Boston taking game six, 9-6, everything was on the line for the deciding game. The Yankees, trailing 4-0 in the fourth inning and 5-2 in the eighth inning, came from behind in storybook fashion to tie the game and send it into extra innings. Wakefield, who had stymied New York in games one and four, came into pitch in relief in the 10th inning. In spite of his earlier successes against the Yankees, Wakefield gave up a series-ending home run to Aaron Boone in the 11th inning. The Yankees won the game, 6-5, and advanced, once again, to the World Series.[2]

To anyone who followed the series closely, our synopsis of the series should seem stiff, cold, and bloodless. It captures little of its drama because it is removed from its historical context. Of course, one might argue that a much more expansive description of the series as it unfolded—one that is game-by-game, inning-by-inning, and pitch-by-pitch—is needed to capture the drama completely. That, we acknowledge, would be a decided improvement, but would still miss the dramatic essence of *this* series. To get at the dramatic essence of this series, one must go beyond the surface structure of events and plumb the early history of baseball.

In 1920, the Boston Red Sox traded a young all-star pitcher, George Herman "Babe" Ruth, to New York for the staggering amount of $100,000. The trade was significant for two reasons. First, in trading away Ruth, Boston traded away someone who would arguably become baseball's greatest player of all time. Second, Boston, which had won five world championships before trading Ruth, had yet as of the 2003 league series to win another, since trading Ruth. In contrast, the New York Yankees, who had never won a world championship before acquiring Ruth, would go on to become the most successful baseball franchise in the history of the game after acquiring the slugger by winning 27 world championships in all. What was the reason for New York's success and Boston's lack of success? The answer that many mavens of baseball gave was the "curse of Ruth."

The curse of Ruth—acknowledged as being a bit of silly frivolity that was dreamed up at some time as an "explanation" of New York's World-Series success and Boston's lack of it—was undeniably a large art of the overall drama between Boston and New York in the 2003 ALCS. Such drama was, of course, not in the surface structure of events as they unfolded, which itself was highly dramatic, but rather in its depth structure—i.e., its history. Fans everywhere were asking themselves, "Could Boston beat New York and go on to win the World Series after so many years of disappointment?" For many, that was certainly just another way of asking, "Could Boston end the curse?" Yet when the series was over, Boston lost still again . . . and they lost to New York . . . and they lost in the seventh game . . . and they lost in extra innings . . . and they lost with their best pitcher in the series on the mound. Thus, when the very canons of probability seem violated, the curse no longer seems silly. Many in Boston and New York doubtless believed that somewhere and somehow Ruth had a hand in the outcome and those refusing to see that were ostriches. Luckily for Bostonians, after being down 3-0, Boston would go on to beat the Yankees the following year in an equally dramatic series and go on to win the World Series to end the curse.

Note that the drama and the enjoyment of the 2003 ALCS were intrinsic to the game, understood rationally and within its historical context.

Annika Sorenstam's "Fun" Friday

It is likewise easy to forget that the pleasure valued on the AR model of sport comes not just from playful frivolity, but also from the demonstration of excellence. On Friday, March 16 of 2001, at the Standard Register Ping Tournament in Arizona, Annika Sorenstam joined an elite group of professional golfers by becoming only the sixth person ever to shoot a round under 60 and the first female to do so. Her achievement was laudable, historical, and marketable—but those things did not prevent it from being fun.

Sorenstam began the day at the Moon Valley Country Club brilliantly. She birdied the first eight holes, parred her ninth hole, and then made four more birdies for an incredible total of 12 under par for the first 13 holes. "I made such an incredible start, and it was such fun, to put it mildly. By the end, I started to get very nervous. But now I'm so proud and happy."[3]

Nerves clearly did play a part thereafter, as she knew she was in the process of making golf history. Though she birdied only one of the five remaining holes, she parred the other four. Overall, she missed only one fairway and reached every green in regulation. Most astonishing, however, was her putting. Outside of the 13 putts for birdie, her longest putt for par was just over three feet. Playing partner Meg Mallon had this to say about Sorenstam's putting: "You can use all the words you want—impressive, simple. She had two tap-ins and one putt from about six feet. The rest were 10 to 25 feet. She put on a putting display, especially on the front side. She hit the right shots. It was the kind of round everyone dreams of playing."[4]

As the crowd got wind of what was happening, it followed her down the stretch in awe. Not only was the crowd in disbelief, so too were Sorenstam's fellow competitors. Judy Rankin, who covered the event for ABC Sports, wrote:

> Watching Sorenstam around the golf course was an electrifying experience for her competitors. They all remarked about how they had a little trouble focusing on their own games because they were focusing on the leaderboard. Those players who had finished their rounds were watching the account on television off and on and going about their business until each time ESPN went to Annika going for another birdie putt. That's when everything completely stopped. So, yes, it's safe to say that her achievement was the type that really inspired every other player to be better than they've ever been before. They now have the realization that such a perfect round *can* happen.[5]

Sorenstam's incredible round is a perfect illustration of beauty as a-temporal spectacle in sport. She began the day with a few birdies to climb atop the leader-board. Fans and players took note. Then, with 12 birdies in 13 holes, she was on pace to do what had hitherto never been done by a woman—break the 60-shot barrier. Fans in attendance thronged around her as she played with such focus that she was mostly unaware of the other players on the course. Soon she was in the heads of other players, as they realized they were a part of some-thing timeless—something that had never been done. On the 18th hole, she placed her approach shot just 10 feet above the pin and then two-putted for an unbelievable round of 59. Golf history was made and was, as she noted, fun. She went on to win the tournament, but after her round of 59, that could only be an-ticlimactic. Winning was not the chief benefit, nor was the financial boost this performance would provide. The greatest benefit was the sheer joy shared by the community of participants and spectators as they experienced such sporting ex-cellence.

Kaz

Another fine instance of joy through spectacle comes through one of the more prominent of many incredible feats of strength by three-time World's Strongest Man, Bill Kazmaier. To those who follow strength sports, his numerous feats of strength are legendary: a bench press of 661 pounds in 1981 (world record), an 887 pound deadlift in 1981 (world record), a 65-pound weight toss over a bar elevated at 18 feet and three inches in 1984 (world record), a 440 pound barbell curl in 1985 (world record), and 40 repetitions with 100 pounds (each arm) in the dumbbell military press in 1989 (world record).

Yet in spite of those seemingly superhuman accomplishments, one episode in the 1980 World's Strongest Man Contest sticks out especially. The fifth event in this contest was the barrel-loading event. Each competitor had to lift and load 12 barrels of beer, each weighing 167 pounds and arranged in two columns of six, on to the rear of a truck placed near the barrels. There were several heats, each featuring two athletes, two trucks, and 24 kegs in all.

As this event was to be a measure not only of power, but also of endurance, the competitors employed one of two strategies. Many grabbed each end of a barrel, carried it waist-high to the truck, muscled it up to a chest-high position, and then pushed it on to the rear of the truck's bed. Others lifted each barrel on to a shoulder, where they ran up to the truck and deposited the barrel on the bed.

Going into the final pairing of competitors, Britain's Geoff Capes and America's Bill Kazmaier, the time to beat was just over one minute. As the heat went off, Kazmaier began in absolutely stunning fashion. He threw the first few barrels, as if they were empty, on to the truck from afar and then shouldered and ran the remaining barrels to the truck for an astonishing time of 49.11 seconds![6] Those persons in attendance, knowing that they had just seen something that no one hitherto in the history of the world could have done, stood in awe. Several said that it was the most impressive deed of strength they had ever seen.

Kazmaier would go on to win the contest, his second of three straight, in dominating fashion. He is hailed by many in strength circles as the greatest strongman to have ever lived. Again, however, the fame and fortune extrinsic to the event fails to capture its real value. For athletes and spectators alike, it is the aesthetic enjoyment derived from athletic achievement, understood in context, which constitutes the greatest good of sports. End-zone antics and gratuitous brawls may fill the highlight reels, but sport's greatest goods for the sportive gourmand are intrinsic to the game.

Notes

1. Joe Torre was their coach at the time.

2. http://mlb.mlb.com/mlb/ps/y2003/home.jsp?view=bos_nyy.

3. Terry McNamara, "With 13 Birdies, Sorenstam Records first 59 for Woman," *New York Times*, 17 Mar. 2001, http://www.nytimes.com/2001/03/17/sports/golf-with-13-birdies-sorenstam-records-first-59-by-woman.html?pagewanted=1.

4. McNamara, "Sorenstam Records first 59 for Woman."

5. McNamara, "Sorenstam Records first 59 for Woman."

6. http://samson-power.com/ASL/kaz.html.

Chapter 14
Playful Integrity

"The only thing that is not worthless is to live this life out truthfully and rightly and to be patient with those who do not." Marcus Aurelius

THE WIN-AT-ALL-COSTS ATTITUDE THAT PREDOMINATES in panagonistic sport, along with the money involved, makes it difficult for some to respect the rules. Cheating is commonplace in collegiate sports—especially at the highest level—as well as in professional sports. This disrespect for the rules to gain an edge on the competition, it is at least implicitly sanctioned, and it extends to treating others involved in sport as means rather than ends. Integrity seems to be a pipe dream on the MC model of sport.

It is tempting to identify panagonism, the obsessive focus on competition and winning, as the root of this problem and to prescribe the solution of nonagonism. On the A/R model, the goal is not winning but enjoyment. Rules and opponents are respected and even valued because they make the game—and therefore the enjoyment—possible. Competition is simply a form of play.

Playing by the Rules

Watching people on a beach on any sunny day gives one pause to reflect upon the extent to which humans, like many other animals, love to play. On the beach, children build sandcastles on and dig waterways into the sand. Young adults pass footballs and toss frisbees to one another. Elderly people, beneath the shade of large umbrellas, play board games like chess or backgammon. In the water, there is laughing and splashing everywhere. So much of human behavior is play-directed that philosopher Johan Huizinga believes human play antedates culture. Humans, he maintains, are not so much rational animals as they are playing animals.[1]

When not spontaneous, human play generally finds expression in rule-governed activities called games. Rules set the parameters of games of all sorts that enable games to be distinguished from other forms of play. Writes philosopher Bernard Suits:

> In games, artificial barriers are erected just so they can be overcome by the use
> of rule-governed skills. Rules are the crux of games because it is the rules of
> any particular game that generate the skills appropriate to that game. Blocking
> in football is a skill required by, and thus generated by, the rules because the
> rules *rule out*, among other things, the use of machine guns by guards and tack-
> les.[2]

In competitive sport, rules determine what physical skills or activities are admis-
sible and inadmissible. Consequently, competitive sport is fundamentally a test
for certain skills within rule-determined parameters. Winning teams or athletes
are generally those that best or most effectively display such skills within the
rules of competition. Athletes and teams are said to play fairly when they spirit-
edly pursue victory to the best of their ability in keeping with the rules of a contest.

That analysis looks quite right, of course, on paper, but a close look at the
actual practice of competitive sport shows something else. At the highest levels
of competition, athletes do not seem so committed to winning *by the rules*. Victory is just too important. Instead, coaches, athletes, and teams often do "whatever it takes" to win,[3] while there is mere lip service paid to fair and honest
competition.

In Division I college football and basketball, for instance, winning generates revenue for athletic departments through prime-time television appearances
for teams—especially bowl appearances for football teams and the NCAA
Tournament for basketball teams. The competition for television revenue, which
ranges from tens of thousands to many millions of dollars for one game, depending upon the significance of the game, puts tremendous pressure on coaches and
athletes, and incites other money-flow schemes. With millions of dollars involved, there is great incentive to cheat in order to win. Coaches that do not win
do not last long. Those coaches that do win earn enormous salaries.

While college coaches and athletes express outrage, when seeing the opposition cheating on the field, they express surprise when others catch them trying
to "bend the rules." Moreover, they customarily participate in cheating off the
field. Cheating has become an accepted part of recruitment procedures by college coaches and assistants. Athletes routinely take the bait—e.g., free cars,
"help" in finding jobs, and under-the-table money. Why is cheating so much a
part of off-the-field recruiting procedures? Why do coaches and players express
little remorse over bending the rules on the field? The answer is simple: The
measure of their success is winning and winning generates publicity, revenue,
and other extrinsic goods for a university. To say that top college programs
"play" sports like football and basketball is practically a misuse of the word.

Is a Win Always a Win?

The narrow focus on victory is so engrained in the MC sports culture, it extends beyond athletes and coaches. Sports commentators are fond of stating things in bottom-line, platitudinous fashion: "If the refs didn't see it, it didn't happen"; "The better team won"; and "A win is a win." Sometimes, however, those platitudes are thrown out as rationalizations that cover questionable, unethical play. Consider, for instance, the last platitude: A win is a win. Is a win, however, always a win?

Philosopher Robert Simon in his book *Fair Play: Sports and Social Values* believes that the answer to that question is "no." What is essential to competitive sport for Simon is that it is "a mutual quest for excellence through challenge." The mutuality of this quest entails a commitment to sportsmanship and sportsmanship entails that not all means of winning are legitimate—not, at least, if "achievement" and "success" are to be meaningful from the perspective of fairness.[4]

Simon gives the example of the 1990 football game where the University of Colorado won a game against Missouri, when officials mistakenly gave Colorado five downs to score a game-winning touchdown in the final seconds. The officials were at fault here and Colorado accepted the win. Should they have? Did they *really* win?

Simon gives another, more difficult, example of a basketball team, unable to hear the buzzer due to the noise of the crowd and overall excitement in the game, which takes to the court late after a time-out. In such a case, the opposition is in a position to take the ball down the court and score before the other team assembles. Such a move, of course, is entirely in keeping with the rules. Should the other team take full advantage of this miscue and score a couple of easy points?

For Simon, the question anyone should ask is this: "Is a victory earned in this way significant, one I should take pride in?"[5] The answer Simon gives is "no." By the yardstick of competitive sport as a "mutual quest for excellence," Simon is right. If the point of sport is simply recreation and pleasure, as it is on the AR model, however, one might conclude that such technicalities are as unimportant. We argue, with Simon, that the salient issue is excellence (*aretē*); if athletes demonstrate excellence, then they may take pride in their performance, whether or not it results in victory.[6]

There are certainly many other examples of athletes and teams committed to do whatever it takes to win a contest. One has only to reconsider Tonya Harding/Nancy Kerrigan incident in 1994, where the latter was clubbed on the knee in an effort to keep her from competing in the upcoming Olympic Games (see chapter 5), or the stabbing of Monica Seles by a fan of Steffi Graf that occurred just months later. The point should now be clear: Winning at all costs ought to be no part of a socially sanctioned conception of competitive sport. It sucks pleasure out of the game and, more important, it threatens the moral dimension of athletic excellence. Integrity, too, is necessary in sport.

Our reasons may seem to be exclusively consequentialist—i.e., winning at all costs has socially harmful consequences. They are not. There is something plainly foul about contests where winning in any manner is acceptable—where players or teams "win ugly" by bending or breaking the rules of fair play. After all, rules make the game possible; in a technical sense it is impossible to play a game and break its rules at the same time. Such a victory is Pyrrhic from an aesthetic and ethical point of view. The victory becomes a celebration of human dishonesty and brutality. Integrity is lost and integrity is not something that is easily regained.

Treating Self and Others as Ends

Myopic emphasis on winning not only disrespects rules, it also disrespects persons. The commitment to win at all costs is perhaps no more evident than in the way coaches and players treat themselves and others in the effort to win. For instance, it is not uncommon in critical football games for one team to make it part of their game plan to injure a star player from the opposing team to increase their chances of winning. A win, gained in this manner, clearly violates the spirit of playfulness as well as the canons of fair play. It also promotes bestiality in a form of human activity that should be pleasant.

It is more the norm than the exception to treat others in sport instrumentally—as means, not as ends. Where winning is the only or even the principal aim of competition, coaches, like generals on a military campaign, must use players in a manner that best makes winning possible. Teammates are friends as long as each contributes significantly toward victory. Opponents are treated as enemies to be soundly wiped out in battle. Recall the angry words of former Miami tight end Kellen Winslow after their loss to Tennessee: "It's war! They're out to kill you, so I'm out there to kill them. We don't care about anybody but this U[niversity]. . . . I'm a fucking soldier!"

What is even more astonishing is the extent to which athletes will put their mental and physical wellbeing on the line in order to secure a victory. Concussions are common among players in football, especially quarterbacks and wide receivers, and numerous concussions have forced many players to consider early retirement. Many who have had numerous concussions, like former quarterback Brett Favre, continued to play at the risk of permanent brain damage, vision impairment, and even death.[7] What is the reward for taking on those and other risks game after game? Only this: Favre was universally admired by his peers as one of the toughest players ever to play the game. Sportswriter Bob Carter, for instance, said of Favre:

Brett Favre never got around to the health regulations for quarterbacks. The longtime Green Bay Packer—the only NFL player to be voted MVP three times by the Associated Press—has played the game much like his rough 'n' tumble life, with a daring style that has set him apart from his peers. . . . Favre is the ultimate risk-reward quarterback, a free-spirited gambler who can drive coaches crazy. Three times he's been tops in the NFL in passing yards and four times in touchdown passes, Favre has become one of the league's best passers, the most durable quarterback in history and the leader of the Pack.[8]

Carter's characterization of Favre is typical. It is not merely Favre's successes over the years that make him so well liked, but instead the manner in which they are achieved—his toughness, his indifference to pain. Over his career, Favre has had a laundry list of injuries, none of which has ever kept him from competing, most often, at a high level. So accustomed to living with pain, he became addicted to the painkiller Vicodin in 1995 and still managed to rally his team to an 11-5 record that year. In addition, he played through the entire 2003 season with a broken thumb on his throwing hand.[9]

We are not suggesting here that there is anything intrinsically faulty about Favre's character, for he was certainly one of the most colorful and most likeable athletes in professional sport. We merely wish to make the point that a conception of competition that rewards athletes like Favre for putting their own physical health at risk for a game is absurd.

Recall philosopher Immanuel Kant's grounding principle of morality, "Act in such a way that you always treat humanity, whether in your own person or in the person of any other, never simply as a means, but always at the same time as an end."[10] In agreement with Kant, there is something morally right, perhaps even beautiful, about treating oneself and all others, not just athletes, with dignity. Players are not pawns to be sacrificed, if needed, in the quest for victory. Opponents are not obstacles to be overcome. Athletes are people, thinking beings, and ought to be treated with due respect. After all, we are, as Maxim Gorki wrote "beasts of the same kidney."[11]

The panagonistic MC model of competitive sport, placing winning ahead of respect for personhood, affords athletes only instrumental status and is inconsistent with the Kantian principle of dignity. That in itself is sufficient reason to reject it. AR sport, with its emphasis on cooperative play instead of competitive victory, regards violation of personhood as anathema.

Respect for others is a necessary component of integrity in cooperative play as well as in competitive sport. The MC model's panagonism encourages disrespect for both rules and persons. The AR model's indifference to victory brings respect for rules and personhood back to the fore. A balanced interest in respect and victory will be a key feature of Aretism, developed in the last part of this book.

Notes

1. Johan Huizinga, "Selections from *Homo Ludens*," *Philosophy of Sport: Critical Readings, Crucial Issues*, ed. M. Andrew Holowchak (Upper Saddle River, NJ: Prentice-Hall, 2002), 7-8.

2. Bernard Suits, "Tricky Triad: Games, Play, and Sport," *Philosophy of Sport: Critical Readings, Crucial Issues*, ed. M. Andrew Holowchak (Upper Saddle River, NJ: Prentice-Hall, 2002), 33.

3. This is a common motivational phrase of many coaches.

4. Robert Simon, "Sportsmanship and Fairness in the Pursuit of Victory," *Philosophy of Sport: Critical Readings, Crucial Issues*, ed. M. Andrew Holowchak (Upper Saddle River, NJ: Prentice-Hall, 2002), 167-169.

5. Simon, "Sportsmanship and Fairness," 169.

6. An analytic victory is where one wins according to the rules but may or may not have demonstrated virtue in doing so. Reid makes the distinction in *The Philosophical Athlete*, 145-146.

7. Kevin Guskiewicz, Nancy Weaver, Darin Padua, and William Garrett, "Epidemiology of Concussion in Collegiate and High School Football Players," *American Journal of Sports Medicine*, 28 Sept. 2000, 643-650.

8. Bob Carter, "Fearless Favre's a Gameday Gambler," *ESPN Classic,* http://ad.abctv.com/classic/biography/s/Favre_Brett.html.

9. Carter, "Fearless Favre's a Gameday Gambler."

10. Immanuel Kant, *Groundwork for a Metaphysics of Morals* (New York: Harper & Row, 1964), §429.

11. Maxim Gorki, "In the Steppe," *Chelkash and Other Short Stories* (Whitefish, MT: Kessinger Publishing, 2005), 129.

Chapter 15
The Aesthetics of Journeying

"The more things a man is interested in, the more opportunities of happiness he has and the less he is at the mercy of fate, since if he loses one thing he can fall back upon another." Bertrand Russell

A DEFINING CHARACTERISTIC OF DEMOCRATIC SOCIETIES is that they allow for diversity of expression through regard for autonomy and free choice. True democracies, as free societies that do more than pay lip service to autonomy, enable individuals to decide for themselves what sorts of goods ought to be included in their society. Competitive sport is generally included as one of those goods, though it is certainly not the most important one, nor is it always clear why it is considered a good.[1]

The overriding value of sport on the Aesthetic/Recreational model derives from its intrinsic beauty and pleasure. Factors that interfere with those goods, including serious competition, are rejected on this model. This fact gave us some pause because we also know that many athletic goods depend on fair competition—in particular the good of challenging presumptions. In chapter 9 we criticized MC sport's tendency to stifle sport's belief-challenging capability by managing it in such a way as to affirm misguided beliefs about aggression, violence, and gender. Can the AR model contribute anything to this challenge?

Enjoyment or Fanaticism?

The interest and influence of fans on modern sport is undeniable, and the reality is that mavens find the MC model of sport highly entertaining. For those reasons, it seems that the AR model's emphasis on enjoyment and pleasure actually endorses some of the MC model's more troubling aspects, including panagonism, violence, and even sexism. Fans clearly enjoy men's sports more than women's, are entertained by violence, and take pleasure in the cut-throat approach to winning exhibited by certain teams. They demonstrate that not just with their wallets, but also by investing the lion's share of their free time following sporting events.

Of course the term "fan" derives from "fanatic" and fanaticism is characterized by unquestioned acceptance of even the most troubling aspects of a given activity. Fanatics live for sport by making a complete investment in it to the exclusion of other worthwhile, often more worthwhile, activities. For such dyed-in-the-wool fanatics, without sport, life lacks meaning. They follow their favorite teams religiously and adopt a cut-throat attitude to it that violently denigrates their team's opponents and even those opponents' fans. Consider, for instance, what one Penn State football fan says about a hit on the Ohio State quarterback, Troy Smith, near the end of their 2010 meeting, which he calls astonishingly the "greatest sports fan moment of my life."

> Ohio State trailed Penn State 17-10 with about 1:30 to play in the fourth quarter. Penn State fans had read this script far too many times from 2000-2005. PSU with a lead late in an epic and extremely important Big Ten game only to give up the lead in the fourth. The student section (including myself and about two rows of friends) was an extremely odd combination of loud and edge-of-your-seat nervous. Where we were positioned, my fellow PSU students and I had a perfect view of the Ohio State backfield as then quarterback Troy Smith took the snap.
>
> To this day, I swear that the Good Lord slowed time down after Smith snapped the football. I say this because I distinctly remember the world around me becoming one of those *Madden Football* montages as Penn State defensive end Tamba Hali broke free. Everybody in the stadium saw what was about to take place; except for poor Troy Smith. The crowd erupted about one second before Hali hit Smith with what can only be called a "life ending" hit. Smith was hit so hard that he was actually flipped head over feet (seriously, check it out). The football came loose, Penn State pounced on it and the game was clinched for PSU.[2]

Note here the young man's MC description: the blatant sensationalism, as the whole game seems to be reduced to one moment; the glorification of the violence of the "life-ending" hit, as if a mere stripping and recovery of the ball, having an identical result, would not have been as significant; and the total investment in victory, as if the play, had the fumble not been recovered by Ohio State, would have been nothing.

To be wholly absorbed by spectacle in competitive sport, however, is socially irresponsible—perhaps even morally objectionable. Not only does it encourage fanatics to adopt a cut-throat attitude toward life, it causes them to neglect social obligations. Children of parents that are consumed by competitive sports, like football or golf, often compete with such sports for their parents' time and attention. Those children, of course, will certainly try and figure out what it is that is so intoxicating about such sports, and might even develop the aggression, individualism, and sensationalism they see in athletes in order to get their parents' attention.

Obsessive spectatorship narrows both parents' and children's range of interests, as it shuts off both from other rewarding experiences, like learning to play a musical instrument, creative playing with other children, working outside on the house or in the garden, or going for a leisurely stroll in the park. It is not unreasonable to suppose that such a narrowing of one's interests makes it much more difficult to be happy, since diversifying interests allows for a wider range and greater number of things to experience. Philosopher Bertrand Russell in *Conquest of Happiness* says that happiness is a function of letting one's interests to be as wide as possible and allowing one's reactions to things and persons to be friendly and not hostile. He says, quite soberly, "The more things a man is interested in, the more opportunities of happiness he has and the less he is at the mercy of fate, since if he loses one thing he can fall back upon another."[3]

Lack of diversity in interests explains why many athletes, upon retirement, experience uncertainty and become depressed—what psychologists call "disengagement trauma" or "a crisis of identity." For instance, retired Oakland Raiders offensive lineman Marvin Upshaw, a perennial all-pro, had this to say after his retirement:

> You find yourself just scrambled. You don't know which way to go. Your light . . . has been turned out. You miss the roar of the crowd. Once you've heard it, you can't get away from it. There's an empty feeling—you feel everything you wanted is gone. All of a sudden you wake up and you find yourself 29, 35 years old, you know, and the one thing that has been the major part of your life is gone. It's gone.[4]

It is perhaps the same with fans who move away from their favorite team or lose their beloved team to another city, as was the case many years ago when the Cleveland Browns' football team was moved to Baltimore. Fanatical fans did not know what to do. It was a true life-crisis. Cleveland, of course, has since been awarded a new franchise and the dog-pound fanatics are back.

Democratically diverse societies offer a significant range of opportunities for personal fulfillment and enrichment. Competitive sport is just one of them and, we have argued, certainly not the most important one. Therefore, morally responsible parents should encourage participation rather than mere spectatorship in sports for willing children, but sports should be one of many childhood interests. Why? First, because there is the risk of disengagement trauma or existential crisis of a certain sort—i.e., the realization that one has spent one's salad years doing something as intrinsically senseless as kicking a ball toward a net. Second, because we all need critical perspective on sports in order to make them an instrument of human improvement rather than reinforcement of human failings. Finally, diversity of interests means breadth of character and allows for

meaningful contributions to personal and social well being at many different
levels.

More than Entertainment

We argued in chapter 9 that MC sport tends to affirm troubling presumptions
such as the natural aggressiveness and superiority of males. Media coverage of
sport only exacerbates that problem, not least because violence and machismo
are marketable. As long as sports are experienced primarily through the media,
participants will tend to imitate what they see and problems like violence and
sexism will continue. A skeptical, but open-minded perspective is needed.

The language of sport is filled with words and metaphors related to violence, war, and sex and those metaphors reveals much about how we think about
sport. Bruce Kidd writes about how use of language depicts sport as be male
preserve:

> The language [of sport] is rife with words and phrases that unconsciously rein-
> force the male preserve: *jock*, the popular metonym for athlete; *tomboy* to de-
> scribe any bright, active girl who likes physical activity and is good at sports;
> and *suck* and *sissy* to condemn anyone who betrays fear or anxiety. These all
> remind us that sports were designed to harden males. We should question the
> use of these terms the way the civil rights movement did with *nigger* and *boy*
> and the women's movement as with *mankind* and *girl*; develop inclusive sub-
> stitutes (such as *athlete* for *jock* and *young athlete* for *tomboy*); and then cam-
> paign to remove the offending terms from usage.[5]

Military or war metaphors are also superabundant and misleading. The same
goes for metaphors relating sport to violence.

The problem is that such language reinforces presumptions about female
weakness even while sport itself tries to challenge them. In a review of gender
biases in language used by the sportive media, sociologists Christy Halbert and
Melissa Latimer identified problems such as asymmetrical gender marking, gendered hierarchy of naming, unequal ratio of praise to criticism, different types of
praise, different character portraits, and gendering the athletic event itself.
Asymmetrical gender marking refers to the tendency to mark off women's events
from men's by prefacing the former as "women's" athletic events and having no
such preface for men's events, presumably because they represent the "standard". Gendered hierarchy of naming is a two-fold tendency. First, there is the
tendency to refer to female athletes as "girls," "ladies," and "women" (the first
two implying immaturity or incompetence), while men are only called "men."
Second, there is the tendency to refer to female athletes by their first name, while
males are designated by their last name. Unequal ratio of praise to criticism is

the tendency to criticize women more and praise them less than men. Most often, when praise is given to female athletes, it is given for their physical appearance, not their capabilities. Women do not "play well," they "look nice" (or hot). Next, men and women are generally given different character portraits. Men are described as "talented', "intelligent," "quick," "risk-takers," and "hard-workers," while women are often said to be "lucky," "nervous," "non-aggressive," "emotional," and "excessively dependent." Last, women's athletic events are often marked off from men's by frequent mention of the more difficult circumstances that attend men's events.[6]

Halbert and Latimer warn that commentators' language is an expression of prevailing attitudes regarding women's sports. Those attitudes mold false views of reality and reinforce negative stereotypes in keeping with the belief-affirming nature of MC sport. The language of sport, they maintain, ought to be free of gender bias. They sum, "Although women have made great strides in sport, their achievements are meaningless as long as those achievements are trivialized or only put in the context of feminine sport, rather than the context of a genderless sports realm."[7]

Going beyond the issue of gender biases in language, there is the problem of equal coverage of women's athletic events. Media coverage at academic institutions and elsewhere is greatly slanted toward covering male athletes and men's athletic events.[8] One study even showed that the *NCAA News*, put out through the NCAA, covered male athletes through articles and pictures at roughly twice the rate as that of female athletes.[9] Overall, there are still disproportionate numbers of female authors to cover sports at academic institutions, and that in itself lends itself to male bias.[10] The justification that men's sports are more popular or entertaining falsely exploits the AL models emphasis on pleasure to reinforce the MC model's endorsement of the status quo. There is no excuse for perpetuating such inequalities, especially in the educational environment.

Halbert and Latimer believe that the media have helped to perpetuate male dominance through excluding women completely from coverage, having little coverage of female athletes (which distorts the public's image of the percentage of women interested and participating in sports), covering only those events such as figure skating and tennis that reinforce stereotypical feminine images of female athletes, and minimizing women's athletic achievements through sports commentaries.[11] NBC's coverage of the 2002 Winter Olympics illustrated the bias in reporting on events. In general, men's events were covered by men alone, while women's events were covered by a woman-man team. The message that sends, whether explicitly or implicitly, is that women alone are incapable of proper coverage of sportive events. The situation improved for the 2010 Winter Olympics, but female coverage still lagged significantly behind male coverage— especially at marquee events or when personal interviews were conducted with significant interviewees.

Television commercials too reinforce the idea female inferiority. In one study of television commercials that accompanied sports programs, 44.9% featured men and women, 38.6% featured men only, 12.6% featured no people, and only 3.9% featured women only. Of the no-people commercials, almost all of 91 had a male voice-over. Of the men-women commercials, women were often portrayed as "sexual rewards for men who purchase the right product" and "supportive props" for men's success in sports.[12]

The excuses that sport and sport spectatorship are recreational, "just for fun," or mere entertainment are all insufficient. Serious or not, sport has great social impact and there is need to eliminate violence and sexism from it in word and deed. Sports that center on or showcase violence should be banned or reformed. Good television ratings are not justification for the brutality of tough-man contests and anything-goes brawls that occur in Ultimate Fighting Championship, Strikeforce, and Mixed Martial Arts. Popularity and spectator appeal in warm-weather markets unfamiliar with the game do not justify the tolerance and even encouragement of fighting in professional hockey.

What Edward R. Murrow said about television in the 1950s applies to sports and their coverage in the media: "This instrument can teach. It can illuminate, and it can even inspire. But it can do so only to the extent that humans are determined to use it towards those ends. Otherwise, it is merely wires and lights . . . in a box."[13]

Sport as a Quest for Knowledge

The aesthetic, recreational aspects of sport have been present since its inception. Even before Homer's Bronze Age warriors held athletic games near the battlefields of Troy, Sumerian kings and Egyptian Pharaohs used athletic spectacle to amaze and inspire their subjects, thereby affirming their privilege and worthiness to lead. Yet once the ancient Olympic Games promoted fair athletic contests that admitted entry even to non-noble contestants, sport began to challenge rather than merely affirm the established social hierarchy. Thus, sport may have contributed to the politicial revolution we now call democracy.[14]

The crucial point is that it was Greeks' capacity to ask authentic questions and seek knowledge openly that led to positive social change. Because Olympia's contests were motivated by authentic questions about which athlete was most preferred by the gods, care was taken to see that plausible candidates were included and that the selection process was free from the usual social biases.[15] As the success of lower-class athletes challenged the nobility's presumed right to lead, the idea emerged that *aretē* was not simply a matter of inheritance, but something that could be achieved by assiduous effort. That led, in turn, to the notion of education for *aretē* that inspired Socrates and Plato and the belief that sports can in some measure contribute to building character.

By reducing sport to commerce or a substitute for war, the MC model eviscerates its knowledge-seeking potential. Sport's tendency to challenge social hierarchies and presumptions are resisted by the idea that athletic excellence is isolated from and irrelevant to real social worth (an idea reinforced, as we saw in chapter 10, by the obsession with quantification and statistics). MC sport, rather, reinforces presumptions about male superiority by privileging masculine characteristics and undermining female athletic achievement. The seriousness of sport as a profitable business is used to justify such practices, without asking whether sport's very profitability depends on its knowledge-seeking nature. Completely predictable contests have little commercial value.

Meanwhile, the AR model shows indifference toward the knowledge-seeking potential of sport by focusing on its autotelic character, particularly the pleasure and entertainment it can produce. As long as sport is viewed as something separate from serious pursuits like education and social reform, its potential to effect positive results in those areas is negligible.

Sport may have helped to create democracy, yet what keeps democratic societies healthy is the sober recognition by its members that they must contribute, even sacrifice, for the good of the whole. To keep a society healthy, its citizens must in some sense give in proportion to the benefits they receive. Consequently, individuals, through their actions, have a responsibility both to other citizens and society itself. Individuals participating in competitive sport, regardless of wealth, are not exceptions.

We have argued that sport, understood as an expression of excellence, is chiefly about development of character and character cannot be developed in isolation from a community of people. As an expression of excellence through development of character, competitive athletic expression is a matter of journeying and such journeying, which results in great self-understanding for aretic athletes, is its own reward.

Notes

1. Our take (see chapter 22) is that competitive sport is a genuine good insofar as it promotes *aretē*, not just a good because it happens to be chosen as one.

2. Zac Wassink, 23 Feb. 2010, http://www.associatedcontent.com/article/2730951/best_sports_fan_moment_ohio_state_at.html?cat=14.

3. Bertrand Russell, *The Conquest of Happiness* (New York: Liveright 1996), 123 and 126.

4. Michael A. Messner, "The Meaning of Success: The Athletic Experience and the Development of Male Identity," *Sport in Contemporary Society: An Anthology,* ed. D. Stanley Eitzen (New York: St. Martin's Press, 1996), 381.

5. Bruce Kidd, "The Men's Cultural Centre: Sports and the Dynamic of Women's Oppression/Men's Repression," *Sport, Men, and the Gender Order: Critical Feminist Perspectives,* eds. Mike Messner and Don Sabo (Champaign, IL: Human Kinetics Books, 1990), 41-42.

6. Christy Halbert and Melissa Latimer, "'Battling' Gendered Language: An Analysis of the Language Used by Sports Commentators in a Televised Coed Tennis Competition," *Sociology of Sport Journal,* 11 (Indianapolis, IN: Human Kinetics Publishers, Inc., 1994), 300-306.

7. Halbert et al., "'Battling' Gendered Language," 307.

8. Daniel L. Wann, Michael P. Schrader, Julie A. Allison, and Kimberly K. McGeorge "The Inequitable Newspaper Coverage of Men's and Women's Athletics at Small, Medium, and Large Universities," *Journal of Sport & Social Issues* Vol. 22, No. 1 (Sage Publications, Inc., 1998), 79.

9. B. Schifflet and R. Revelle, "Gender Equity in Sports Media Coverage: A Review of the *NCAA News*," *Journal of Sport & Social Issues,* 18, 1994.

10. Wann et al 1998, 86.

11. Halbert et al., "Battling' Gendered Language," 299.

12. Michael Messner, Darnel Hunt, and Michele Dunbar, "Boys to Men: Sports Media Messages about Masculinity." *Children Now,* www.childrennow.org, 1999, 9-10.

13. Edward R. Murrow speech quoted at the end of the movie *Good Night and Good Luck.*

14. For a full account of this argument, see H. Reid, *Athletics and Philosophy in the Ancient World: Contests of Virtue* (London: Routledge, 2011) chapters 1-3.

15. On the knowledge seeking function of Olympic sport see H. Reid, "Sport, Philosophy, and the Quest for Knowledge" *Journal of the Philosophy of Sport* 36, 2009, 40-49.

Chapter 16
Beauty as Unity

"The way a team plays as a whole determines its success. You may have the greatest bunch of individual stars in the world, but if they don't play together, the club won't be worth a dime." Babe Ruth

OME OF THE DOMINANT THEMES of Martial/Commercial sport, examined in the second part of this book, have been the obsession with statistical analysis, myopic promotion of individualism, and the lack of respect for others that comes with self-promotion. The MC attitude toward competitive sport, we have argued, perpetuates those problems, because of its blind fixation on winning at all costs and its commitment toward panagonism. We have concluded thus far not that winning is unimportant in competitive sport, only that a society that values winning at any cost is an unhealthy society with unhealthy ideals.

The Aesthetic/Recreational model of sport, as we have begun to see in this part, values respect for rules and for others as a precondition of enjoyment and play. This respect reflects the AR model's overall emphasis on the community rather than the individual—an emphasis that contrasts with the MC model's problem of self-promotion or ego-puffing. Now we turn to the related issue of individual versus community in sport. The questions of this chapter are, "To what extent are competitive athletes beholden to their communities?" and "What does it mean to play together as a unified team?" In addressing these questions, we draw from the AR model's commitments to egalitarianism, cooperation, and team play.

Individual versus Community

November 18, 2003, was, perhaps, a turning point in professional sport. Former Tampa Bay Buccaneer wide receiver Keyshawn Johnson was officially deactivated. Johnson had stated openly to his teammates during the year that he did not plan to be with the team at the end of the season. He felt that he was being underutilized and that the team was suffering because of that. There were many instances, in front of players and fans alike, where he let the coach know of his disappointment and underutilization. Spokespersons for the team stated that Johnson was let go because he was a distraction to the team. He had been missing training sessions and team meetings and openly showed his disgust for the coach John Gruden.[1]

Why was that event a turning point in professional sport? What is so significant about Johnson's deactivation? Players, fans, and owners are coming belatedly to learn what the best coaches have always known: ego-puffed players, however talented, are in the long haul a detriment to their team. Johnson's deactivation was a signal to the rest of the league and to all of sport that at least one team thinks it is easier to win consistently without such players, however gifted. The underlying premise is that a team of talented players—who are committed to their coach, their fellow players, a system of team play, their sport, and their fans—will generally outperform a team of superstars, each of whom is chiefly committed to himself.

This argument against self-preoccupation, given in chapter 11, seems forceful. Still it does not go far enough. It is measured too narrowly by the harm such players do to a team through less wins and more losses over time. It does not address the harms such individualistic players do to themselves, their sport, or even society. To see those harms as problems of sufficient weight, in what follows, we phrase the difficulty not in terms of self-preoccupation but in terms of community-concern: Why is it that so many athletes have such a barefaced disregard for others—players, coaches, and fans—in competitive sport today? Furthermore, why is it that people tolerate that disregard?

Causes and Effects

Chapter 11 identified a large contributing cause of this problem as the manner in which players are marketed before they make it to the professional ranks. They are scouted and assessed principally as individuals, not so much as members of a team. It is too often assumed that raw talent and athletic potential will make players a factor at the next level. When they turn professional, the lure of a multimillion-dollar salary entices them to market themselves as individuals, not as members of a team. A talented wide receiver, as was Johnson, is attractive to a contending team in need of receivers. Unfortunately, those fishing for talent seem seldom to pause to consider whether players like Johnson will be an asset or a distraction to the team.

Playing on and for a team is important, but increasingly players strive to make themselves visible in team sports through exceptional play, showboating, taunting, and even fighting opponents, managers, or teammates. What is most unsettling is that players are generally praised, even rewarded by reporters, critics, and fans, for drawing attention to themselves, their peers, and, at least ostensibly, their coaches. As such, personal victory trumps team victory. When things are going well for the team, ego-puffed players are the first to let everyone know just how their play has led to such success. When things are going badly, it is, of course, not they who are to blame. Football analyst and former player Merril Hoge had this to say about Johnson, before his deactivation from Tampa Bay:

> Often times, it's during adversity that you find out what a person is truly made of. And, true to character, when something doesn't go right, Keyshawn Johnson has repeatedly been the first guy to beat his chest and say, "What about me?" In the midst of a three-game skid, what the Bucs players should be saying is, "What about the team?"[2]

Johnson's case is merely a prime example of a widespread sports disease that has a variety of symptoms and causes including the previously discussed fixation on (often meaningless) statistical data, equation of success with winning, and the focus on manliness, strength, speed, and domination. It should be clear by now just why those features are problematic, so there is no need of redundancy. What we need now is to see what sports would look like if community should be privileged over individuality; it need not be a game of hacky-sack.

An Organic Ideal

Let us begin with an ancient model. In Book VI of *Republic,* Plato states that the best-running city-state is very much like an individual person—i.e., like an organic being. When a person hurts his finger, it is not merely the finger that feels pain; the entire organism, body and soul, suffers it. A city-state with good government and good laws suffers similarly, whenever any one of its citizens is harmed or does harm. Socrates says: "What greater evil can there be for a city-state than that which breaks it apart and makes it many instead of one? Or what greater good can there be than that which binds it together and makes it one?" The best city-state, like the best person, is most noticeably one, not many. The goodness of both, in consequence, resides in their unity.[3]

Plato then argues that the unity of a city-state is best achieved when all citizens, as parts, recognize just how they can contribute to the good of the whole. That can involve many citizens sacrificing their aim of doing what they most want to do, a purely self-regarding aim, for a goal that is chiefly other-regarding, doing what they can to contribute to the most unified, best-running city-state. It need not be, of course, that doing what one wants and doing what one ought to do for a well-running city-state are at odds. It is Plato's emphasis that is significant: To ensure the most stable and unified city-state, each citizen must subordinate self-concern to other-concern. Only in such a manner can the city-state achieve stability and unity. Only in such a way will the citizens of a community achieve the greatest possible happiness, though, he admits, not everyone will be assured of outstanding happiness.[4]

Plato in *Republic* is making both evaluative and pragmatic claims. The evaluative claim is that the well-being of the city-state is, in some sense, more important than the wellbeing of its citizens. Since that is a philosophical choice, we will not linger on it. The pragmatic claim, however, is one on which it is worth lingering. It states paradoxically that to attain utmost stability, unity, and happiness in a city-state, each citizen ought to subordinate self-concern to community-concern.

How does that model apply to competitive sport? We offer some examples for illustration. Like other successful professional franchises, the Detroit Red Wings—while under coach Scotty Bowman, the most successful coach in NHL history—embraced an organic conception of successful team play. To fit in, every person associated with the team (owners, coaches, players, and even team physicians and equipment managers) did what they could do for the success of the team. All persons, failing to do their part for the team, like the injured finger that brings pain to the person as a whole, harmed the team as a whole through the factionalism they brought. Such players were quickly released. Thus, the driving concern for the Red Wings when they considered adding an employee—superstar player or otherwise—was and still is this: How well will this athlete fit into our community?

Another example is football's New England Patriots—winners of three Super Bowls in four years (2002, 2004, and 2005). Their coach Bill Belichick is arguably the most innovative and intelligent coach in the NFL today and his team plays innovative and intelligent football. All players contribute in whatever way they can and no one is allowed to place himself before the team. Consequently, New England sports no superstars—at least none that they will admit to having—and yet it is recognized as one of the most dominant teams to have ever played the game. What is the reason? It is their unquestioned commitment to team play. On account of their commitment to team play, Resolution 202 was submitted to the 107th Congress on February 4 of 2002 by Senators Kennedy, Kerry, and Reed after New England's first Super Bowl victory. I include the whole resolution, which speaks for itself.

RESOLUTION

Congratulating the New England Patriots for winning Super Bowl XXXVI.

Whereas, yesterday, the New England Patriots pulled off a thrilling 20-17 victory over the St. Louis Rams in Super Bowl XXXVI;

Whereas the victory is the first world championship for the Patriots, and it could not have come at a more poignant time for our country;

Whereas at a time when our entire country is banding together, the Patriots set a wonderful example of self-sacrifice and unity, showing us all what is possible when we work together, believe in each other, and collaborate for the greater good;

Whereas coach Bill Belichick stressed teamwork, saying that only by working together could the Patriots overcome their opponent, the best team in the NFL's regular season, the St. Louis Rams;

Whereas the team was led by Tom Brady, Ty Law, Tedy Bruschi, Mike Vrabel, and Troy Brown, but played together to forge a victory for the whole team;

Whereas the Patriots showed their true spirit, using running back Kevin Faulk, receiver Troy Brown, and intelligent play from Brady to drive from inside their own 20 yard line to give kicker Adam Vinatieri the chance to win the game with only 7 seconds left on the clock;

Whereas the Patriots won the game as the clock expired;

Whereas all of us in Massachusetts, and indeed all who live in New England, are proud of the Patriots and their extraordinary season;

Whereas eight years ago Bob Kraft bought the Patriots, and today he brings the Lombardi trophy home to fans who have been waiting for 42 years; and

Whereas in Massachusetts, April 15 is Patriot's Day—a day when we celebrate the brave men and women who fought for our nation's independence—but, for generations of New England sports fans, yesterday will always be our Patriot's Day: Now, therefore be it resolved,

That the Senate commends the World Champion New England Patriots for their extraordinary victory in Super Bowl XXXVI.

Such resolutions merely express an ideal, but ideals can be expressed, if only imperfectly, in concrete action. One example from professional cycling is the widespread practice of dividing the prize money awarded to winners of races, like the Tour de France, among all participating team members, including mechanics and masseuses. In fact many putatively individual athletes, like cyclists, depend on a team of athletic and non-athletic supporters for their success. It is a reality of sport that is often deliberately ignored on the MC model.

Beauty as Unity

If Plato's insights pertain to competitive sports, and we believe they do, it follows that the very best teams are functioning "units," whose players lose themselves in the team. Such players are motivated by an integrative ideal. In the most general terms, integration means that the community comes first. Players put the well-being of their team ahead of personal concerns. In doing so, they find that their own well-being is preserved. They come to find that caring and cooperative play—a feature of AR sport—tends to lead to winning—irrelevant to AR sport—and winning tends to mitigate other problems.

Unity through integration is more than a team construed as a collection of players with varied talents. Unity through integration is a wholesale commitment to a specific system of play, where competitors at times might have to compromise certain specific talents for the good of the team. When former hockey superstar Brett Hull, who has over 700 goals in his career, came to Detroit, he knew quite well that he was expected to put as much effort into defensive play, penalty killing, and passing as into scoring goals. He made the adjustment and was rewarded with a Stanley Cup.

Two-time women's basketball Olympic gold medalist Natalie Williams eloquently says this of team play:

> A team is a beautiful thing. A bunch of unique peeps all coming together to play. Being part of a team is absolutely the best part about playing basketball. But, it can also be the hardest part. Mish-mashing 10 to 12 players—all with different tastes, values and vibes—can be tricky. There is always going to be a girl on the team that you're not cool with. The key to making the most of your game is figuring out how to get along with everyone on the team—as if you were a big family. Great players learn to respect all their teammates and opponents in the same way that they respect themselves.[5]

In keeping with the aesthetic ideals promoted in this section, it is clear that Williams sees beauty not only in unity—i.e., playing as a team—but also in integrity. Williams' final sentence, "Great players learn to respect all their teammates and opponents in the same way that they respect themselves," is just a reiteration of Kant's principle of human dignity and, of course, gives a complete answer to the first of two questions posed at the start of this chapter.

It might seem strange to promote unified team play as an aesthetic ideal—as if to make here some evaluative claim. One response, at least for the time, is not of the evaluative sort. It is, quite simply, that concern for unity translates into a winning attitude and a winning attitude increases the likelihood of inspired, winning play in a season and over the years. A winning attitude cannot be sustained through habitually entertaining questions such as, "Will the addition of such-and-such person help us to win the championship this year?" There's an unhealthy urgency to that question that comes from its implicit instrumentality: There can be no winning attitude, when players are treated like dispensable commodities to be bought and sold at a moment's notice—an unsavory feature of MC sport.

Finally, unity in sport as an aesthetic ideal even transcends unified team play. It forces mavens of sport to consider the very value competitive sport has in free societies across the globe. This issue will be addressed in Part VI, which explores the normative dimension of competitive sport and proposes, in keeping with the philosophical intuitions heretofore implicit, a new model of it.

Notes

1. "Johnson's Time in Tampa Appears Over," *ESPN.com News Services,* 20 Nov. 2003, http://sports.espn.go.com/nfl/news/story?id=1664796.

2. "Johnson's Time in Tampa Appears Over," 20 Nov. 2003.

3. Plato, *Republic*, trans. G.M.A. Grube (Indianapolis: Hackett Publishing Company, Inc., 1992), 462a-e.

4. Plato, *Republic,* 420b.

5. Natalie Williams, "Doing the Right Thing," www.gogirlworld.org/binary-data/GGW_ARTICLE_PDF/pdf/69.pdf, 2.

Chapter 17
Economy of Performance

"However beautiful the strategy, you should occasionally look at the results."
Winston Churchill

CHAPTER 11 EXAMINED SELF-PROMOTION OR EGO-PUFFING in sport, which turned out to be less innocuous than it might seem. At the end of that chapter, there came the suggestion that ego-puffing is a consequence of commercially-driven sensationalism in competitive sport—a tendency both to judge athletic competitions more by gut-level feel or titillation rather than reason, and to value risk-taking and showmanship more than skill, integrity, and drive. If competitive sport is only about entertainment, as is the case with MC sport, then promoters ought to do whatever they can to maximize profits.

As we shall see in this chapter, however, economy in sports more than a matter of dollars and cents. For Aesthetic/Recreational sport, economy is about beauty rather than money. Drawing upon Kaelin's suggestion that natural grace, an aesthetic feature of sport, is maximum economy, this chapter argues that an appropriate remedy for the commercially-driven sensationalism in competitive sport, in part, is the adoption of a more "economical" view of competitive performances that allows reason a privileged place in their practice and enjoyment.

Best on Athletic Economy

The notion that beauty in sport is linked, if not equivalent, to athletic economy was put forth by David Best in "The Aesthetic and Sport." For Best, the aesthetic is more a way of perceiving an object or action than any objective feature of it. Yet aesthetic judgments are not inescapably subjective, for they happen only against a background of objective features and can be evaluated only by reference to them.[1] For instance, the powerful surge and seeming effortlessness of former hurdling superstar Edwin Moses, as he economically negotiated hurdle after hurdle derive their aesthetic value from his technical mastery. With Moses, efficiency of form, conceptual comprehension of the task, and fluidity of motion were plain for all to see though the beauty of his motion.

The aesthetic, for Best, is not end-directed and any object or event can admit of aesthetic evaluation, though some objects or events more readily admit of this than others. It follows that evaluating the aesthetic element of sportive activity cannot be a matter of perceiving it relative to some practical end. For example, to evaluate a painting as a potential investment or to buy it principally because it matches one's couch is not to appreciate it aesthetically. Likewise to view basketball star Sheryl Swoopes gliding effortlessly around two defenders on her way to a beautiful lay-up as nothing more than a two-point play is a failure of aesthetic sensitivity.

Yet to see Swoopes' move as nothing more than an aesthetic event is a failure of sportive understanding. That is so because, in art, means equals end and the aesthetic is everything, while those things are not the case with sport. No sport is completely aesthetic, not even those such as rhythmic gymnastics or diving, where the aesthetic has a prominent part. Winning is always a part of competitive sport and there are numerous ways to win.[2]

Where there is no separation of means and end, every aspect of some aesthetic object or event is critical in its assessment.[3] Therefore, the aesthetic in art or in sport, for Best, is a sort of economy of effort—an ability to achieve one's end perfectly through one's actions. In such perfect economy, one's actions become identifiable with the end. Critical assessment of the aesthetic, then, involves perceptual analysis of any deviation from this economical path Beauty in sport ought not to be separated from competitive efficiency.

There are many examples that illustrate this principle. In running, too much of an upward bounce in a marathoner's stride is deviation from economy and, thus, deviation from the aesthetic. In cycling, Reid notes that too much side-to-side motion as an athlete climbs a steep hill is energy wasted. In basketball, a slam-dunk on a clean breakaway, when a sure and easy lay-up would accomplish the same thing, is a deviation from the aesthetic. The slam may be emphatic and may rouse a quiet crowd, but it is certainly not the most economical activity. The lay-up is easier to perform and preserves a player's energy for activity on the defensive side of things. Slam-dunks are marketable, but not necessarily beautiful.

A Cue from Aesthetic Sports

Competitive sports are often categorized as aesthetic (e.g., diving, gymnastics, and figure skating), where competition is a matter of performing toward some ideal, and non-aesthetic (e.g., baseball, hockey, and soccer), where obstacles and rules dictate criteria for successful performance. In aesthetic sports, victory is awarded the athlete or team that most closely approximates the aesthetic ideal. An example is the springboard diver who, after a tricky reverse, three-and-one-half somersault tuck, vertically enters the pool with scarcely a splash and performs the dive with efficiency and elegance. In non-aesthetic sports, victory is awarded that athlete or team that follows the rules and best overcomes the obstacles artificially set up by the game. In football, for instance, the aim is to get the ball into one's opponent's end zone (or as close to it as possible to set up a field goal) and prevent them from getting the ball into one's own end zone. Just how that is done is of little consequence so long as the rules are followed. There is no aesthetic ideal to follow or approximate. Many touchdowns are scored inefficiently and inelegantly.

Though this distinction can be made between aesthetic and non-aesthetic sports, it seems that when non-aesthetic competition is at its best, competitors and teams perform at a level of aesthetic economy that is the very heart of aesthetic sports.

Consider the following comparison between the aesthetic sport of springboard diving and the non-aesthetic sport of rowing.

First, note in this interview with a former Olympic springboard diver how the notion of beauty, in the form of performing the ideal dive, acts as a motivator in training intensity.

> My coach wrote up every single one of my dives on a piece of paper, all the bad things about my dive and all the good things about my dive. I read his corrections every day, before every workout. I set a goal to change something on that piece of paper every day. That's why it wasn't boring for me to do the same dive 100 times, because each time I looked at it in a different way. . . . For me the dive is good, but there is always something to improve.[4]

Second, compare the springboard diver's account to the thoughts of world-class senior rower, Malcolm Gefter. Note how the aesthetic dominates his thinking, even though rowing is considered a non-aesthetic sport.

> The aesthetic and appreciation come in pushing the boat with the huge effort level of leg drive and upper body, and watching the boat skip through the water without wobbling, without creating a big wake, without disturbing the water. That is a beautiful thing to observe. And the whole pursuit is one in which the aesthetic qualities translate into speed. Because the harder you try to row without doing it gracefully, the slower you go.[5]

Team rowing is a particularly elegant and fitting example. The crew consists of two, four, or eight rowers, each with one oar only. Though considered a non-aesthetic sport, rowing requires a perfectly coordinated effort among these crewmembers, each of whom needs a body effectively adapted to the demands of the sport, and efficiency of stroking translates into increased speed and an increased probability of winning.[6] It's obvious that rowing, though a non-aesthetic sport, has much in common with aesthetic sports.

Finally, economic considerations are prevalent among the best athletes even in relatively simple sports. The sport of Strongman, Holowchak notes, invites strength athletes to push, pull, or endure heavy objects in a variety of ways. He notes that Strongman is all about economy of movement in a variety of unusual events from tire-flipping, where tires can weigh up to 1000 pound, to hefting round stones that weigh up to 600 pounds. The best strongmen are not only the strongest, but also the most economical, in that lack of economy over the course of a competition leads to crippling exhaustion or even injury.

The three examples, though many more can be given, underscore the aesthetic link between economy and unity.

The aesthetic link between economy and unity is especially difficult to achieve in team sports, where utmost economy can be achieved through a perfectly coordinated effort by a team that follows a viable game plan or system of play. Utmost aesthetic economy comes when a team plays not as a group of talented individuals, but as a unit. Football's New England Patriots come quickly to mind. For unity to occur through team play, athletes have to subordinate personal aims to group aims or, better yet, make the aims of the group their own. As we saw in the previous chapter, teamwork is usually victim of the MC model's preoccupation with marketing and profits.

It is worth repeating in this context that it is not the presence of money and professionalism that undermines the aesthetic in sport. Let us return, for illustration, to the person that considers a painting because it matches his couch. He certainly looks at a painting differently than one who appreciates it as a work of beauty. Still the painting retains its aesthetic value even if it is purchased for the wrong reason. What is dangerous is for the artist to begin creating her work for commercial rather than aesthetic purposes. In sport, the artists are the athletes, but the reward system needs to be set up to reward excellence rather than trumpery.

Notes

1. David Best, "The Aesthetic in Sport," *Philosophy of Sport: Critical Readings, Crucial Issues*, ed. M. Andrew Holowchak (Upper Saddle River, NJ: Prentice-Hall, 2002), 117-119.

2. Best, "The Aesthetic in Sport," 111-112.

3. Boxill argues that sport is a form of art in that it, like art, is a vehicle for self-expression. She maintains that it is "the single most available means of self-expression for both men and women." Jan Boxill, ""Beauty, Sport, and Gender," *Philosophy of Sport: Critical Readings, Crucial Issues*, ed. M. Andrew Holowchak (Upper Saddle River, NJ: Prentice-Hall, 2002), 127-37. Cordner states sport is not art in that works of art are necessarily "objects of contemplation", while sport can be, but need not be, an object of contemplation. Christopher Cordner, "Differences between Sport and Art," *Philosophy of Sport: Critical Readings, Crucial Issues*, ed. M. Andrew Holowchak (Upper Saddle River, NJ: Prentice-Hall, 2002), 138-52.

4. Terry Orlick et al. "Mental Links to Excellence," *The Sport Psychologist*, 1988, 2, 112.

5. Tony Chamberlain, "For Gefter, It's a Stroke of Pluck," *The Boston Globe,* October 17, 2003.

6. Often a coxswain steers the boat and coordinates this effort from the back of the boat.

PART IV
How Should Sports Be Reformed?

Chapter 18
The Aretic Model

"And as in the Olympic Games it is not the most beautiful and the strongest that are crowned but those who compete (for it is some of these that are victorious), so those who act win, and rightly win, the noble and good things in life."
Aristotle

CRITICS FOR DECADES HAVE COMPLAINED of the win-at-all-costs attitude that predominates in what we have dubbed Martial/Commercial sport. Mariah Burton Nelson, for instance, writes:

[It is] characterized by obsessive ranking of teams and individuals according to playing statistics or earnings; authoritarian, derisive relationships between coaches and players; antagonism between opponents; and the inevitable question, "Who won?" the language of the military model says it all: A quarterback's arm is his weapon. Opponents are to be feared and destroyed. Teams battle for honors.[1]

She then argues for reform of competitive sport in the direction of an Aesthetic/Recreational model of cooperative competition.

Gail Whitaker observes that current critics of competitive sport either accept its brutal physicality wholesale or denounce it completely. There is nothing in-between.

Historically we have been torn between two extreme and equally debilitating views of our embodiment. On the one hand, for too long we have been defined and identified in offensively physical terms—that is, both as mindless and as exclusively sexual beings. On the other hand, our frequent response to those characterizations has been to disconnect ourselves from our physicality altogether by retreating into a world that values only intellectual pursuits (and denounces sport as vulgar and excessive). We desperately need a middle ground between these two approaches, a way of exploring, developing, and celebrating our embodiment without abandoning our intelligence or prostituting our feminist convictions. I maintain that sport can provide such a middle ground if we go about it conscientiously, making the personal growth and enrichment of every participant our central and primary focus.[2]

Whitaker argues for medial reform.

The complaints of Nelson and Whitaker are just some of the many underscored throughout this book. Yet do the problems inherent to the MC model call for a wholesale rejection of sport as we know it? If not, to what extent is reform needed?

In this chapter, we follow the lead of critics like Nelson and Whitaker and argue for a new model of competitive sport that seeks a middle ground between the brutishness and unimaginativeness of MC competition, the focus of Part II, and the creative, cooperative, and non-competitive ideals of AR sport, covered in Part III. We call this model Aretism.

Following a tradition of thinkers like Bernard Suits, Paul Weiss, Drew Hyland, Joan Hundley, Allan Bäck, and Robert Simon, each of whom link the practice of competitive sports with a striving for excellence, "Aretism" is the philosophical view that Holowchak has developed in several publications[3]—and has key affinities to those views of Reid.[4] It draws plentifully from the ancient Greek conception of *aretē*—with the general meaning of "excellence," but often translated as "virtue" when used in ethical discourse—to understand this view fully, we often look back to the ancient Greeks. In this chapter we show how Aretism constitutes an Aristotelian mean between the MC and AR extremes.

The Aristotelian "Mean"

The ancient Greek philosopher Aristotle argued in his ethical works that there is no such thing as *aretē* in an unqualified sense. Friendship, generosity, justice, magnanimity, and courage, he deemed virtues (i.e., parts of *aretē*), but only when considered in due proportion and in specific circumstances. For example, generosity practiced to an extreme will soon place a benefactor in abject poverty and he will be no longer of benefit to anyone, not even himself. Likewise, courage without caution in dire and dangerous circumstances can put someone is a position to lose his life to no fruitful end. In short, any excess or defect of virtue in a given situation can easily turn to vice. Excess of generosity is wastefulness; lack of generosity is stinginess. Excess courage is foolhardiness; defect of courage is cowardice. Thus, vice for Aristotle is not only lack of a particular virtue but also too much of one. Vice, then, is simply failure to hit the mean (i.e., the midpoint between deficiency and excess) properly in given circumstances, while *aretē* comes in hitting the mean through use of reason, and doing so habitually.[5]

There is more to it. Being virtuous or hitting the mean in a given situation varies from person to person, since no two people have the same character—i.e., the same temperament and life history. So, virtue requires acute self-knowledge. Hitting the mean is therefore is very difficult for any person to do, since it requires both internal, psychical stability and perception sharp enough to see things as they really are in order to make right decisions.

Much of what Aristotle has to say about virtue seems directly applicable to athletic success.[6] Great athletes too need self-knowledge and a keen perception of circumstances in order to excel. Consider, as examples, golf legend Tiger Woods and former hockey great Wayne Gretzky. Woods has unparalleled ability to be self-critical and Gretzky "saw" the ice like perhaps no one else. Aristotle himself admired the ancient pentathlete that achieved. through moderation, a balanced and versatile fitness applicable to a variety of events.[7]

Aretism is a mean that reflects Aristotle's ideals of moderation, balance, rationality, and versatility. Instead of wholesale abandonment of the MC and the AR models of competitive sport, we use the Aristotelian framework to develop a model that "hits the mean," as it were, to find the middle ground that Whitaker had in mind. In consequence, the remainder of this book offers readers a model that seeks to reconcile, in a manner of speaking, the brutal and the beautiful, the panagonistic and the non-agonistic, in an Aristotelian or medial fashion.

The first step is to oppose features of the MC model of competitive sport with features of the AR model. The second step is to establish a middle ground between each of the contrary characteristics—i.e., to effect a compromise between them. In doing so, we arrive at a conciliatory model—what might be called the "Medial/Aretic" model of competitive sport. Referring back to the characterization of MC and AR sports we sketched in chapters 6 and 12, the Aretic model is characterized by the following general values and features, listed below in contrast with their corresponding "extremes."

M/C Model	Aretic Model	A/R Model
Extrinsic Goods	Intrinsic & Extrinsic Goods	Intrinsic Goods
Panagonism	Agonism	Non-agonism
Belief-Affirming	Knowledge-Seeking	Knowledge-Indifference
Individualism	Meritocracy	Unity
Commercialism	Education	Pleasure/Beauty

Figure 19.1. Aretic Model of Competitive Sport.

When examining the sketch, it becomes obvious that there ought to be no assumption that the contrary AR features are unconditionally more choice-worthy (e.g., unity or pleasure) than those of Aretic sport. The AR ideals are not being endorsed. Moreover, there is no assumption that the traditional MC ideals (e.g., individualism or commercialism) are inherently vicious. Seeking the mean, for us, is conciliatory and, thus, much more realistic than wholesale reform. Wholesale reform is too demanding and likely not a better solution than the values proposed by "mediation." Competitive sport is essentially agonistic and the AR model fails, in part, since it fails to capture that feature of it.

As is the case with Aristotle's own catalogue of virtues and the various vices of extreme he lists, not all extremes from the middle are equally undesirable; some are worse than others. For instance, with respect to courage in battle, Aristotle believed that foolhardiness was preferable to cowardice. It is better to die foolishly in battle than to live like a coward in hasty retreat.[8] Again, it is more vicious to be spendthrifty than stingy, when it comes to money. The spendthrift, in time, does neither others nor himself good, as he is sure to waste all of his money.[9] Likewise, it seems obvious that the AR ideal of *unity* is preferable to the MC ideal of *individualism*, while the MC value of *panagonism* is perhaps preferable to the AR ideal *nonagonism*, given the nature of competitive sport. Our task is to use those extremes as guidelines to develop an improved model of sport. Let us consider each of Aretism's features in turn.

Intrinsic vs. Extrinsic Goods

First, whereas MC sport's goods were extrinsic and AR sport's goods were intrinsic, the "goods" of Aretic sport are, in a sense, both intrinsic and extrinsic. Following Aristotle, we recognize that persons ought to seek *aretē* foremost, but also that other goods extrinsic to sport, such as health and wealth, can be valuable instruments of virtue. Some amount of health and even wealth are needed for the exercise of *aretē*. Competitive sport, practiced thoughtfully and with concern for bodily wellbeing, can help to make virtuous action possible.

Even as Aretism uses sport instrumentally to cultivate *aretē,* however, *aretē* itself demands that persons never be used instrumentally as means to any end, including victory. The philosopher Immanuel Kant, as we have seen, maintained that certain moral principles, as it were, duty-bound all beings capable of reason. One such principle was that every rational being is duty-bound to treat all other rational beings with dignity and respect. Whether that principle is rationally binding in the manner Kant believed is debatable, but the issue of *prima facie* due respect for other human beings seems required by any sober account of moral virtue. What binds all human beings binds athletes.

MC sportive practice is characterized by a means-to-end approach that exploited oneself and others in the consuming quest to win. Acting without prudence, athletes use their bodies as tools. They regard opponents, teammates, even officials and the rules of the game as obstacles to their own aims. Such instrumentalism is then sold to hungry consumers. Because AR sport, by contrast, values only intrinsic goods, its participants view themselves, others, and even their activity as ends in themselves.

Aretism's mean between these extremes is, consistent with Kant's moral views, to treat self and others only as ends, but to allow the sport itself to be used instrumentally as a means to cultivate virtue.

Pangonism vs. Nonagonism

Second, whereas MC sport is panagonistic—i.e., characterized by a win-at-all costs attitude—and AR sport is non-agonistic—i.e., indifferent to victory— Aretic sport is moderately agonistic. In Aretic sport, athletes acknowledge that one cannot compete sincerely without aiming for victory, but they also recognize that the real prize is *aretē*. Since victory without *aretē* is worthless and *aretē* can be demonstrated without achieving victory, the emphasis is on participation and struggle, but struggle is emphasized in an aidful manner. There is no shame in losing, but there is shame in competing at anything less than the best of one's ability.

Aretism rejects the MC notion of contest as battle as not only conceptually perverted, but also morally harmful since it promotes violence as entertainment. However, the AR ideal of non-competitive play is also problematic, because it is limitless; competitive sports, as rule-governed activities, have well defined limits. The correct Aretic approach, assertive play, allows for creative and assertive expression of athletic talents, within the context of competition, which has victory as its end.

We observed in chapter 10 the way that MC panagonism reduces assessment of competitive sport to quantifiable outcomes—i.e., to statistics generated by measurable aspects of performance. Not only does that tendency isolate players from their teams, it isolates athletic excellence from any kind of social context, thereby effectively dehumanizing athletes and symbolically excluding them from the larger context of a community of persons.

Moreover, according to the panagonist ideals, the key AR value of enjoyment in sport becomes importantly limited by whether or not one's favorite team wins. So too does the fun of participation. D. Stanley Eitzen states, "When 'winning is the only thing' the joy of participation is lost. I have observed that organized sports from youth programs to the professional level are mostly devoid of playfulness. When the object is to win, then the primacy of the activity is lost."[10]

Perhaps the most telling objection to MC sport's win-at-all-costs attitude comes from Mike Messner who writes, "Very few people ever reach the mythical 'top,' but those who do are made ultravisible through the media. It is tempting to view this system as a 'structure of failure' because, given the definition of *success*, the system is virtually rigged to bring about the failure of the vast majority of participants."[11] He adds: "[T]he irony of the situation . . . is that the athletes are seeking to get something from their success in sports that sports cannot deliver—and the *pressure* that they end up putting on themselves to achieve that success ends up stripping them of the ability to receive the one major thing that sports really *does* have to offer: fun."[12]

Aretic sport focuses on the commitment to winning characteristic of *aretē*, not winning itself. Those athletes who demonstrate virtue in competition—i.e., those athletes that leave everything on the playing field while competing with full respect for their opponents—are full participants and worthy winners, regardless of results.

Belief-Affirmation vs. Knowledge-Indifference

Third, whereas MC sport is belief-affirming and AR is indifferent to knowledge, Aretic sport is knowledge-seeking. It recognizes that athletic competitions have some social worth, but locates the value of athletic competition not in the game, but in the athletes' *aretē* and the eventual effect of *aretē* on society. As we saw in chapter 15, sport has the capacity to encourage questioning and improve understanding. Aretic sport carries with it a spirit of learning—about oneself, one's relation with others, and about the world beyond.

The paradigm example of MC sport's failure to seek knowledge is its perpetuation of the myth of male superiority. Not only does MC sport endorse "manly" virtues to sometimes foolish extremes—e.g., when courage is lauded as playing through pain to the point of risking permanent physical debilitation. Women are disassociated from such virtues by softening the demands of their events or describing their athleticism in derogatory ways such as "emotional" or "brutish." The AR model is indifferent to such issues—rejecting, as it does, the idea that social understanding or any extrinsic good should be sought through sport.

Since the Aretic model is knowledge-seeking, we shall learn from female athleticism that virtues, like courage, are not gender-specific. The Aretic model acknowledges "manly" virtues in women every bit as much as the "feminine" virtues in men. Its conception of *aretē* is androgynous. Thus, courage, when stripped of its martial link with war, is a self-regarding type of fortitude, pluck, spirit, or endurance when facing a sportive challenge. Consider tennis star Billy Jean King, who faced chauvinist Bobby Riggs in the 1973 "Battle of the Sexes." King beat Riggs in three sets, and "laid to rest notions that testosterone was a prerequisite for athletic ability and intestinal fortitude."[13]

Individualism vs. Unity

Fourth, whereas MC sport is individualistic and AR sport is community-conscious, Aretic sport is community-conscious, yet meritocratic. It aims to reward those athletes that have distinguished themselves from fellow competitors through competition, but it acknowledges the contribution of the team and respect for all persons and sport itself. Aretism always recognizes excellence in the context of community, both its dependence upon others and its obligation to benefit others. *Aretē* is not something kept to oneself. At the same time, Aretism does not pretend that the contribution of athletes to societal well-being is the same as that of nurses, academicians, or local business owners. Rather it uses sport to cultivate the virtues that make nurses, academicians, and business owners useful to their communities to help make athletes useful too.

Rather than accepting the AR model's notion that competition threatens the interests of the group or the MC model's numbers-driven delusion that athletic success is essentially individual, Aretism views competition itself as cooperative. Following the lead of Boxill, Whitaker, Nelson, and especially Bob Simon, the Aretic model states that competition is a cooperative journey for excellence, where athletes express themselves in the spirit of integrative, competitive play that seeks neither to dominate nor to be dominated.

This meritocratic attitude is a combination of feminine and masculine attitudes. Mike Messner elaborates:

> [O]bservations of young children's game-playing show that girls bring to the activity a more pragmatic and flexible orientation toward the rules—they are more prone to make exceptions and innovations in the middle of the game in order to make the game more 'fair' and maintain relationships with others. Boys tend to have a more firm, even inflexible orientation to the rules of a game—they are less willing to change or alter rules in the middle of the game; to them, the rules are what protects any 'fairness.'[14]

The Aretic model maintains that right justice is the proper mean between group and individual interests. At the most fundamental level, right justice entails welfare rights, respect for the dignity of each person, and other ethical principles in agreement with Aretism. There are also considerations of desert that factor in effort and talent—i.e., meritocracy. In other words, justice is properly served only when the interests of all competitors are equally promoted within the rules of competition, aretically construed.

Overall, the Aretic model asks for integration with sport, others, and self. Consequently, individuals' success can never be ascertained in isolation from others' success and the overall success of their sport. Athletes' personal success is intimately linked with the success of their team and successful team play is competition that strives to include committed play or involvement by all members of a team and all opponents at some level.

Commercialism vs. Pleasure/Beauty

Finally, whereas the overriding focus of MC sport is commercial and AR sport is recreational, Aretic sport is educational. Its goal is to improve persons and societies by creating an arena within which *aretē* may be cultivated, tested, and publicly appreciated. The final arbiter on issues like doping and ergogenic aids on the Aretic model is, as we saw in chapters 7 and 8, their educational promotion of *aretē*.

The link between athletics and education for *aretē* is Aretism's most direct inheritance from ancient Greek culture. In Ancient Greece, competitive sport was a way to demonstrate excellence. Athletic *aretē* was thought to be earned by enduring struggle and hardships, and it could be carefully cultivated through training. The word "athlete" derives from the Greek word *athlein*, which means chiefly "to suffer" or "to endure" and secondarily "to contend for a prize." Greeks, as we mentioned in the introduction, introduced competition into nearly in all walks of life.

Plato's famous Academy was set up in a public gymnasium, not just because that was a good place to find young men willing to learn, but also because the gymnasium was already recognized as a place for education. The philosophical debate he introduced there reflected the competitive nature of athletic activities and probably complemented rather than replaced them.[15] It is that philosophical link between athletics and *aretē* that Aretism seeks to revive.

What is perhaps not typically Greek about Aretism is its focus on striving for and attainment of *aretē* rather than victory. Athletic *aretē* demands a commitment to play hard to the best of one's capacity, but also a commitment to play fair, with full respect for the dignity of self, others, and even the sanctity of sport as a social institution. Thus, it is not victory that is most praise-worthy, but the manner in which athletes conduct themselves while competing—specifically the *aretē* demonstrated in the pursuit of victory.

Aretē in competitive sport, then, is not just the *aretē* of any particular athlete or any distinct manner of doing something with an eye to excellence in athletic competition. *Aretē* in competitive sport is the culture of excellence within sport—the values that all athletes, who consent to engage in fair and honest competition with others, at least implicitly ought to embrace. Aretism, thus, has an ineliminable ethical component, the topic of the next chapter.

Notes

1. Mariah Burton Nelson, *Are We Winning Yet? How Women are Changing Sports and Sports are Changing Women* (New York: Random House, 1991), 9.

2. Gail Whitaker, "Sport Promotes Positive Social Values," *Sports in America: Opposing Viewpoints,* ed. William Dudley (San Diego: Greenhaven Press, Inc., 1994), 185.

3. M. Andrew Holowchak, "Excellence as Athletic Ideal: Autonomy, Morality, and Competitive Sport," *International Journal of Applied Philosophy* 15:1, 2001, 153-164; "'Aretism' and Pharmacological Ergogenic Aids in Sport: Taking a Shot at the Use of Steroids," *Journal of the Philosophy of Sport* XXVII (Champaign, IL: Human Kinetics Publishers, 2000), 35-50; and "Liberalism and the Moral Atrophy of Sport: Autonomy and Social Irresponsibility," *Contemporary Philosophy,* Vol. XXII, No. 1 & 2, 30-36.

4. Heather Reid, *The Philosophical Athlete* (Durham, NC: Carolina Academic Press, 2002); "Was the Roman Gladiator an Athlete?" *Journal of the Philosophy of Sport* 33:1, 2006, 37-49; "Athletic Competition as Socratic Philosophy" (AUPO *Gymnika*) 35:2, 2006, 73-77; "Sport and Moral Education in Plato's *Republic,*" *Journal of the Philosophy of Sport* 34:2, 2007, 160-175; "Sport, Philosophy, and the Quest for Knowledge," *Journal of the Philosophy of Sport* 36:1, 2009, 40-49; "Athletic Virtues East and West," *Sport Ethics and Philosophy* 4:1, 2010, 16-26; *Athletics and Philosophy in the Ancient World: Contests of Virtue* (London: Routledge, 2011).

5. Aristotle, *Nicomachean Ethics,* trans. Terrence Irwin (Hackett Publishing Company, Inc., 1999).

6. For a detailed application of Aristotle's ethics to athletics see H. Reid, *Athletics and Philosophy in Ancient Greece and Rome: Contests of Virtue* (Routledge, 2011), chapter 6.

7. Aristotle, *Rhetoric,* trans. H.J. Freese (Cambridge: Harvard University Press, 1982), 1361b10.

8. Aristotle, *Nichomachean Ethics,* III.6-9.

9. Aristotle, *Nicomachean Ethics,* IV.1.

10. D. Stanley Eitzen (ed.), *Sport in Contemporary Society: An Anthology* (New York: St. Martin's Press, 1996), 190.

11. Mike Messner, "The Meaning of Success: The Athletic Experience and the Development of Male Identity," *Sport in Contemporary Society: An Anthology,* ed. D. Stanley Eitzen (New York: St. Martin's Press, 1996),374.

12. Messner, "The Meaning of Success," 377.

13. http://sportsillustrated.cnn.com/siforwomen/top_100/3/.

14. Messner "The Meaning of Success," 374.

15. Heather Reid, "Plato's Gymnasium," *Sport, Ethics and Philosophy,* Vol. 4, No. 2, 2010, 170-182. Reprinted in , *Athletics and Philosophy in Ancient Greece and Rome: Contests of Virtue* (Routledge, 2011), chapter 5.

Chapter 19
Aretism and Values

"Karate-Do is not only the acquisition of certain defensive skills, but also mastering the art of being a good and honest member of society. . . . The pervasiveness of this traditional goal of moral virtue is such that, even today, the primary requirement for a black belt in many schools of the martial arts is having 'a good moral character.'" Daeshik Kim and Allan Bäck

THE LAST CHAPTER AIMED TO SHOW THAT Aretism constitutes an Aristotelian mean—i.e., ethical midpoint between the panagonistic extremes of the Martial/Commerical model of sport and the Aesthetic/Recreational model, characterized by its emphasis on intrinsic goods such as beauty and unity. Aretism is not just the product of an ancient method for moral reasoning; it is also an intrinsically moral ideal that makes normative demands upon competitive sport.

In order to understand the relationship between Aretism and moral values, however, we must not only analyze why the MC model is seriously flawed, we must also sketch out the sort of ethical underpinning our alternative model ought to have. To do those things, we begin by analyzing four competing conceptions of morality and then turn to two distinct views of how values in the practice of competitive sport are related to moral values in society. We end by outlining the normative implications of Aretism's conception of competitive sport as a socially integrative institution.

Four Views of Moral Values

Moral relativism is the view that moral truths or values vary in different societies. What those truths or values are and should be for a given society is to be resolved by that society or some empowered part of it (e.g., a deliberative council). Consequently, what one society claims to be morally true cannot be meaningfully challenged by another, since moral truth in one society is simply a product of its particular cultural conditions, which may vary over time. If moral relativism is right, there can be no meaningful debate between the societies to re-solve any moral issue.

Moral skepticism, in contrast, is the view that doubts, in some measure, the possibility that there can be moral knowledge at all. Radical moral skepticism holds that there are no moral truths or values and, thus, moral inquiry is bootless. That is, of course, an apparently self-defeating claim. Is not knowing that there are no moral truths a matter of knowing at least one moral truth—i.e., that there are no moral truths? Soft skepticism addresses that objection by regarding all moral claims as suspicious simply because it acknowledges rival moral tradi-tions. Thus, the soft skeptic maintains that one could defend the claim "It is al-ways morally impermissible to lie" as well as the contradictory claim "It is some-times morally permissible to lie," and so suspension of judgment is warranted.

Moral perspectivism is the related view that there can be no truth outside of a particular perspective (e.g., a generic human point of view or a particular cul-tural, gender-based, or linguistic perspective). It is similar to soft moral skepti-cism in that it acknowledges the possibility of varying moral traditions. It differs, however, in that it does not view those traditions as incompatible ways of view-ing a moral system and, hence, as cause for concern, but rather as different and complementary ways of seeing reality.

Moral realism, finally, is the view that there are moral truths or values—fixed, unchanging, and absolute—and they are to some extent discoverable. Moral realism is a very attractive view intuitively, but it is not without problems. Just what are those truths, if they exist? To whom are they binding (e.g., all crea-tures capable of rationality, humans only, etc.)? Moreover, moral realism seems to presuppose a one-size-fits-all conception of rationality that is unalterable and fixed for all time.

Each of the four views has been advanced by philosophers in an attempt to justify moral claims—at least, to some extent. In the rest of this chapter, we shall try to show why a form of realism—a very soft form—is the alternative that best aligns with Aretism. First, we need to say something about two different percep-tions that concern how moral values relate to social institutions such as competi-tive sport.

Externalism and Internalism

Externalism is the view that the values of institutions like competitive sport are merely the values of that society in which such sport is practiced. It denies that sport can have its own system of values independent of or, at least, somewhat autonomous from the values of a particular society. On this view, sport itself will have nothing unique to offer society other than the values society has already contributed to sport.

Internalism, in contrast, is the view that the values of competitive sport can have a significant degree of autonomy from the prevailing views of society. The values of competitive sport might even conflict with the views of society. According to internalists, competitive sport has an inner morality, but still nothing to offer society because its unique moral values remain confined within the practice.

In defending Aretism as a form of moral realism that can have positive effects on society, we also need to show why strict internalism and externalism are both wrong. We do so by critically evaluating Bob Simon's argument for the inner morality of sport in his second edition of *Fair Play: The Ethics of Sport.*

Simon argues that sport has a unique set of values internal to its practice. He writes, "These values are internal in that they arise from the core character of competitive sport and are not mere reflections of wider social values, which can in principle and sometimes in practice diverge significantly from those found in competitive sport."[1]

Just what are these values? Simon lists many different types. There are values such as excellence, discipline, and dedication. There is respect for the rules of the game. There are the excellences of particular sports that guide evaluation of the play of oneself and others. Last, there is sport as the mutual quest for excellence itself.[2]

What exactly does Simon mean? He does not say that all of the values that characterize competitive sport at a given time are unique to sport and he does not deem it necessary that there is any one value that is unique to sport through all time—i.e., strict internalism. What he seems to be stating is that sport is defined at particular times by clusters of values that are unique to sport within a given society.

How is that to be cashed out? Suppose that American sport in 2010 is uniquely defined by such values as discipline, hard work, and financial gain and that each of those values can be found in American society as parts of other practices, i.e. academics or business. So, we might say that American society—embracing the values of discipline, hard work, and financial gain, as well as, say, truth, justice, and apple pie at some particular time—is defined by those values. If so, then the values of sport are simply a subset of those values of society and sport can claim no peculiar inner logic. The fact that sport does not embrace all of society's values hardly proves that the values of sport are not reducible to social values. If that were true, then Simon's internalism would really be a form of externalism.

Yet that is not what Simon has in mind. On his view, there is nothing to prevent conflicting values in different practices within a society. The values of academic scholarship, for instance, could differ from those values of sport at a given time. It might be that academic scholarship is characterized by such values as non-competition and self-sacrifice, in contrast to sport's values such as competition and self-promotion. On such an account, it would then not make much sense to say that American society itself embraces non-competition and competition as well as self-sacrifice and self-promotion. That would make light of what a value is. Rather one would want to say that values have worth only in particular contexts—i.e., in particular practices. For Simon, practices create a place for values. One might even go so far as to say practices create values. For Simon, "values" are context-dependent (i.e., something can be a value in one context or practice and fail to be a value in another).

Simon considers a teacher who will not allow students to persuade one another through the threat of violence in her classroom, but insists upon rational discussion between them. In doing so, she is "rejecting some values, such as intimidation, as a means of settling disagreements."[3] Labeling "intimidation" as a value is, to say the least, is a very broadminded use of the term "value." On the other hand, it is hard to see how "respect for the equal moral standing of others" could be practice-dependent in any viable moral system.

Simon acknowledges the tension. "On the one hand, the claim is that there is an inner morality of sports that is independent of and can even conflict with prevailing social values; on the other, it is claimed that such values are nonpartisan and, in some sense, neutral. Are these claims mutually compatible?" He falls back on the notion that some values are more fundamental, at least procedurally, in that the very practice of moral education could not exist without them. They include commitment, discipline, respect for others, and an appreciation of excellence. They are, he asserts, the "core values" of scholarship and sports that the practice of each reinforces. Simon's reinforcement argument is itself a justification of the inclusion of sport in moral education.[4]

Aretism simply takes that value-based justification for sport as a form of moral education and makes it normative. In agreement with Simon, Aretism assumes the inner morality of sport ought to be just the same as the inner morality of all properly run social practices. This view rejects strict internalism, the view that that sport has its own core set of values, independent from society. It also rejects the strictly externalist claim that sport values are reducible to the values of any particular society. Aretic values—such as regard for truth, justice, courage, generosity, friendliness, and wisdom—do not seem to us to vary from culture to culture, but are, at least, species-fixed or, at best, universally embraceable by all creatures capable of rationality.

Thus, Aretism is a virtue-ethics form of soft moral realism, one which posits the existence of moral universals such as virtue without trying to define them so strictly that one culture's conception of virtue gets imposed on all others. Virtue, it will be noted, is central not just to the Western ethical traditions rooted in ancient Greece, but also the Eastern ethical traditions rooted in the ancient Chinese philosophies of Lao-tzu and Confucius.

As Reid noted in a comparison of Greek and Chinese conceptions of virtue, however, the two traditions share many values relevant to athletics. Both agree that virtue is cultivated through training, which may involve effort and struggle, but at its highest level appears effortlessness. Both traditions warn that the pursuit of external goods like fame and fortune interferes with the acquisition of virtue, but they consider wealth and honor appropriate rewards for achieving it. Both traditions understand virtue as a form of excellence available to males and females alike. Both conceptions of virtue take account of both individual achievement and community engagement.[5]

Aretic Integration

We have seen with our sketch of the MC model that competitive sport can have harmful consequences for social morality. Sociologist Michael Messner maintains that the skills essential for survival in panagonistic sport can have troubling social consequences.

> Within the hierarchical world of sports, which in many ways mirrors the capitalist economy, one learns that if he is to survive and avoid being pushed off the ever-narrowing pyramid of success, he must develop certain kinds of relationships—to himself, to his body, to other people, and to the sport itself. In short, the successful athlete must develop a highly goal-oriented personality that encourages him to view his body as a tool, a machine, or even a weapon utilized to defeat an objectified opponent. He is likely to have difficulty establishing intimate and lasting friendships with other males because of low self-disclosure, homophobia, and cut-throat competition. And he is likely to view his public image as a 'success' as far more basic and fundamental than any of his interpersonal relationships.[6]

What is noteworthy is that there is nothing essential to sport that precipitates those consequences. If we regard sport as external to moral values, we might think there is nothing to be done except withdraw oneself from the practice. We believe, however, that sport can be practiced in such a way that it benefits society by cultivating positive moral values among participants.

Aretism asserts that many of the core values of competitive sport are not exclusive to sport, but rather common among all human beings. By emphasizing universal values, competitive sport can substantially contribute to moral betterment within a community, a society, and the global human community. Athletes, committed to excellence through competitive athletics, strive for moral and social betterment on three levels: excellence through personal integration, excellence through social integration, and excellence through global integration.[7]

Global Integration

Taking the last first, aretic athletes attain a type of cosmic or global integration by deliberately engaging in competitive sport in a manner consistent with the set of universal ethical values that define its practice and all human practices over time—values such as friendliness, courage, justice, patience, sedulousness, and commitment. Athletes ought to understand that their own athletic expression in sport, as a celebration of human perseverance and creativity, takes on social meaning because it reinforces those values.

By the same token, victories that reinforce vices—such as deception, disrespect, and dishonesty—are socially harmful even if they result in victory and the extrinsic goods that accompany it. It is sometimes noted that doped athletes that were caught long after their victories were able to bask in the glory of victory and sometimes even allowed to keep their prizes. Aretism not only rejects the value of such extrinsic goods, it holds athletes and officials accountable for the damage wreaked by such scandals—whether it is local or global. In a strict sense, morally suspect actions are their own penalty: The damage done is internal, as harmful deeds over time impact the psychical well-being of the agent in the same way that improper eating over time impacts a person's physical wellbeing.

International events like the World Cup and Olympic Games confer a special opportunity and responsibility upon athletes and organizers to set a good example for the world. The first fundamental principle of Olympism from the IOC's *Olympic Charter* states, "Olympism seeks to create a way of life based on the joy of effort, the educational value of good example and respect for universal fundamental ethical principles."[8] Yet rhetoric can only go so far; athletes must demonstrate excellence (i.e., virtue) in action if sport is to achieve its Aretic potential.

Social Integration

At the level of social integration, competitive sport, ought to be founded on recognition of and respect for others. While competitively and creatively distinguishing themselves from competitors in a particular sport, athletes simultaneously acknowledge the contributions of other athletes that also accept sport as a social institution and who commit to virtuous activity. Socially integrated athletes recognize the essentially cooperative nature of competition and therefore agree to conduct themselves in a manner respectful and appreciative of the efforts of other competitors. In the words of Kant, others are to be treated as ends and not means. Skier Picabo Street beautifully characterizes the aretic spirit of social integration.

[I]t has been important for me to have a connection to the people who watch me. . . . In general, I think, women in sports are more concerned about making that kind of connection with their fans. We feel a sense of responsibility to them and I think that is one of the most important contributions from women to this generation and those to come. I hope that, as competition among women continues to grow fiercer and more women enter the sports world as top competitors, we don't lose sight of our responsibilities and our abilities to be role models for other women as well as for men.[9]

Daeshik Kim and Allan Bäck capture the essence of other-concern in the proper practice of the martial arts.

[T]he goal of traditional martial arts training is to acquire virtue. This goal does not merely center around personal development and enrichment, but is supposed to be other-regarding and to benefit others: Karate-Do is not only the acquisition of certain defensive skills, but also mastering the art of being a good and honest member of society. . . . The pervasiveness of this traditional goal of moral virtue is such that, even today, the primary requirement for a black belt in many schools of the martial arts is having "a good moral character."[10]

Aretic competitors and spectators recognize and celebrate the cooperative nature of competition. Competitors ought not to be regarded as obstacles to victory; instead they ought to be embraced for their contribution to the shared project of cultivating *aretē*. A poem from the International Olympic Committee describes the spirit perfectly:

You may be my opponent, but you are not my enemy
Because your resistance gives me strength.
You determination gives me courage.
Your spirit lifts me up.
And, even as I try to defeat you, if I manage
I will not humiliate you.
On the contrary, I will honor you
Because, without you, my own humanity is diminished. [11]

Personal Integration

Last and least controversially, Aretism requires personal integration. Personal integration involves athletes' own autonomous striving for a greater sense of self—i.e., a personal commitment to excellence. Through integrative participation, athletes come to see sport as a vehicle for both physical and moral self-improvement. Athletes actualize physical and mental capacities that they never realized they had. Working through failure teaches perseverance. Obstacles offer opportunities for imaginative deliberation on possible solutions. Peggy Flemming, former Olympic gold-medal winner in figure skating, writes:

> In 1961, the entire U.S. figure-skating team died in a plane crash on the way to the world championships. I was only 11 and unaware of the gap that this would create in our sport on a national level. Because all my potential role models were gone, I had to draw on inspiration from what I had seen of ballet, music, and art. I had to look inside myself for what I thought my style should be.[12]

Upshot

The focus on and tripartitioning of excellence into its personal, social, and global aspects is what distinguishes Aretism from other normative accounts of sport. Mariah Nelson—author of *Are We Winning Yet?*—has this to say about sport as a type of integration in what she proposes as her "partnership" model.

> I use the term "partnership model" to emphasize that teammates, coaches, and even opposing players view each other as comrades rather than enemies. Players with disparate ability levels are respected as peers rather than ranked in a hierarchy, and athletes care for each other and their own bodies. . . ."To compete" is understood from its Latin source, *competere*: "to seek together." . . . Like early physical educators, partnership athletes maintain that sport should be inclusive; in balance with other aspects of life; cooperative and social in spirit; and safe.[13]

Nelson's partnership model is very much in the spirit of Aretism.

Moreover, in keeping with the arguments in Parts II and III, *aretē* combines the seriousness of purpose found in MC sport, with the aesthetic component emphasized in AR sport. Sport is excellent in large part because sport is meaningful and beautiful. From the simplest to the most complex movements and arrangements of movements involved, what often moves people most in sport is not its brutality or the anything-goes, pan-agonistic commitment to victory of many competitors, but rather an appreciation of the aesthetic subtleties of athletic excellence and of the dedication required to achieve that level. Competitive sport requires passion, diligence, focus, drive, planning, patience, and a commitment to work with others, even opponents, toward a goal.

To love sport genuinely is to recognize that sport is more than mere contending for a prize. It transcends mere winning and losing. Sport is a means of cultivating the moral values of excellence and excellence—following Plato, Aristotle, and the Greek and Roman Stoics—is essentially integration: personal, social, and global.

Notes

1. Robert Simon, *Fair Play: The Ethics of Sport,* Second Edition (Boulder, CO: Westview Press, 2004), 203.

2. Simon, *Fair Play,* 203.

3. Simon, *Fair Play,* 206-207.

4. Simon, *Fair Play,* 206-208.

5. For a comparison of these virtue-ethical traditions in their relation to sport see Heather Reid, "Athletic Virtues East and West," *Sport, Ethics and Philosophy* 4:1 (2010) 16-26.

6. Michael A. Messner, "The Meaning of Success: The Athletic Experience and the Development of Male Identity," *Sport in Contemporary Society: An Anthology,* ed. D. Stanley Eitzen (New York: St. Martin's Press, 1996), 379.

7. See M. Andrew Holowchak, "Excellence as Athletic Ideal: Autonomy, Morality, and Competitive Sport," *International Journal of Applied Philosophy* 15:1, 2001, 153-164; "'Aretism' and Pharmacological Ergogenic Aids in Sport: Taking a Shot at the Use of Steroids," *Journal of the Philosophy of Sport* XXVII (Champaign, IL: Human Kinetics Publishers, 2000), 35-50; and "Liberalism and the Moral Atrophy of Sport: Autonomy and Social Irresponsibility," *Contemporary Philosophy,* Vol. XXII, No. 1 & 2, 30-36.

8. International Olympic Committee, *Olympic Charter* (Lausanne, 2007), 11.

9. Christina Lessa, *Stories of Triumph: Women Who Win in Sport and in Life* (New York: Universe Publishing, 1998), v.

10. Daeshik Kim and Allan Back, *Martial Meditation: Philosophy and the Essence of the Martial Arts* (Akron, OH: The International Council on Martial Arts Education, 1989), 146.

11. International Olympic Committee, "Adversary", Celebrate Humanity Ad Campaign, 2004.

12. Lessa, *Stories of Triumph,* iv.

13. Mariah Burton Nelson, *Are We Winning Yet? How Women are Changing Sports and Sports are Changing Women* (New York: Random House, 1991), 9.

Chapter 20
Aretism and Education

"Putting winning and losing in a saner perspective may reduce the motivation to resort to cheating, distasteful forms of gamesmanship, and trash talking and other forms of taunting. And, while the desire to win is a necessary ingredient of competitive sport, realizing that winning is not the be all and end all of athletic excellence may help to foster the cooperation that is part of a healthy competition and prevent it from degenerating into alienation." D. Stanley Eitzen

T HE PRECEDING CHAPTERS HAVE POINTED OUT something rather obvious to many—there are numerous problems with competitive sport as it has been and continues to be practiced today. These problems, we have argued, have roots in a Martial/Commercial conception of competitive sport, where victory and money are the final measures of performance and worth. Our argument throughout has been that victory secured in MC fashion comes at too high a price. Athletic competitions that turn a blind eye to cheating, encourage ego-puffing to the detriment of teammates and fellow competitors, and promote spectacle and instrumentality at the expense of athletes' physical health are socially irresponsible and morally suspect practices.

The main purpose of this book is to offer solutions to those prickly problems by proposing that we open ourselves up to the Aesthetic/Recreational dimension of athletic competitions and rethink the worth of competitive sport. We argue that sporting practices ought to be reshaped according to a medial, Aretic model that is ultimately educational. In this chapter, we offer concrete examples for initiating Aretic reform within youth and scholastic sports.

Problems with Youth Sports

The place to begin Aretic reform in sport is at the most basic level. Since the late nineteenth century, competitive sport has been promoted as a vehicle for teaching boys just those values that are needed to be successful in later life. The prob-

lem with this sports-builds-character approach is that character has been evaluated mostly according the Lombardian ethical principle: You are nothing unless
you win. Lombardianism, a feature of the MC model, dominates competitive
sport all the way down to the youth level. Athletes who buy into it, even the most
successful ones, often see themselves as utter failures, as it is impossible to win
always or often. Even the brightest stars, the greatest victors, fade with time. In
short, a win-at-all-costs attitude in sport is very likely inversely related to happiness in life.[1]

Presently, organized sports for children are very popular—especially in
more affluent American neighborhoods. The reasons are many. First, many families have both parents working and this creates a need for supervised programs
for their children. Sports programs fit the bill. Second, parents today want to be
able to account for their children at all hours of the day, and organized sports
allows for such accountability. Third, organized sports is believed to channel
children's energy in a constructive way and keeps them away from more dangerous activities—especially in the least affluent neighborhoods. Fourth, parents
and coaches generally receive vicarious gratification through watching children
compete successfully—often at the expense of those children.[2] Fifth, as was the
case in the 1900s, parents today still believe that competitive sport is helpful
preparation for the predatory rigors of today's competitive society. Finally, professional sport today has a visibility it never had and with visibility comes the
promise of exceptional financial security for anyone who can make it as a pro.
Many parents view organized sports are an investment in their child's athletic
future for their own financial independence. An athletic scholarship can save
families hundreds of thousands of dollars in education costs. It's no wonder sport
for youth is taken so seriously.

However, the growing popularity of youth sports has had some unhappy
consequences in recent years. In extreme cases, there have been numerous instances of parents or coaches responding aggressively, even violently, to controversial calls by officials or verbal reproaches by other parents. A few examples
will suffice. About 25 years ago, Michael Babicz was hospitalized for a broken
jaw he received by two brothers after he made a questionable call in a softball
match. In Lidenhurst, England, a woman was arrested in 1998 for assaulting a
referee who, she claimed, missed a call in her daughter's soccer game. More
recently, in Salt Lake City, two women beat a third woman unconscious after a
youth baseball game. Most astonishing of all, on July 5 of 2000 Thomas Junta
beat to death hockey coach Michael Costin in Massachusetts, because the latter
was conducting a practice session that was too rough for the kids.

Even with the international exposure of the incident involving Junta, Fred
Engh, president of the National Alliance for Youth Sports, said, "Since the Massachusetts [i.e., Costa] incident, the rash of violence has only continued. We'd
love to be able to say that, with all that we do, these kinds of incidents were in

decline but that just isn't the case." In a recent poll, over 60 percent of parents reported having seen at least one violent event at a youth-sports event. The National Association of Sports Professionals—representing over 19,000 coaches, umpires, and referees—has reported a marked increase in the incidences of violence by parents at youth sports events. The National Association of Sports Officials has reported nearly 150 cases of acts of violence directed toward officials in the year 2000.

The best explanation for the increase in violence is that youth sports is not, as it ought to be, regarded as a form of education. Rather it has adopted wholesale the MC model. Parental involvement in children's sports and the win-at-all-costs attitude of some coaches come at too large of a price. Today, the neighborhood pick-up game—which was unscored, untimed, and unsupervised and a key feature of Holowchak's early-life exposure to baseball—is nearly obsolete. In place of playing for fun, there are highly bureaucratized sport programs for youth that expose children to the serious side of competition at a very young age and often require many hours of rigorous training or practice. In many youth leagues, parents, with little knowledge of biomechanics and child psychology, take to coaching children in a dictatorial fashion. Fun and education take a back seat to winning, as coaches, in an effort to make up for some defect in their own childhood, push children too far.[3]

In some cases, children are pushed to their physical limits. Some are even encouraged to play through pain. They are told that "playing through the pain" will make them tougher—that it will build character. What should have been fun becomes work. K.L. Siegenthaler and G. Leticia Gonzalez write: "[T]urning children into miniadults at an early age may rob them of spontaneous play, which is also an important teacher of valuable social lessons. Additionally, by transforming play into work, athletes sometimes become stressed due to external pressure to win, or may become bored and stop participating."[4]

Below is an account of high-school student, Emily, who talks of her frustration with the competitive element of organized sports:

> For years I played goalie on a soccer team and was pretty good, despite my height. I remember how excited I would get because I was helping my team. But I'll never forget the day I wasn't put in goal. It was the championship game, and I was just 'too short' to play. After that I was crushed and didn't play for another three years. . . .
>
> Some parents will push their kids way too hard. At soccer fields, you can hear parents screaming. At basketball games, parents yell at the refs, and it's the same at the baseball field. Some kids are punished just for losing a game. The children become angry and frustrated with the sport. . . .
>
> But parents, coaches, and fans need to remember that it's just a game.[5]

As Emily's words show, unfortunately it is the children, in many cases, who have greater wisdom about what is best for them than their parents or coaches.

A study by the American Footwear Association lists the most important reasons why children quit playing a sport.

- I lost interest.
- I was not having fun.
- It took too much time.
- The coach was a poor teacher.
- There was too much pressure.
- I wanted non-sport activity.
- I was tired of it.
- I needed more time to study.
- The coach played favorites.
- Sport was boring.
- There was too much emphasis on winning.[6]

According to Ronald Kamm, adults impose their standards on children without consideration, if those standards are good for the children. "Parents push their kids to ever greater heights without considering what is best for the child. In its most extreme form, children may be forced to train or play when injured. Many children, hungry for love and approval, go along with the program."[7]

What happens to children that are pushed too hard? Many suffer from low self-esteem and excessive anxiety, which, unsurprisingly, often leads to a heightened tendency to aggress in later life.[8]

Proud Parents and Careful Coaches

What can Aretism do to reverse that trend? We need to develop in children a gender-free, cooperative, and moderate notion of competitive sport. In other words, we need to instill ideals in children that are more aesthetic and recreational, than martial or commercial. They will be exposed to the martial elements of consumerism soon enough.

Here are some practical suggestions for improvement or reform, many of which are already being practiced in some youth-sports programs around the globe:

- Coaches and parents need to remind themselves that youth sports are first and foremost for the benefit of children. Thus, parents should allow children to decide for themselves which sport they want to play.
- Youth competitions ought to be set up so that enjoyable learning, rather than winning, is the ultimate aim. Assertive play is one thing and is consistent with the goal of education; aggressive or violent play should never be applauded or condoned.

- Coaches and parents ought to emphasize the aesthetic ideals of cooperation and teamwork. As reformists Aubrey Fine and Michael Sachs mention, "we," the single most important word that children playing sport should learn, always comes before "I."[9]
- Coaches and parents ought to also emphasize the personal development of each child through sport. Children ought to be rewarded for improvement on their own past performance, and not expected to equal the performances of the best person or anyone else on a team.
- Children ought to be encouraged to make new friends through youth sports. Parents too should see that as an opportunity to model social skills by making friends with other parents—both on the same team and the other team—as well as with officials and coaches.
- Coaches ought to tailor involvement to meet the educational needs of all individuals of a team. Parents ought to be supportive of this aim—even if their own child is a "budding superstar."
- Parents and coaches ought not to get overly exited or upset about the outcome of any competition. Effort, not outcome, should be applauded. Fun should be encouraged. Parents and coaches ought to lead by example.
- Children ought to be taught how to commit to their sport, team, and teammates—regardless of the outcome. There will be times when continuing to play a game is not much fun (for instance, when one team is getting badly beaten by another). Yet this is a fine opportunity for children to build character through not giving up and sticking it out with their teammates, however lopsided the final result becomes. This develops a notion that success is often more a matter of commitment to others or a worthwhile cause than of winning outright.
- Coaches and parents ought to positively reward children for effort and commitment, regardless of outcome.
- Coaches and parents ought to introduce children to positive role models in sports and distance them from negative role models. They also ought to distance children from some of the practices of professional sports that highlight MC play (e.g., showboating, emphasis on winning, violence).
- Children's sports ought to be gender-neutral. Discriminating between boys and girls because of perceived differences in abilities at a young age due to sex is more a matter of prescribing differences, not finding them. In fact, we believe that youth sports should remain gender integrated for as long as competitive standards allows.

There is perhaps truth in the old saw that old ideas do not die until those persons that hold them do. For the present, maybe it is best to set the modest, but realizable goal of teaching children to play sports with commitment, care, fun, creativity, imagination, and respect for themselves, others, and even their sport—to play in the Aretic manner. One rule and only one rule ought to be enforced: All children must enjoy and learn from their sports experience. If Aretic aims can be met for children's play, there will be a base, at the adult level, for Aretic reform of competitive sport in years to come.

Higher Education

Our claims about reforming youth sports will not meet the resistance that our claims about reforming scholastic sports will. Our position there is blunt and controversial: If competitive sports are to be a part of formal education, they must either consciously direct themselves toward the goal of cultivating virtue or be abolished outright at academic institutions. We make that claim because the MC, win-at-all-costs model has taken over competitive sports programs at many, if not most, high schools, colleges, and universities in America. Top-level collegiate football and basketball programs are run almost exclusively according to a commercial paradigm that is at odds with the mission statements and educative ideals of the very institutions that sponsor them.

Our recommendation that such programs be reformed or abandoned, however, does not reject sports' educational potential. We believe that intramural competitions, where the emphasis is on committed participation and fun, or even non-scholarship extramural competition, might bring athletics back in line with educational objectives. Student-athletes themselves regard sport as a means to scholarship dollars (i.e., instrumentally) and a professional career. They are unfazed that their institutions are using them to promote commercial interests and that shows dearth of aretic sensibility.

We recognize that such reforms are unlikely to happen anytime soon, if at all. Competitive sports at academic institutions, especially Division I universities, are fueled by corporate dollars, television revenue, and merchandise sales. Fan appeal is at fever pitch and a successful program increases new student applications as well as alumni giving.[10] Thus, whatever the long-term educational benefits of our suggestion are, it seems unlikely that they will be implemented soon.

A more humble and realistic recommendation in the direction of aretic reform, therefore, is compliance with Title IX—which mandates gender equity at academic institutions—something which has not occurred in any meaningful sense thus far. On account of the lack of penalization for non-compliance of Title IX, former chief executive officer of the Women's Sports Foundation, Donna Lopiano, argued as far back as 1993 that reform at academic institutions must come through encouraging the Department of Education's Office of Civil Rights to demand obedience to the law by filing as many lawsuits as possible.[11] She also maintained that revenue must be justly distributed among athletic programs in a manner compliant with Title IX and that all income and expenditures associated with collegiate athletics must be easily accessible to anyone through print and electronic media.[12] Access to income and expenditures was put into law with the Disclosure Act in 1994, yet full compliance with Title IX is still far from being realized after nearly 40 years.

Gender equity in education—including sports—is hardly a pipe dream. All it takes is full recognition that women deserve equal access to sports education (and not just academic subjects) plus a commitment to working toward those aims. The Olympic Games, which arguably face a difficult challenge promoting gender equity on a global scale, have nevertheless made great strides since their reemergence in 1896, and that despite founder Pierre de Coubertin's opposition to women in sport and enduring religious and social oppression of females worldwide.

The IOC has publicly committed itself to promoting women in sports. Article 7 of the "Mission and Role of the IOC" says sport ought "to encourage and support the promotion of women in sport at all levels and in all structures with a view to implementing the principle of equality of men and women."[13] The IOC has taken a proactive approach by implementing rules and quotas to back up their rhetoric. The results speak for themselves. Female participation in the modern Olympic Games has steadily increased from 1.6% of athletes, competing in three events at Paris 1900, to around 42% of athletes, competing in 137 events in 2008.[14]

The movement has not shied away from challenging gender stereotypes. Since 1984, women's events have been added in such traditionally masculine sports as shooting, judo, ice hockey, weightlifting, and wrestling. Boxing is planned for London 2012. Since 1991, all new sports added to the Olympic Games must include women's events. There remain few women's-only or men's-only sports. Men and women compete on equal terms in equestrian events.

The IOC is also promoting women in sport management. National Olympic Committees and International Sports Federations are required to set the objective of reserving at least 20% of decision-making positions for women. Compliance is still low, although more than half of NOCs and IFs have achieved the mark of 10%.[15] Female membership is also increasing on the IOC itself. Although it was not until 1981 that Pirjo Haggman of Finland and Flor Isava-Fonseca of Venezuela become the first female members of the IOC—an organization that is today over 100 members—women now comprise 15% of the members. There has never been a female president of the IOC and women are underrepresented in the four positions of vice-presidency, but such statistically modest progress is huge compared with the rest of the sporting world—including scholastic sports in the USA, which are supposed to be regulated by Title IX.

In the Olympic Movement, legislation has been complimented by education. The IOC sponsors a variety of educational programs and holds a world conference on women and sport every four years. They take up issues such as development of educational resources on gender equity, representation of women at National Olympic Committees and International Federations, and advocacy of females in meetings and seminars at National Olympic Committees and International Federations. The 2008 edition took place in Jordan and involved more than 600 participants from 116 countries.[16] Overall, we believe that the Olympic movement is headed in the right direction and professional sports would benefit greatly by following its lead.

There is no reason why gender equity cannot be achieved in scholastic sport, as it is a reality in nearly every other aspect of education. The obstacle seems to be the notion that sports is not really educational in the same way that traditional academic subjects are supposed to be. Females are marginalized and excluded from scholastic sports and that is evidence that the value of those sports lies in entertainment and revenue-generation—i.e., that the MC model is in effect today. Aretism, by contrast, values sport fundamentally for its educational value and education should never be denied on the basis of gender.

One can rejoin that males and females need different types of education. Philosopher Jan Boxill has noted that many regard "competition" as the kind of education appropriate only for males.

> One of the most controversial, and perhaps most misunderstood, features of our society is "competition." Competition is seen to be driven by selfish motives and involves competitors treating others as means, as enemies to be defeated, or as obstacles thwarting one's victory or success—all of which are to be removed by any means possible. Competition places an emphasis on winning, leading to the "win-at-all-costs" syndrome. These characteristics are associated with men. On the other hand, co-operation, the unselfish treatment of others as partners sharing in the ends, places no emphasis on winning. These characteristics are associated with women. It has been stated, "Athletic competition builds character in our boys. We do not need that kind of character in our girls."[17]

From the Aretic point of view, however, something worth having is valuable for males and females alike. Especially in today's world, where women compete in the job market and even on the battlefield with men, there is no reason to deny them learning opportunities in competitive sport.

Typically "masculine" values, such as courage and assertiveness, ought to be promoted among females, typically "feminine" values, such as cooperation and grace, ought to be promoted among males. Said former Olympic skating champion Peggy Flemming of her grace, while skating:

> I'm very flattered when I'm referred to as a "feminine" skater. Elegance and grace are what I have always admired in women, no matter what their profession, and I'm proud to have brought that side of my personality to my sport. . . . Sports are not just a display of athletic power; they are a tool to help develop self-esteem and a healthy image. They also teach respect for discipline and responsibility.[18]

Respect, discipline, and responsibility are not gender-specific. If a competitive task is worth doing, it is worth doing with excellence. Even Plato recognized that, as he prescribed the same education, including gymnastics, for males and females guardians, because he understood *aretē* to be a quality of the soul and he knew that souls were genderless.[19] Aretism, likewise, does not consider virtue to be gendered.

Returning to the larger picture, Aretic reform of sport in education, the changes suggested thus far seem quite reasonable and, we hope, just. By beginning with youth sports, we can effect change in attitudes and ultimately administration of sports at the high-school and college level. Since the Aretic model values sport ultimately as education, reform in those areas might not be so difficult. Professional sport is another matter. To that issue we now turn.

Notes

1. Michael A. Messner, "The Meaning of Success: The Athletic Experience and the Development of Male Identity," *Sport in Contemporary Society: An Anthology*, ed, D. Stanley Eitzen (New York: St. Martin's Press, 1996), 374.

2. K.L. Siegenthaler and G. Leticia Gonzales, "Youth Sports as Serious Leisure," *Journal of Sport & Social Issues*, Vol. 21, No. 3 (Sage Publications, Inc., 1997), 306.

3. Joan Hundley, "The Overemphasis on Winning: A Philosophical Look," *Philosophy of Sport: Critical Readings, Crucial Issues*, ed. M. Andrew Holowchak (Upper Saddle River, NJ: Prentice-Hall, Inc. 2002), 208-9.

4. Siegenthaler et al., "Youth Sports as Serious Leisure," 302.

5. Janice E. Smith, "Organized Sports for Young People: Sports Today." http://home.earthlink.net/~jesmith/Sports.html (April 4, 2001), 1.

6. Aubrey H. Fine and Michael L. Sachs, *The Total Sports Experience for Kids* (South Bend, IN: Diamond Communications, Inc., 1997), 26.

7. Ronald L. Kamm, "Out of Williamsport, Into the Parent Trap," http://www.mindbodyandsports.com/youth.html, 1997, 1.

8. Jon C. Hellstedt, "Kids, Parents and Sport: Some Questions and Answers," *The Physician and Sportsmedicine,* 16 (4), 1998, 60-62.

9. Hellstedt, "Kids, Parents, and Sport," 24.

10. Though, paradoxically, most programs lose money.

11. Donna A. Lopiano, "Political Analysis: Gender Equity Strategies for the Future," *Women in Sport: Issues and Controversies*, ed. Greta L. Cohen (London: Sage Publications, 1993), 112.

12. Lopiano, "Political Analysis," 113-114.

13. International Olympic Committee, *Olympic Charter* (Lausanne, 2007), 15.

14. International Olympic Committee, "Factsheet on Women in the Olympic Movement," Lausanne, December 2009.

15. International Olympic Committee, "Factsheet on Women in the Olympic Movement," Lausanne, December 2009.

16. International Olympic Committee, "Factsheet on Women in the Olympic Movement," Lausanne, December 2009.

17. Jan Boxill, "Title IX and Gender Equity," *Journal of the Philosophy of Sport* XX-XXI (Champaign, IL: Human Kinetics Publishers, 1993-1994), 25.

18. Christina Lessa, *Stories of Triumph: Women Who Win in Sport and in Life* (New York: Universe Publishing, 1998), iv.

19. Heather L. Reid, *Athletics and Philosophy in Ancient Greece and Rome: Contests of Virtue* (Routledge, 2011), chapter 5.

Chapter 21
Aretism and Society

"I have made good judgments in the past. I have made good judgments in the future." George W. Bush

ONE OF THE IMPLICIT THEMES OF THIS PROJECT is that the historically entrenched Martial/Commercial conception of competitive sport, characterized panagonistically by a win-at-all-costs attitude, has been harmful to society. In arguing for aretic reform, we are asking even professional sport to be aware of its social consequences. As it did in Ancient Greece, sport ought to put itself in the service of community. Key social values such as justice and fairness ought to be exemplified and promoted by the public practice of sport, including the market-driven sports entertainment industry.

The contribution that sports have made to race relations in America, although far from perfect, is generally recognized as positive. For instance, the most plausible explanation for the overrepresentation of black athletes in sports like football and basketball is that sports offer opportunities that are unavailable to them elsewhere in society.[1] The excellence displayed by black athletes in sport has helped to open doors to social opportunity by changing attitudes about race. Although issues remain, racial integration of sports has benefitted not just minorities, but society at large.

We believe that it is time for sport to provide a similar social service with respect to gender. Part of the issue is simply fair distribution of social goods—one of which is sport. We need to ask not only what sport can do for women, but also what women's involvement in sport can do for society. This chapter argues for mutual recognition of and respect for the talents of both male and female athletes through aretic reform. The differences between the sexes in sport are not cause for discrimination or repudiation of any one sex, even at the highest levels. Rather gender diversity in sport provides an opportunity to acknowledge the beauty of human diversity through athletic expression. Thus, we hope here to make a modest, but significant, contribution to the push for female equality and just distribution of goods as they pertain to competitive sports in democratically oriented societies today.

The Problem of Sexism in Sport

Sexism in sport is not a women's issue, it is a social issue that harms both genders. Sexism affects the genders differently and the Aretic reforms championed here are not based on a genderless notion of sport. Men and women, we have been arguing all along, are unquestionably unlike each other in certain obvious respects. There is no reason to mandate that the sports they play must be the same and that they must be played under precisely the same guidelines and rules. In addition, there is no reason to think that sport itself ought to reflect the traditional ideals of any one sex to the exclusion of the other.

Instead of a genderless ideal for competitive sport, Aretism is an androgynous ideal that values both male and female perspectives and seeks to promote each equally for the betterment of both. Aretism entails a radical rethinking and redefinition of many of the key concepts related to the practice of sport; concepts such as "success," "empowerment," and "competition."

First, consider what Mike Messner says of success:

> Social scientific research has suggested that the contemporary sense of failure and inadequacy felt by many American males is largely the result of unrealistic and unachievable social definitions of masculinity and success. This research has suggested that there is more to it than that. Contemporary males often feel empty, alienated, isolated, and as failures because the socially learned means through which they seek validation and identity (achievement in the public worlds of sports and work) do not deliver what is actually craved and needed: intimate connection and unity with other human beings.

Messner's quote illustrates the way that MC sport worsens the problem of frail male identity, which for many men reaches a crisis at mid-life.[2] Studies on children show that success is perceived by them to be not a matter of winning, but realizing personal goals.[3] That seems the right goal for adults as well. Success ought to be redefined in terms of achieving realizable personal goals—that do not separate individual ideals from communal values. Sport can provide a good model for that if emphasis is removed from defeating others and refocused upon personal achievement—i.e., *aretē*.

Next, there is the issue of empowerment. Sport gives individuals a sense of involvement, identity, and worth—all of which are empowering values. Yet the traditional notion of empowerment also includes domination and other MC elements that make competitors behave like predators. That leads to emasculation, not empowerment. Television commercials related to sports, for instance, often focus on speed, danger, and aggression and, therefore, play on men's insecurities, instead of their strengths. Commercials are effective at convincing men to purchase a particular product to help overcome their fears, embarrassments, and shortcomings, but they are not "empowering." Rather than promoting athletic virtues, they engender worry about being a geek or a nerd that is not cool, aggressive, or attractive to women.[4]

To engender Aretic reform, empowerment ought to be redefined in a manner that excludes those MC elements and aims at virtue—an androgynous ideal. Anne Barstow argues, "Power can be seen as power with rather than power over, and it can be used for competence and cooperation, rather than dominance and control."[5] David Whitson agrees, "We need to introduce boys and girls alike to the empowering experiences of skill and strength that are offered in many kinds of nonconfrontative sports, and we need to celebrate these more than we do fighting skills."[6] The Aretic model endorses an androgynous redefinition of empowerment that helps to individuate athletes in terms of their excellences, not their gender.

Last and perhaps most importantly, the notion of "competition" must be challenged and stripped of its MC implications. Competition today is viewed through a strongest-will-survive or win-at-all-costs perspective. Sport is often seen as reflecting the cutthroat, predatory environment of the everyday business world. Kathryn Pyne Addelson elaborates:

> Organized sports were developed in a society in which men's work in business and politics was considered to be a competitive battle in which the victor showed himself fitter than the vanquished and thus deserving of the spoils. Even if some of those sports do give boys skills to survive in our present world of business and politics, it is far from clear that citizens in a democracy should be encouraged to have that kind of character.[7]

As Addelson correctly warns, the militaristic attitude that today's competition engenders probably has little to do with business success or moral character and more to do with rationalizing people's brutish inclinations. It is society at large that suffers from these attitudes.

Equal Participation

Sociologist Bruce Kidd calls the inequalities plaguing females who equal opportunity in sports and careers the "problem of distribution." He argues that in preaching that "the qualities males learn from sports are masculine," we thereby celebrate the achievements of males in sports, while we reduce women to the role of spectator. Thus, "sports validate the male claim to the best jobs and the highest status and rewards."[8]

The huge difficulties in coming to grips with gender-based inequality in sports are, in general, reducible to the problem of social androcentrism. A varie-

ty of approaches to this issue have been proposed. They fall between two extreme positions. On the one hand, conservatives believe that things are fine just
the way they are. That is clearly false. Things are certainly better for women than
they have been in the past, but there needs to be more push for equality between
sexes at all levels in free societies. Assimilationists, on the other hand, argue for
radical social equality, where sexual differences, as they contribute to social
roles, are no more relevant than eye color. Forced equality would require instan-
tiation and enforcement, which might lead to a great loss of autonomy and, therefore, be at odds with the principles of democratic ideals. Moreover, it seems
quite likely that few people would be happier in a society void of gender distinctions. Humans make out gender distinctions to be greater than they are, because
they like to think that gender distinctions are greater than they are.

How, then, should we try to reform sport? Attempts to achieve equality by
constraints placed upon the most popular sports would be unpopular solutions.
Men's professional basketball, baseball, and football are huge money sports in
America. They are also sports with tremendous fan appeal. If the "goods" of
society are to be determined by members of that society, placing constraints on
such sports seems undemocratic. Nonetheless, the most popular sports have
gained their great appeal, in part, through clever marketing strategies that have
blocked off many women's sports and certain other sports from public enjoyment. By not having exposure to a full variety of sportive involvement, most
females and many males have been denied some measure of expression of their
personhood.

There is no simple solution to this vexing problem. The best chance of long-
term success, we have argued, is to begin from the bottom and work upward.
Cities and towns, when possible, should have numerous and varied athletic programs for youth. Boys and girls should be equally encouraged to participate and
they should at least begin by competing together in the same programs. There
should be equal money spent on programs for each sex.

At the journalistic level, the media should give men's and women's events
equal exposure. The commercial argument that fan appeal should determine exposure begs the question. The relationship between fan appeal and exposure is
reciprocal: fan appeal not only determines exposure, it is in large measure determined by exposure. The broadcast appeal of women's Olympic events, such
as gymnastics, figure-skating, and most recently, beach volleyball, could not
have been predicted by the MC sports paradigm. Without something closer to
equal exposure, equal participation in sport will remain elusive.

In modern democratic societies, women are expected to have full participation. Nowadays females participate at almost every level, even in the military.
Joan Hundley argues, and we agree, that equality of participation in sports would
itself significantly conduce equality of participation in society. She writes:

[E]qual participation by women in athletics on all levels, including youth sport programs as well as professional athletics, would be significant in the undermining of the patriarchal nature of modern society. It stands to reason that if women are considered equals within the athletic arena, men could no longer use sport as a proving ground for masculinity; this would also undermine the notion of sport being a safety valve for masculine expression.[9]

Partnership

The model of gender equity in aretic sports and democratic societies is not one of tolerance or even accommodation, but rather equal partnership. Philosopher John Dewey has said, "[I]t is no exaggeration to say that the measure of a civilization is the degree in which the method of cooperative intelligence replaces the method of brute conflict."[10] Men and women must work together to reform sport in a way that gives both sexes equal opportunity of participation and expression; without forcing either to conform to the MC manner of its practice.

Sport is a human creation, so women ought to be granted full partnership with men in managing it. Competitive sport ought to be cooperative and not based on the traditional, masculine principles of competition. Jan Boxill writes:

Once we recognize that men and women are partners rather than adversaries, then we can achieve a great deal through cooperative endeavors. . . . We need to educate all people that sports participation has value, not just for men, but for all of us. It is not simply a male activity. Through education we will come to realize that strength is important in some sports, but is overrated and not the decisive factor in most sports.[11]

Boxill insists that equality of sportive participation must begin with education, which entails a big change in the manner in which societies think about women. More importantly, it requires a changed attitude concerning what it means to be male in this age of so-called equality. It is that last issue that has not been straightforwardly addressed.

Phyllis Ghim Lian Chew also sees gender equality as a cooperative quest. She maintains that there are noticeable differences between the sexes, which she captures straightforwardly and in yin-yang fashion by referring to a masculine principle and a feminine principle. The masculine principle is based on focus—an analytic interest in things and objects—while the feminine principle is characterized by context—an attempt to keep the whole in perspective.[12] In today's world, she states, there is an imbalance of principles, whereby masculine priorities of authority, control, victory, ownership, law, courage, strength, power, and competition play themselves out in an end-justifies-the-means mentality. "'Winning' and 'losing' or being 'first' and 'last' are important results in a patriarchy. .

. . The concept of superiority, might and aggression appears of supreme importance and it does not appear to be losing its grip."

What are at stake are world peace and a new-world order, and those things will come about, she believes, only through a conception of gender equality that entails complementarity, not sameness. "Men and women should be viewed as a single organism, each with unique and diverse characteristics which come together in harmony."[13] In short, the MC depiction of traditional competitive sport, for Chew, is symptomatic of a global incongruity concerning principles.

A Humanistic Model

To initiate Aretic reform of competitive sport, males and females must work together for the benefit of their collective communities. Current sportive practice glorifies aggression and other MC ideals that place females at a distinct disadvantage, and promote insecurity among males. Bonnie Beck's insistence that we adopt a more humanistic model of competitive sport comes because of her ardent belief that female assimilation into the current male, physicalist model perpetuates female oppression. Sport today, she says, is often brutal and violent, and it reinforces the injustice of male dominance and superiority.[14] The 2003 WNBA championship series between Detroit and Los Angeles was played out in just this martial fashion (see chapter 5).

The virtues demanded by Aretic sport are neither masculine nor feminine but rather humanistic. In Aretism, it is not the end that counts in sport, but how that end is reached. It was delightful to watch Martina Hingis play tennis, whether she won or lost, since she was an intelligent and unrelenting competitor, who, while playing by the rules, employed a wide range of tactics to gain advantage in a tennis match. Again, who will ever forget the unmatched artistry of running back Barry Sanders as he would turn back from a sweep, cut up the field, twist one way and then turn another to avoid this tackler and the next, and then scamper for 50 or 60 yards downfield to the utter frustration of opponents? Moreover, the 1999 Women's World Cup soccer championship between the United States and China left spectators speechless—almost hoping that no one would win a match so evenly contested. Last, hockey mavens recall the Detroit Red Wings' dedication to a specific system of team-styled hockey that earned them four Stanley Cups in 11 years (1997, 1998, 2002, and 2008). Those are humanistic examples of excellence of sport.

Nevertheless, an abundance of empirical data reveals the reluctance of men to accept women as equal partners in competitive sport. Part of the problem is the presumption that athletic women just do not quite measure up when compared to men. Men are stronger, faster, and more aggressive, and thereby better suited for competitive sport. Yet as female participation increases, men are coming to find that women can be tenacious competitors in physical sports. Women too are strong, fast, and aggressive. Yet they have other athletic interests and gifts—such as grace, balance, and fluidity of expression—that have not always been valued in sport.

Maybe males do not care to be graceful, balanced, and fluid, because it is, in Schwarzneggerian terms, too "girly-mannish" and, therefore, threatens their masculinity. Athletic excellence is androgynous, not sexist. The traditional MC notion of competitive sport is stiflingly narrow and a horrid reflection of masculinity today. The idea that "real men" watch football, love cars, and drink beer is degrading to men. Masculinity is much more complex than that.

Regard for personhood and egalitarian principles of justice require that all willing and able citizens have equal access to the goods of their society. No democratic society should discriminate against anyone because of race, philosophical or religious conviction, or gender. In consequence, even if it could be shown that men are undoubtedly superior to women in the majority of competitive sports, that would still not be a justification for labeling sport as "male preserve" or for prohibiting women from equal access to competitive sports.

The key to successful acceptance of the MA model comes through convincing men that they have little to lose and much to gain in accepting women as equal partners in competitive sport. Bruce Kidd states:

> It is necessary to assure males who resist integration on the basis of ability that we are strong enough to survive an "invasion" of outstanding female athletes. Where the implementation of affirmative action programs will bring about cuts in existing male opportunities, we should strive to find additional resources and make more efficient use of the existing ones. The most difficult task will be persuading other men that gender-divided sports are not just a "women's problem" but in dialectical interaction harm us as well. Once there's a shared understanding of that, the critical redesign of sports can really begin.[15]

For centuries, men have had privileged access to competitive sport and the many benefits that often accompany it. If sport builds self-esteem and confidence, engenders goal-setting and goal-meeting skills, improves physical fitness, facilitates camaraderie, and helps give athletes a sense of identity, should not females have the same access to those benefits? Kathryn Pyne Addelson agrees. She says, "If sports build character in citizens of a democracy, then those 'basics' must include access to sports resources for men and women."[16] She adds that a revised notion of "competition" is necessary for equality. The notions of sport as combat and of combat as male territory, by definition, rule women out from competition[17] and that is clearly unjust.

An Opportunity for Equality

Failure to accept female athletes in competitive sport is perhaps chiefly, if not exclusively, reducible to men's lack of self-understanding and that lack of self-understanding is fear-based. Men still shut themselves off from female competitive sport simply because they are afraid of women and what women represent. That fear is not so much founded on women discovering something about themselves through competitive sports; it is instead the fear that men will not be men, if women can compete equally as well in competitive sports—the fear of emasculation.

In ancient Greece too, there was a fear of female athleticism. The mythical athlete Atalanta was said to race the suitors who wanted to marry her, kill them when they lost, and then place their heads on posts lining the race-course. The tribe of Amazon warriors was tricky and formidable in battle. Achilles is said to have fallen in love with the Amazon queen right at the moment he killed her. As we noted earlier, females were marginalized and excluded from athletics in ancient Greece, but they still managed to use sport to make the case for equality. The Spartan princess Cyniska won an Olympic crown in horse racing (as the owner of the horses) and erected a statue of herself alongside the male athletes in the sacred grove. By one account Cyniska's feat showed that Olympic crowns (at least in horse racing) were not true indicators of *aretē*;[18] by another it showed that females too could demonstrate *aretē* if given the chance.

Aretism embraces the second interpretation of Cyniska's challenge and calls for sport to be opened to females so that they can demonstrate their *aretē* and reshape our understanding of *aretē* to be androgynous—a humanistic rather than a gender-specific ideal. It is important to underscore what is at issue here. Women are not asking for a period of domination over men in compensation for the many hundreds of years of being dominated by men. Women are asking only for equal status as human beings.

Still, many men are not yet ready to accept equality of gender, however much they might preach its merits. What they fail to recognize is that resistance to female athletes and insistence on sport being male preserve is ultimately damaging to men. Bruce Kidd talks of sports "poisoning the athletes' dealings with other men." First, sports limit men's expression of affection for other men. Instead of allowing for a straightforward expression of fondness, through sports we are taught to express feelings of affection through teasing or mock fighting. Second, sports also teach men that masculinity is power in two unhealthy senses: While competing, men occupy space and they forcefully operate on objects, including others, in that space.[19]

Sociologist Don Sabo argues that, while the participation of women in athletic sport does more to androgynize than masculinize women, it functions to compartmentalize men.

Traditional sport endorses stereotypical gender expectations and idealizes manliness. For boys, sport socialization represents a *continuation* of previous gender learning; traditionally masculine expectations often become exaggerated as boys spend more time in the athletic subculture. In contrast, when girls enter the "masculine" world of sport, their experiences are apt to have an androgynizing effect on gender identity development. Athletic involvement for girls is a source of social and psychological counter-point, but for boys, just another variation on a theme. Theoretically, therefore, gender socialization in sport is often one-sided and narrowing for boys and multifaceted and expansive for girls.[20]

Mike Messner writes of men's need to confront the social element of Martial values through a more cooperative, nurturing ethic that can be cultivated through sport:

If many of the problems faced by all men (not just athletes) today are to be dealt with, class, ethnic, and sexual preference divisions must be confronted. This would necessarily involve the development of a more cooperative and nurturant ethic among men, as well as a more egalitarian and democratically organized economic system. And since the sports world is an important cultural process that serves partly to socialize boys and young men to hierarchical, competitive, and aggressive values, the sporting arena is an important context in which to begin to confront the need for a humanization of men.

Yet he believes that humanization of men through infusion of "cooperative and egalitarian values into sports is likely to be an exercise in futility." Real social changes need to be made for that to work. One such change with the potential for substantial improvement of male insecurity, he maintains, would be a push for equal involvement in parenting.[21] In short, men need to be socialized in tenderness, not merely toughness. Sports, we believe, can help.

Overall, aretic reform of sport is an extraordinary opportunity for male change—especially in the areas of growth and self-understanding. It is not weakness, but strength, to come to a full recognition that women have as much right as do men to express and discover themselves through competitive sport. In fact, justice demands that. It is not weakness, but strength to acknowledge that each sex needs some degree of same-sex intimacy and that violent physical play is a socially irresponsible and harmful form of fulfilling that need. Sport has social consequences and Aretism insists that we do what we can to make those consequences positive.

Notes

1. By "overrepresentation" we mean that the percentage of athletes of color in sports is higher than the percentage of people of color in that society.

2. "The Meaning of Success: The Athletic Experience and the Development of Male Identity," *Sport in Contemporary Society: An Anthology*, ed. D. Stanley Eitzen (New York: St. Martin's Press, 1996), 385.

3. K.L. Siegenthaler and G. Leticia Gonzales, "Youth Sports as Serious Leisure," *Journal of Sport & Social Issues*, Vol. 21, No. 3 (Sage Publications, Inc., 1997), 301.

4. Messner et al., "Boys to Men," 10.

5. D. Margaret Costa and Sharon R. Guthrie, *Women and Sport: Interdisciplinary Perspectives* (Champaign, IL: Human Kinetics Publishers, 1994), 177.

6. David Whitson, "Sport Promotes Negative Male Values," *Sports in America: Opposing Viewpoints*, ed. William Dudley (San Diego, CA: Greenhaven Press, Inc., 1994), 178.

7. Kathryn Pyne Addelson, "The Meaning of Success: The Athletic Experience and the Development of Male Identity," *Sport in Contemporary Society: An Anthology*, ed. D. Stanley Eitzen (New York: St. Martin's Press, 1983), 154.

8. Bruce Kidd, "The Men's Cultural Centre: Sports and the Dynamic of Women's Oppression/Men's Repression," *Sport, Men, and the Gender Order: Critical Feminist Perspectives*, ed. Mike Messner and Don Sabo (Champaign, IL: Human Kinetics Books, 1990), 36-37.

9. Joan Hundley, "The Overemphasis on Winning: A Philosophical Look," *Philosophy of Sport: Critical Readings, Crucial Issues*, ed. M. Andrew Holowchak (Upper Saddle River, NJ: Prentice-Hall, Inc. 2002), 217.

10. John Dewey, *Liberalism & Social Action* (New York: Capricorn Books 1963), 81.

11. Jan Boxill, "Beauty, Sport, and Gender," *Journal of the Philosophy of Sport* XI (Champaign, IL: Human Kinetics Publishers, 1995), 30.

12. Phyllis Ghim Lian Chew, "The Challenge of Unity: Women, Peace and Power," *International Journal on World Peace*, Vol. XV, No. 4, 1998, 31-32.

13. Chew, "The Challenge of Unity," 30-41.

14. Bonnie Beck, "The Future of Women's Sport: Issues, Insights, and Struggles," *Jock: Sports and Male Identity*, eds. Donald Sabo and Russ Runfola (Upper Saddle River, NY: Prentice-Hall Trade, 1980), 301.

15. Kidd, "The Men's Cultural Centre," 1990, 43.

16. Kathryn Pyne Addelson, "The Meaning of Success: The Athletic Experience and the Development of Male Identity," *Sport in Contemporary Society: An Anthology*, ed. D. Stanley Eitzen (New York: St. Martin's Press, 1996), 373-388.

17. Addelson, "The Meaning of Success," 149.

18. Xenophon, *Agesilaus*, 9.6.

19. Addelson, "The Meaning of Success," 140.

20. Donald Sabo, "Psychosocial Impacts of Athletic Participation on American Women: Facts and Fables," *Sport in Contemporary Society: An Anthology*, 5th, ed. D. Stanley Eitzen (New York: St. Martin's Press, 1996), 32.

21. Michael A. Messner, "The Meaning of Success: The Athletic Experience and the Development of Male Identity," *Sport in Contemporary Society: An Anthology*, ed. D. Stanley Eitzen (New York: St. Martin's Press, 1996), 386-387.

Chapter 22
Is Sport a Good?

"The strange paradox of sportsmanship as applied to athletics is that it asks the athlete, locked in a deadly serious and emotionally charged situation, to act outwardly as if he was engaged in some pleasant diversion." James W. Keating

WHEN EUTHYPHRO, IN PLATO'S DIALOGUE of the same name, settles on a definition of "piety" as "what all the gods love," Socrates asks his arrogant young interlocutor whether piety is loved by all the gods, because it is pious, or piety is pious, because it is loved by all the gods.[1] The implication of the former is that there is something special about piety that makes it deserving of all the gods' love. Piety is an unqualified good and, thus, choice-worthy by gods and men alike. The implication of the latter is that there is nothing special about piety other than the chance fact that all the gods happen to love it. Piety is a qualified or contingent good. Like, say, chocolate ice-cream, it is dubbed "good" or "valuable" only because many or most persons happen to like it. The young cockalorum, unable to grasp what Socrates has said, is flummoxed.

Most of today's politically-minded philosophers and political theorists categorize the key virtues of Greek and Roman societies—justice, wisdom, courage, and self-control—as "contingent goods" or "values." John Rawls, for instance, argues that a politically correct notion of democratic justice entails only that its citizens are allowed to have some notion of good, but allows for that notion to be revisable through rational discussion. For them, the key issue is justice and justice is a political, not a moral, issue. Morality, then, is answerable to justice.[2]

The Aretic approach that we champion is otherwise. Following the Greek and Roman philosophers Socrates, Plato, Aristotle, Epictetus, and Seneca, we begin with assumption that people are social animals and that their end or good exists as a social form of living, where individuals are to be construed as fundamental parts of a social or political unit. That is not to say that political units or systems are more ontologically fundamental or axiologically greater than the people that comprise them. It is merely to assert that persons ought not to be construed, like many liberal thinkers construe them, as isolated or asocial individuals—i.e., as atoms.

Being social or political animals, we assume also that the exercise of *aretē*—being just, honest, friendly, generous, magnanimous, courageous, self-controlled, *inter alia*—is the chief, if not sole, human good and refusal to exercise *aretē*, the chief, if not sole, human vice. For Socrates, Plato, and the ancient Stoics, a life devoted to the pursuit of *aretē* and avoidance of vice was as good, as pleasant, or as happy a life as any person, capable of full rationality (or nearly so) could have. Nothing could add to or detract from the pleasantness or happiness of someone who was perfectly Aretic. Things like health and wealth were conveniences and worth pursuing in their own right, but not unqualified goods.

Aristotle disagreed. For him, there were psychical goods, the virtues, but there were also bodily goods (e.g., health, height, and looks) and external goods (e.g., wealth and good fortune)—all three of which were needed to be happy. Happiness, thus, consisted of full *aretē* and some small stock of bodily and external goods. A person fully virtuous, but lacking the right amount of "lesser goods," could never be miserable, due to his *aretē*, but could never be happy either, due to want of the lesser goods. One lacking full *aretē*, irrespective of an adequate stock of lesser goods, would always be miserable, due to lack of *aretē*.[3]

What did those ancients think about sports activities—especially competitive sport? Given Socrates', Plato's, and the Stoics' insistence that *aretē* was sufficient for happiness and Aristotle's take that it was the key needed component of a happy like, it should come as no surprise that none of those thinkers or schools thought competitive sport was good in itself. In its all-consuming professional guise, they thought sport was wasted energy that led to self-absorption and emphasis on external goods, not political assimilation and participation, or most important, *aretē*.

In this final chapter, we explore the issue of whether and to what extent sport is a component of the good life by examining the views of two contemporary thinkers, Bernard Suits and Thomas Hurka, on the issue.

Games as Metaphysics of Leisure

Philosopher Bernard Suits opened the door for a viable role for competitive sport by arguing that autotelic activity—i.e., activity done for its own sake—is the only good, the real human end, and game-playing is the most satisfying form of autotelic activity. In chapter 15 of his brilliant work *The Grasshopper*, Suits says that game playing is the ideal of human existence.[4]

Suits has readers imagine a Utopia, where all instrumental human activities (i.e., types of work) are unneeded and have been eliminated. Machines, activated by mental telepathy, now do the work of humans—presumably because any other means of activation would be a form of work. So efficient do they work that the number of goods they produce is plethoric and there is a superabundance of each type of good. Furthermore, psychotherapy and the social sciences have made such advances that all interpersonal problems have been solved. There is such psychological wellbeing and adjustment that people no longer need affection, approval, attention, and admiration. The advances of psychotherapy also make moral principles superfluous. Art too is unneeded and unpracticed, since the motivation for its creation—human aspirations, frustrations, hopes, fears, triumphs, tragedies, and the like—do not exist in Utopia. Science, philosophy, and all other forms of investigative inquiry do not exist in any significant sense, for Utopia is a society where all the important questions are already answered. Finally, even love, friendship, and sex disappear.[5]

In the end, Grasshopper, the main character in the book,[6] argues that the only meaningful activity left is that of game-playing. Game-playing is what remains as the human ideal, after all instrumental activities are abstracted away. As pure autotelic activity, "Game playing makes it possible to retain enough effort in Utopia to make life worth living," since there is "nothing to strive for because everything else has already been achieved." Grasshopper adds, "Game playing performs a crucial role in delineating that ideal—a role which cannot be performed by any other activity, and without which an account of the ideal is either incomplete or impossible."[7]

What precisely is autotelic activity? Suits defines the ideal of human existence, pure autotelic activity, as "that thing or those things whose only justification is that they justify everything else; or, as Aristotle put it, those things for the sake of which we do other things, but which are not themselves done for the sake of anything else."[8] If some action, α, is undertaken for the sake of some end, τ, then it is τ that is what one is really striving for, not α. It is τ that makes α worth doing.

What is *pure* autotelic activity? It turns out to be game-playing, which he defines as follows:

> To play a game is to attempt to achieve a specific state of affairs [prelusory goal], using only means permitted by rules [lusory means], where the rules prohibit use of more efficient in favor of less efficient means [constitutive rules], and where the rules are accepted just because they make possible such activity [lusory attitude].

Put succinctly, "[P]laying a game is the voluntary attempt to overcome unnecessary obstacles."[9] Such voluntary activity, Suits argues, is the only true, humanly meaningful autotelic activity, and that he attempts to show through his notion of Utopia.

Grasshopper and his interlocutor, Skepticus, go on to consider whether game playing is the only possible occupation in Utopia. Grasshopper proceeds as follows. He assumes that someone in Utopia wants to build a house the old-fashioned way—i.e., through what was once deemed work. Since houses are in abundance in Utopia and readily available in every size, shape, and form, the desire to build one is merely the desire to bring about some end through over-

coming unneeded obstacles. That, however, is just to be playing a game. He also
assumes that someone wants to solve a scientific problem. Since all scientific
problems are solved in Utopia, the desire to solve a problem is again the desire
to bring about some end through overcoming unneeded obstacles. Therefore,
like one who persists in a crossword puzzle without using the answer-key, he too
would be playing a game.[10] Suits sums:

> I am truly the Grasshopper; that is, an adumbration of the ideal of existence,
> just as the games we play in our non-Utopian lives are intimations of things to
> come. For even now it is games which give us something to do when there is
> nothing to do. We thus call games 'pastimes', and regard them as trifling fillers
> of the interstices in our lives. But they are much more important than that. They
> are clues to the future. And their serious cultivation now is perhaps our only
> salvation. That, if you like, is the metaphysics of leisure time.[11]

In sum, though there may be other ways of passing the time in Utopia, like loaf-
ing or traveling, game-playing is the chief and most satisfying form of autotelic
activity in Utopia. It gives meaning to human lives that otherwise would be vac-
uous and absurd. Without games, life palls.

There are difficulties with Suits's view of game-playing as the supreme
good, which Holowchak has articulated elsewhere,[12] but *The Grasshopper*
makes one point cogently: People are passionate about the games they play and
many of the other things they do, like work, they seem to do for the sake of having time to play games. The same seems to be true of competitive sport.

Modern vs. Classical Notions of Value

In an important paper, "Games and the Good," Thomas Hurka develops the thesis that "skill in games is worth pursing for its own sake and can add value to
one's life."[13] That allows for a justification of the admiration we feel for the
excellence exhibited in athletic and non-athletic games. It also leaves room for
competitive sport, being a good. Hurka's views, he expressly says, are significantly influenced by Suits's *Grasshopper*.

We value achievements, Hurka begins, and some more than others. What
we value about achievements, especially the better ones, is in large part their
difficulty—i.e., how complex they are and how much skill and ingenuity they
require. "So reflection on our intuitive understanding of the value of achievement suggests a first reason for holding that difficult activities are such a
good."[14]

Hurka's next step is to argue that achievements are especially valuable, if
they are "rationally connected to reality." Here he considers Robert Nozick's
famous thought experiment of an experience machine, which allows, through
electrical stimulation, for any pleasurable experience. Nozick says that a life of

such electrically generated pleasures is less than ideal, because it is disconnected from reality.[15] So achievement is good because it is knowledge-generating[16]— and that is a feature of sport.

Finally, Hurka argues that mundanely repetitive, imprecise, and narrow-content achievements are of lesser value than complex, precise, and wide-content achievements. Complex hierarchical achievements allow for multiple levels of failure and, thereby, make success more difficult. Complex hierarchical achievements also demand greater skills—both deliberative and physical. Such achievements are typical of not all games, but good games.[17]

In contrast to Suits, who claims that playing games is the greatest good, Hurka argues that playing games, good games, is a lesser good. Good games are a species of good, because they are complex and difficult and they develop skills that are transferable to other scenarios. Good games link persons to other, more fundamental goods.[18]

Hurka's point is that games, considered in themselves, are trivial pursuits, because the ends pursued are trivial. They are not, strictly speaking, instrumentally valuable, because the ends, at which they aim, are valueless in themselves. Consider the competitive sports of sprinting and powerlifting. No sensible person would believe that running a 100-meter race is important because it is crucial for one at the starting line to move his body to the finish line, 100 meters away. The same can be said for sinking a 500-pound barbell to one's chest for the sake of pressing it off one's chest. The two activities are set up artificially and each, considered alone, seems patently absurd. If the two ends were important, as Suits would say, one would certainly find more efficient ways to do them. One could transport oneself from the start to the finish line, 100 meters away, by a motorcycle, if efficiency of transportation itself were the issue. One could have a hydraulic machine move a 500-pound barbell on and off one's chest, if moving a barbell on and off one's chest were the issue. Thus, on account of the trivial nature of games like competitive events, the honor due a great competitor, who covers the 100-meter distance in world-record fashion, or another competitor, who presses up a world-record weight, is certainly not the same as the honor due a great statesperson, who accomplishes a peace treaty between warring nations, even if the effort expended by all persons is roughly the same. Peace between warring nations is a good thing. Moving one's body 100 meters and pressing up a ponderous barbell are not.

Nonetheless, the sort of lesser good that is competitive sport, as a species of game, is not a good of the Aristotelian sort, as what is characteristic of good for Aristotle is its achievement. Actualization is everything for Aristotle. For Hurka, the actualization of a certain end in a game is significant, insofar as the end of a game is a key component to its structure, yet it is subordinate to the process of participation.[19] In short, for Hurka, willing and committed participation is itself achievement—even if the end aimed at is not achieved. That, for Hurka, marks an important difference between the ancient notion of "value" and the modern notion of "value." While achievement was needed for Aristotle, participation is sufficient for moderns. Good games—games that are connected to reality and sufficiently complex—allow for meaningful participation.

Competitive Sport and the Good Life

This comparison has left us with two important questions. Is sport a good? If so, is it, as Suits asserts, the chief good or is it, as Hurka asserts, a lesser good, if the game contested is a good game?

Though Suits' *Grasshopper* is compelling, there is no reason to believe that games are the sole or even the most significant human good. That is not to say that game-playing is not a lesser good and a (potentially at least) vital part of the good life.

Following Hurka, we acknowledge that good games, because they offer challenges and opportunities for achievement that people otherwise might not have, are a species of good. We acknowledge that it is willful, committed participation in certain activities, certain competitive sports among them, that yields achievement.

Yet, following Aristotle and the Greek and Roman Stoics, we believe that activities like competitive sport are worthless in themselves, unless they are done with one eye toward virtuous activity and political integration. A professional athlete, who absorbs herself in engaging and difficult competitive sports throughout her salad days to the exclusion of virtuous activity outside of sport, is no better than someone, recognizing the value of health or wealth, strives exclusively for health or wealth to the exclusion of more significant, socially beneficial activities. To be happy and live a good life, one must aim foremost at virtuous activity, which has an ineluctable social dimension. That is not to say that competitive sport is unqualifiedly a good of a lesser sort, but merely to acknowledge, as does Hurka, that *certain* competitive sports, practiced aretically, are sufficiently complex and challenging to promote virtue.

There is a second reason to consider competitive sport a socially significant activity. Competitive sport could be a vehicle for channeling human assertiveness in ways that promote moral betterment and world peace.

In a paper entitled "Violence and Aggression in Contemporary Society," philosopher Jim Parry argues that assertion, aggression, and violence in competitive sport allow opportunities for reflection on moral education and moral development. Competitive sports, he asserts, are "laboratories for value experiments."[20]

> I find it an attractive and intriguing idea, worthy of further consideration, that the competitive sports situation challenges individuals to develop and use their power and aggressiveness; but not, finally, to use this power to control and sub-

jugate the other. May we see more assertive and aggressive people, and less violent ones. And may sport be an agent of moral change.[21]

Frans DeWachter too sees sport as a possible vehicle for moral progress—specifically, regarding education in resolution of conflict and peace. "The question is not whether sport is functional for peace. That seems to me to be a question that is too ambitious. The realistic question is whether sport education can be functional in the context of peace education." Citing four objectives related to peace education that could be instrumental to that end—reduction of militaristic attitudes, diminution of aggressiveness, eradication of "enemy images," and development of conflict-resolving skills—he encourages work in each of those areas.[22]

Sociologist Mike Messner writes that sport could have a key role in the proper socialization of boys.

> If many of the problems faced by all men (not just athletes) today are to be dealt with, class, ethnic, and sexual preference divisions must be confronted. This would necessarily involve the development of a more cooperative and nurturant ethic among men, as well as a more egalitarian and democratically organized economic system. And since the sports world is an important cultural process that serves partly to socialize boys and young men to hierarchical, competitive, and aggressive values, the sporting arena is an important context in which to begin to confront the need for a humanization of men.[23]

The issue of sportive activity for moral betterment and social improvement is engaging. As one can imagine, however, there is not an abundance of contemporary philosophical and sociological work on this issue.[24] People are soured perhaps by what they have seen in the past under the rubric "morality and sport," such as the politically vicious fascism that sullied athletic competition at the 1936 Olympics in Berlin (see chapter 4). Their attitude today seems to be that sport is or, at least, ought to be value-neutral. They seem content to let sports promoters and athletes do their own thing.

There is a third, naturalistic reason to consider playing games, in general, and competitive sport, in particular, as socially significant. Playing behavior is observable in a large number of species of animal. Some biologists believe that certain animals invent games—often of the difficult and dangerous sort. Because their games are difficult and dangerous, those biologists believe that animals' games must have significance for adaptation to changing circumstances and overall evolutionary success.[25] What is *aretē*—i.e., human excellence—if not the ability to adapt successfully to changing circumstances? Again, insofar as certain types of game playing promote *aretē*, they improve not just individuals, but the species at large.

In this book, we have been very critical of sport in the modern world. We observed the manipulation of sport throughout Western history to serve a variety of human ends, many far from noble. We stated that the Martial/Commerical approach to sport, predominant today, has dangerous social consequences. We stated that the Aesthetic/Recreational alternative is too self-absorbed to contribute meaningfully to social good.

Our solution to the problems of MC sport is a new model of sport that derives from an ancient link between athletics and human virtue, known to the Greeks as *aretē*. We believe that an Aretic approach to sport can benefit athletes, institutions, and even society at large. By making *aretē*, rather than profit or enjoyment, its guiding principle, we allow sport to have an educational function that justifies its social purpose.

Notes

1. Plato, "Euthyphro," *Five Dialogues*, trans. G.M.A. Grube (Indianapolis: Hackett Publishing Company, Inc., 2002), 9d-e.

2. John Rawls, *Justice as Fairness: A Restatement* (Cambridge, MA: Belknap Press, 2001).

3. See M. Andrew Holowchak, *The Stoics: A Guide for the Perplexed* (London: Continuum International Publishing Group, 2008).

4. Bernard Suits, *The Grasshopper: Games, Life and Utopia* (Orchard Park, NY: Broadview Press Ltd., 2005), 29-32.

5. Suits, *The Grasshopper*, 149-54.

6. This is a spin from one of Aesop's fables.

7. Suits, *The Grasshopper*, 149-54.

8. Suits, *The Grasshopper*, 149.

9. Suits, *The Grasshopper*, 154-55.

10. Suits, *The Grasshopper*, 157-58.

11. Suits, *The Grasshopper*, 159.

12 M. Andrew Holowchak, "Games as Pastimes in Suits' Utopia: Meaningful Living and the 'Metaphysics of Leisure,'" *Journal of the Philosophy of Sport*, vol. 34, no. 1, May, 2007.

13. Thomas Hurka, "Games and the Good," http://www.chass.utoronto.ca/~thurka/docs/pass_games.pdf, 1.

14. Hurka, "Games and the Good," 4-6.

15. Robert Nozick, *Anarchy, State, and Utopia* (New York: Basic Books, 1974), 42-45.

16. Hurka, "Games and the Good," 6-8. That too is a feature of Aretic sport.

17. Hurka, "Games and the Good," 8-9.

18. Hurka, "Games and the Good," 9-10.

19. Hurka, "Games and the Good," 13-14.

20. Aggression he defines as assertive behavior that need not be violent, and violence as behavior that aims at harming another. Jim Parry, "Violence and Aggression in Contemporary Sport," *Philosophy of Sport: Critical Readings, Crucial Issues*, ed. M. Andrew Holowchak (Upper Saddle River, NJ: Prentice-Hall, 2002), 264.

21. Jim Parry, "Violence and Aggression in Contemporary Sport," 263.

22. Frans DeWachter, "Education for Peace in Sports Education," *Philosophy of Sport: Critical Readings, Crucial Issues*, ed. M. Andrew Holowchak (Upper Saddle River, NJ: Prentice-Hall, 2002), 447-48.

23. Mike Messner, "The Meaning of Success: The Athletic Experience and the Development of Male Identity," *Sport in Contemporary Society: An Anthology*, ed. D. Stanley Eitzen (New York: St. Martin's Press, 1996), 386.

24. See also M. Andrew Holowchak, "Aggression, Gender, and Sport: Reflections on Sport as a Means of Moral Education," *Philosophy of Sport: Critical Readings, Crucial Issues*, ed. M. Andrew Holowchak (Upper Saddle River, NJ: Prentice-Hall, 2002), 466-75, and Heather Reid, "Sport, Education, and the Meaning of Victory," http://www.bu.edu/wcp/Papers/Spor/SporReid.htm.

25. Jack Lucentini, "Dolphin Games: More than Just Child's Play? *World Science*, http://www.physorg.com/news8138.html, 13 Nov. 2005.

Index

About the Authors

M. Andrew Holowchak teaches philosophy at Rider University in Lawrence, New Jersey. He has published some sixty peer-reviewed papers in areas such as ethics, psychoanalysis, ancient philosophy and science, philosophy of sport, and social and political philosophy, and has authored eighteen books including *Freud and Utopia: From Cosmological Narcissism to the 'Soft Dictatorship' of Reason*; *Happiness and Greek Ethics*; *Critical Reasoning & Philosophy*; *Ancient Science and Dreams: Oneirology in Greco-Roman Antiquity*; *Philosophy of Sport: Crucial Readings, Critical Issues*; *The Stoics: A Guide for the Perplexed*, as well as two philosophical novels, *Life of a Jellyfish* and *Hotel Bob*. When not teaching or writing, Holowchak enjoys strength training (former super-heavyweight powerlifting champion), biking, gardening, travel, cooking, brewing beer, and polite conversation. He lives in Lindenwold, New Jersey, with his wife, Angela, and their several cats.

Heather L. Reid is professor of philosophy at Morningside College in Sioux City, Iowa, and director of the Morningside in Italy study abroad program. She researches and publishes in the areas of ancient philosophy, philosophy of sport, ancient sport history, and Olympic studies. She is the author of *The Philosophical Athlete* and *Athletics and Philosophy in the Ancient World: Contests of Virtue*. She serves on the editorial boards of the *Journal of the Philosophy of Sport* and *Sport, Ethics and Philosophy*, and is coeditor of the Ethics and Sport book series. A national intercollegiate champion and Olympic hopeful in her youth, Reid is still an active cyclist who leads bicycle tours in Italy each summer.